Towards a Global Core Value System in Doctoral Education

Towards a Global Core Value System in Doctoral Education

Edited by Maresi Nerad, David Bogle,
Ulrike Kohl, Conor O'Carroll, Christian Peters
and Beate Scholz

First published in 2022 by
UCL Press
University College London
Gower Street
London WC1E 6BT

Available to download free: www.uclpress.co.uk

Collection © Editors, 2022
Text © Contributors, 2022
Images © Contributors and copyright holders named in captions, 2022

The authors have asserted their rights under the Copyright, Designs and Patents Act 1988 to be identified as the authors of this work.

A CIP catalogue record for this book is available from The British Library.

Any third-party material in this book is not covered by the book's Creative Commons licence. Details of the copyright ownership and permitted use of third-party material is given in the image (or extract) credit lines. If you would like to reuse any third-party material not covered by the book's Creative Commons licence, you will need to obtain permission directly from the copyright owner.

This book is published under a Creative Commons Attribution-Non-Commercial 4.0 International licence (CC BY-NC 4.0), https://creativecommons.org/licenses/by-nc/4.0/. This licence allows you to share and adapt the work for non-commercial use providing attribution is made to the author and publisher (but not in any way that suggests that they endorse you or your use of the work) and any changes are indicated. Attribution should include the following information:

Nerad, M. et al (eds). 2022. *Towards a Global Core Value System in Doctoral Education*. London: UCL Press. https://doi.org/10.14324/111.9781800080188

Further details about Creative Commons licences are available at http://creativecommons.org/licenses/

ISBN: 978-1-80008-020-1 (Hbk.)
ISBN: 978-1-80008-019-5 (Pbk.)
ISBN: 978-1-80008-018-8 (PDF)
ISBN: 978-1-80008-021-8 (epub)
DOI: https://doi.org/10.14324/111.9781800080188

Since 2019, from the events leading to this book until its publication in autumn of 2022, during just three years, major catastrophes have accelerated world crises of such scope we have not fully come to terms with:

- a health crisis – the COVID-19 pandemic;
- a man-made crisis – the constant wars in Yemen, Syria, Afghanistan, and now the outrageous war against Ukraine;
- a long-looming environmental crisis – an accelerated climate change which gets pushed into the background by responses to the wars.

These crises force us to reflect on our fundamental values. As scholars who create new knowledge in a complicated and complex world, applying a *global core value system* in doctoral education is the way forward for the current and next generations of researchers and their advisors. By not retreating into the academic ivory tower but instead accepting leadership roles based on these global core values, the worldwide doctoral education community can set global value standards in their contribution to solving health, political and environmental crises.

Contents

List of figures and tables   ix

Acknowledgements   x

List of contributors   xi

Comparative international terminology   xxi

Prologue The thinking doctorate and the factory model of production: cautionary tales from the South   1
Jonathan D. Jansen and Cyrill A. Walters

PART I Guiding principles and essential policy recommendations

1. The doctoral-education context in the 21st century: change at every level   18
Barbara Grant, Maresi Nerad, Corina Balaban, Rosemary Deem, Martin Grund, Chaya Herman, Aleksandra Kanjuo Mrčela, Susan Porter, Janet Rutledge and Richard Strugnell

2. Guiding principles   43
Maresi Nerad, David Bogle, Ulrike Kohl, Conor O'Carroll, Christian Peters and Beate Scholz

3. The Hannover Recommendations   51

PART II Contentious issues in doctoral education

4. On quality assurance in doctoral education   57
Maresi Nerad, Janet Rutledge, Richard Strugnell, Hongjie Chen, Martin Grund and Aleksandra Kanjuo Mrčela

5. Supervision in context around the world   82
Ronel Steyn, Liezel Frick, Reinhard Jahn, Ulrike Kohl, William M. Mahoney, Jr, Maresi Nerad and Aya Yoshida

6. Funding of doctoral education and research   110
Marc Torka, Ulrike Kohl and William M. Mahoney, Jr

7   Capacity building through mobility and its challenges   133
    Devasmita Chakraverty, Maude Lévesque, Jing Qi,
    Charity Meki-Kombe and Conor O'Carroll

8   Global labour market developments   171
    David Bogle, Igor Chirikov, Miguel S. González Canché,
    Annamaria Silvana de Rosa, Nancy L. Garcia, Stefaan Hermans,
    Joyce Main and Suzanne Ortega

9   Social, ethical and cultural responsibility as core values
    for doctoral researchers in the 21st century   201
    Roxana Chiappa, Daniele Cantini, Yasemin Karakaşoğlu,
    Catherine Manathunga, Christian Peters, Beate Scholz and
    Betül Yarar

PART III Ways forward

10 Reflections from early-career researchers on the past,
    present and future of doctoral education   241
    Shannon Mason, Maude Lévesque, Charity Meki-Kombe, Sophie Abel,
    Corina Balaban, Roxana Chiappa, Martin Grund, Biandri Joubert,
    Gulfiya Kuchumova, Lilia Mantai, Joyce Main, Puleng Motshoane,
    Jing Qi, Ronel Steyn and Gaoming Zheng

11 Ways forward   257
    David Bogle, Ulrike Kohl, Maresi Nerad, Conor O'Carroll,
    Christian Peters and Beate Scholz

Index   261

List of figures and tables

Figures

5.1 Basic structure of US PhD Programmes
6.1 EUA 2018 Doctoral Survey: to what extent are doctoral candidates at your institution financially supported by the following sources (stipend, grant, salary, scholarship, fellowship, etc.)?
6.2 R&D Expenditures (in million US Dollars)
6.3 Total researchers (FTE)
6.4 Awarded doctoral degrees
7.1 Political instability and its impacts upon academics and doctoral students

Tables

1.1 Increase in PhD production 1991–2016
8.1 Skills developed by doctoral candidates (Bogle et al., 2010)
10.1 Early-career researchers' areas of interest

Acknowledgements

We thank the Volkswagen Foundation (VW) (VolkswagenStiftung) and especially its past Secretary General Dr Wilhelm Krull for their generous support of this dual project, of an international workshop on assessing doctoral-education changes during the last 20 years, as well as funding an international conference on the same theme. The Volkswagen Foundation opened its beautiful conference centre at the Herrenhausen palace in Hannover with its baroque garden providing a conducive environment.

We express thanks to the University of Bremen, particularly its former Vice Rector for Research, Professor Andreas Breiter, for taking on the administrative task of administering the VW grant and selecting Dr Christian Peters, Managing Director of the Bremen International Graduate School of Social Sciences, as the main implementor of the many facets of this dual project. Without Christian, who is a member of our editing team, his many special skills including IT expertise and the competent support of Barbara Dzaja, then Office and Faculty Assistant at BIGSSS, the workshop and conference would not have proceeded so smoothly and enjoyably.

We are grateful to Professor Jonathan Jansen and Cyrill Walters from South Africa for making time to came to Hannover, Germany, where Jonathan delivered a memorable keynote speech which we include as the prologue to this book. Jonathan Jansen, who is a household name in South African political and educational circles, holds many roles as the first black (coloured) Vice-Chancellor of the University of the Free State, Distinguished Professor of Education at Stellenbosch University, current President of the Academy of Science of South Africa, author of numerous books and weekly columnist of a South African national newspaper.

Our warm thank-you goes to the 41 workshop participants including 11 early-career researchers who gave freely and generously of their time before the workshop to collectively produce working papers and when it came to producing this book, who again big-heartedly responded to many e-mails and requests despite their busy lives as senior or junior professionals connected to doctoral education.

Maresi Nerad, David Bogle, Ulrike Kohl, Conor O'Carroll,
Christian Peters and Beate Scholz.

List of contributors

Editors

Maresi Nerad is Founding Director of the Center for Innovation and Research in Graduate Education (CIRGE), Professor Emeritus for Higher Education at the University of Washington in Seattle and Affiliate Faculty at UC Berkeley's Center for Studies in Higher Education. She serves on international university advisory boards and review committees related to doctoral education in the US and worldwide, writes together with current and former students, and advises and coaches on a broad range of issues in doctoral education worldwide.

David Bogle (I.D.L. Bogle) is Pro-Vice-Provost of the Doctoral School (Graduate Dean) at UCL. He is also Professor of Chemical Engineering with research interests in Process Systems Engineering and Systems Biology. He chairs the Doctoral Studies Policy Group of the League of European Research Universities (LERU) and sits on a number of advisory boards for doctoral education across Europe.

Ulrike Kohl is director of ErwuesseBildung Luxembourg, a non-profit association in the domain of personal and professional development and training. She formerly worked as Head of HR in one of Luxembourg's research institutes and during 17 years at the Luxembourg National Research Fund where she coordinated the activities on doctoral training and research careers. She contributed to the set-up of the Luxembourg National Quality Framework for Doctoral Training in 2015. She is a part-time coach and research career consultant.

Conor O'Carroll is an Independent Consultant on Higher Education and Research Policy at SciPol. He is active in the development of European policy on researcher careers with a particular focus on doctoral education and training and led the development of the European Innovative Doctoral Training Principles.

Christian Peters is a political scientist and Managing Director of the Bremen International Graduate School of Social Science (University of Bremen/Jacobs University Bremen). Besides managing a research unit with more than 70 early-career researchers, he has interests in populism studies, the political impact of new media technology and the relationship of religion and politics.

Beate Scholz is founder and director of Scholz CTC GmbH. As strategy consultant, trainer, coach, reviewer and researcher, she focuses on researchers' career development with special attention to doctoral education and equal opportunity. She works internationally with individual researchers and research policymakers as well as with universities, research funders and research performing institutions. Scholz was in charge of moderating the Herrenhausen Conference.

Contributors

Sophie Abel is a doctoral candidate at the Connected Intelligence Centre at the University of Technology in Sydney, Australia. Her research focuses on how writing analytics, the use of text analytics techniques to provide automated feedback on writing, can be used in doctoral writing training programmes to develop evaluative judgement and encourage one to think critically about their writing.

Corina Balaban is an honorary research associate at the Manchester Institute of Innovation Research at the University of Manchester, UK. Her PhD thesis compared flagship models of doctoral education in the EU and the US.

Andrés Bernasconi is Professor of Education and Director of the Center of Advanced Studies in Educational Justice at the Pontificia Universidad Católica de Chile. Interested in higher-education policy, university governance and the academic profession, Bernasconi has served as Provost, Vice-President for Research and Graduate Programmes, Vice-Dean and Dean at three universities.

Daniele Cantini is a social anthropologist currently working at the University of Halle, Germany. He earned his PhD in social anthropology at the University of Modena in 2006. He lived and conducted fieldwork for several years in some Middle East countries, including Egypt, Israel/Palestine, Jordan, Lebanon and Syria. He taught at universities in Germany (Halle) and Italy (Milano-Bicocca, Modena), lead a research project funded by the German Ministry of Education and Research and participated in several others, with funding from France, Italy and the United States. He authored *Youth and Education in the Middle East: Shaping identity and politics in Jordan* (London: I.B. Tauris & Co., 2016).

Hongjie Chen is Professor at the School of Education at Peking University and director of the Chinese Center for Doctoral Education. He has written several publications about doctoral education in China and Germany. He is currently working on a project concerning the reform of the doctoral grant system in China.

Manuel S. González Canché is associate professor in the Graduate School of Education at the University of Pennsylvania, USA. He brings an innovative set of tools – including econometric, geospatial and network analysis methods – to study the structural factors that influence minority and at-risk students' likelihood of success, including less access to financial, academic and social resources. He aims to identify plans of action capable of closing these social and economic gaps. His work has already challenged traditional ideas about access, persistence and success in higher education and has led to a better understanding of the effect of location, influence and competition.

Devasmita Chakraverty is Associate Professor at the Ravi J. Matthai Centre for Educational Innovation at the Indian Institute of Management in Ahmedabad. Her research interests include examining the impostor phenomenon ('impostor syndrome'), workforce development in STEM and medicine and understanding the experiences of underrepresented minority groups. Her research focuses on the US, India and Germany.

Roxana Chiappa completed her PhD in higher education from University of Washington, Seattle (2019) with a dissertation that analysed the effects of social class of origin on the career of doctorate holders in Chile. Currently, her research is looking at the role of academic elites in allowing the entrance of women and PhDs from the working class into the academic profession in the fields of economics, law and industrial engineering. Roxana is affiliated to the University of Tarapacá (Chile), the Rhodes University (South Africa), the Centre for Social Conflict and Cohesion Studies, COES (Chile) and the Center for Innovation and Research in Postgraduate Education, CIRGE (US).

Igor Chirikov is Student Experience in the Research (SERU) Consortium Director and Senior Researcher at UC Berkeley. SERU Consortium is an academic and policy collaboration of research universities worldwide, aimed at generating comparative data on undergraduate and graduate student experience. Chirikov's research interests include student learning outcomes and international higher education.

Rosemary Deem is Sociologist, Emerita Professor of Higher Education Management and Doctoral School Senior Research Fellow at Royal Holloway (University of London). Founding Director of Lancaster University Graduate School, 1998–2000. 2006 Elected Fellow of UK Academy of Social Sciences. Member of three UK Research Assessment Education sub-panels (1996, 2001, 2008). Joint-Editor of *The Sociological Review*, 2001–5. Coeditor, *Higher Education* (Springer) since 2013. Appointed OBE in the Queen's Birthday Honours list for services to higher education and social sciences, 2013. 2015–18 chair, UK Council for Graduate Education. She researches doctoral education, higher-education inequalities, academic work, higher-education leadership, governance, management and higher-education policy.

Annamaria Silvana de Rosa is Founder and Director of the European/International joint PhD in Social Representations and Communications led by Sapienza University of Rome in Italy. She is Rector's Delegate in the EUA-Council of Doctoral Education and her publications also concern the distinct forms of internationalisation of doctoral education.

Liezel Frick is Associate Professor in the Department of Curriculum Studies and Director of the Centre for Higher and Adult Education at Stellenbosch University in South Africa. Her research focuses on doctoral education, with a pedagogical focus on doctoral creativity, supervision and the student experience. She is also cochair of the International Doctoral Education Research Network (IDERN).

Nancy L. Garcia is Full Professor of Statistics at University of Campinas (UNICAMP) working in the field of Probability and Statistics. She was formerly Coordinator of the Mathematics Committee of Coordination for the Improvement of Higher Education Personnel (CAPES). Garcia is currently Vice-Rector for Graduate Studies at UNICAMP and vice-president of the Brazilian Mathematical Society.

Barbara M. Grant is Associate Professor at the University of Auckland in New Zealand. She is currently exploring doctoral students' experiences of publishing during candidature, doctoral identity work in thesis acknowledgments and doctoral supervision work of academic women in NZ universities. She has published extensively on doctoral supervision/education.

Martin Grund is an experimental psychologist who investigates how brain–body interactions shape conscious tactile perception. Besides his basic research at the Max Planck Institute for Human Cognitive and Brain Sciences, he tries to make academia a place that integrates and enables the diversity of our society. In 2016 he was the spokesperson of the Max Planck PhDnet and cofounded N^2, the network of more than 16,000 doctoral researchers at Germany's non-university research organisations. Since 2019, he has headed the Science Forum Middle Germany. He is an advisor, speaker and author on science communication and science policy.

Chaya Herman is Associate Professor at the Department of Education Management and Policy Studies at the University of Pretoria. She specialises in doctoral education and higher-education policy and has conducted national and international studies on the topic.

Stefaan Hermans is Director of Policy Strategy and Evaluation in DG Education, Youth, Culture and Sports at the European Commission. He formerly served as Head of Cabinet to the Employment, Social Affairs, Skills and Labour Mobility Commissioner and has developed initiatives to make research careers in the EU more attractive as Head of Unit in the Research and Innovation DG in 2018 and 2013.

Reinhard Jahn was Professor and Director of the Max Planck Institute for Biophysical Chemistry in Göttingen with research focusing on molecular neuroscience until his retirement in 2018. He was Dean of the Göttingen Graduate School for Neurosciences, Biophysics and Molecular Biosciences, funded in the German Excellence Initiative and worked on committees proposing reforms of the academic career system.

Jonathan D. Jansen is Distinguished Professor of Education at the University of Stellenbosch and President of the Academy of Science of South Africa. He was recently Fellow at the Center for Advanced Study in the Behavioral Sciences at Stanford University before serving as Vice-Chancellor and Rector of the University of the Free State for seven years.

Biandri Joubert is a PhD student in the field of international trade law (Specifically SPS measures as non-tariff barriers to trade) at Northwest University in South Africa. As a Zimbabwean in South Africa, Joubert provides insight into doctoral research in South Africa as a citizen of a southern African country.

Lilia Mantai is Academic Lead in Course Enhancement at the University of Sydney Business School. She got her PhD from Macquarie University for research on researcher development of doctoral students in 2017 and received an HDR Excellency award. Mantai was also awarded the status of Senior Fellow of Advance HE (formerly the Higher Education Academy) for her contributions to higher education.

Charity Meki-Kombe is Lecturer and Researcher at Mulungushi University, Zambia. She took up the stated position after completing a two-year postdoctoral research fellowship with the University of Pretoria, South Africa. Her primary research interest relates to policy/programme implementation and evaluation, doctoral education (its value and students' experiences) and higher-education policies and programmes. She has consulted and undertaken national and international research projects on these topics.

Yasemin Karakaşoğlu holds the chair for Intercultural Education at the University of Bremen. As a Turcologist and educational scientist, her research interests focus on teacher training and school and university policies in a diversity and discrimination sensitive perspective. Karakaşoğlu was VP of International and Diversity from 2011 to 2017 and is Member of the executive committee of the German Academic Exchange Service DAAD.

Aleksandra Kanjuo Mrčela is Professor of Sociology at the University of Ljubljana, Head of the Doctoral School at the University of Ljubljana and Member of the Steering committee of the European University Association Council for Doctoral Education (EUA–CDE). Her teaching and research is in economic sociology and the sociology of work and gender studies. She is an editor of *Social Politics: International studies in gender, state and society*, Oxford University Press.

Gulfiya Kuchumova is an early-career researcher who recently completed her PhD at Nazarbayev University, Kazakhstan. In her PhD research project, she examined doctoral-education reforms and practices in Kazakhstan, focusing on research methods courses, supervision and cocurricular research activities. Her research interests also relate to exploring university–industry research partnerships, faculty engagement in research collaborations and graduate employability.

Marketa Lobkovitz is an associate professor of Mathematical Linguistics at the Charles University, Prague, Czech Republic. Her current research interests focus on lexical semantics, dependency syntax, treebanking and formal modelling of natural languages. She is a member of the Rector's Board responsible for doctoral education at the Charles University.

Maude Lévesque is Part-time professor at the University of Ottawa. She is also PhD Candidate in Social Work at the University of Ottawa in Canada jointly with the EuroPhD programme in Social Representations and Communication at the University of Rome in Italy. She specialises in social gerontology and professional distress in healthcare workers and recently completed an exchange with the Social Psychology laboratory of the University of Aix-Marseille in France.

William M. Mahoney, Jr is Associate Dean for Student and Postdoctoral Affairs at the University of Washington Graduate School and Associate Professor of Pathology at their School of Medicine. As a cardiovascular developmental biologist, he directs the Molecular Medicine and Mechanisms of Disease (M3D) PhD programme. He has a longstanding interest in STEM professional development, focusing on graduate students, postdoctoral fellows and junior faculty.

Joyce B. Main is Associate Professor of Engineering Education at Purdue University. She examines the factors that influence PhD degree completion and the career trajectories of doctorates in the United States. She was awarded a 2017 National Science Foundation CAREER grant to model the longitudinal career pathways of engineering doctorates.

Catherine Manathunga is Professor of Education Research in the School of Education at the University of the Sunshine Coast in Australia. She is a historian who brings an innovative perspective to higher-education research. Catherine has research projects on doctoral education, academic identities and the history of universities in Ireland, Australia and Aotearoa, New Zealand.

Shannon Mason is Associate Professor in the Faculty of Education at Nagasaki University in Japan. Her interests revolve around the lived experiences of doctoral and early-career researchers and demystifying the processes of academia, including scholarly publishing, peer review and science communication. Her current study is focused on the experiences of doctoral researchers who are also navigating motherhood.

Puleng Motshoane is a doctoral candidate researching how higher education meets the needs of a transformed South Africa. She has authored book reviews on doctoral education and coauthored a chapter about holistic supervision development in doctoral studies. Motshoane has coedited *Postgraduate Studies in South Africa: Surviving and succeeding*, in which she contributed a chapter on the benefits of being part of a doctoral team. Her recent publication is about crossing the border from candidate to supervisor. Additionally, she is a member of the International Doctoral Education Research Network.

Suzanne Ortega serves as President of the Council of Graduate Schools (CGS). The only US higher-education association devoted solely to graduate study, CGS has nearly 500 US and Canadian members and nearly 30 international affiliates. A sociologist by training Ortega's research focuses on social inequality, mental health and graduate education.

Susan Porter is Dean and Vice-Provost of Graduate and Postdoctoral Studies at the University of British Columbia (UBC), with oversight of 9,000 graduate students and 900 postdoctoral fellows. She focuses on 'reimagining' graduate education for the twenty-first century. She is also a clinical professor in pathology and laboratory medicine and President of the Canadian Association for Graduate Studies.

Ana Proykova is the Universities for ScieNce, Informatics and Technologies in e-Society (UNITe) Science Director and Professor at the Sofia University. UNITe aims to improve the possibilities of researchers in geographically distributed regions in Bulgaria. UNITe facilitates the inclusion of responsible research and innovation in the doctoral curriculum in the universities involved in the consortium.

Jing Qi is Lecturer and Researcher at RMIT University in Australia. She has published in the areas of global education, teacher education and doctoral education. Her current research focuses on capacity building of doctoral candidates by understanding the politics governing doctoral education and harnessing the global and local stock of knowledge for innovative knowledge production.

Janet C. Rutledge, an electrical engineer, serves as Vice-Provost and Dean of the Graduate School at the University of Maryland in the US. She has chaired the Graduate Record Examination (GRE) Board, served on the Board of the Council of Graduate Schools and serves on the TOEFL Board. She has been involved in national efforts to increase PhD completion rates, track career outcomes and improve diversity and inclusion.

Ronel Steyn is PhD Scholar in Higher Education Studies at Rhodes University in South Africa. She is exploring changing doctoral-education practices in South African research-intensive universities and the structural and cultural mechanisms that condition them. Previously, she worked as head of the postgraduate development programme at Stellenbosch University.

Richard (Dick) Strugnell is a Professorial Fellow and coleads the Doherty Institute PhD programme at the University of Melbourne. From 2007 to 2017, he was Pro-Vice-Chancellor (Graduate Research) at the University of Melbourne, which manages Australia's largest doctoral-education cohort. He has interests in the development of doctoral candidates for life beyond the academy, equity and internationalisation of graduate research including the establishment of joint PhDs.

Marc Torka is a sociologist of science and higher education at the Department of Sociology and Social Policy at the University of Sydney. He is Principal Investigator of the project 'International comparison of doctoral training practices' in Germany, Australia and the US, funded by the German Research Foundation.

Cyrill Walters is Postdoctoral Fellow in Higher Education at Stellenbosch University. She also teaches on the MBA programme at Stellenbosch University Business School. She is currently working on projects ranging from decolonisation within South African universities, the intersection of race/gender in higher education as well as complexity theories within leadership. She is coauthor of a forthcoming book on the uptake of decolonisation within South African universities (Cambridge University Press, 2022).

Betül Yarar is Senior Researcher for the Intercultural Education at the University of Bremen. She is specialised in sociology, cultural studies and gender studies. Her recent publications are mainly on the issues related to gendered body politics, politics of culture and the AKP's politics in Turkey in the context of neoliberalism and neoconservatism.

Aya Yoshida is Professor in the School of Education at Waseda University in Japan. Her research focuses on liberal education and graduate education. She is an editor of *The Trilemma over Graduate Schools in Humanities and Social Sciences*. She has served as Director of the Japan Society of Educational Sociology and as a council member of the Science Council of Japan.

Gaoming Zheng is Assistant Professor at the Institute of Higher Education Research at Tongji University in China and affiliated researcher at the Higher Education Group at Tampere University in Finland. Her research interest covers quality assurance of doctoral education, Europe–China higher education cooperation and international joint doctoral-education provision. Her publication, 'Towards an analytical framework for understanding the development of a quality assurance system in an international joint program' was awarded with Best Paper Prize at 2016 Eu-SPRI Forum 'Science, Innovation and the University'.

Comparative international terminology

In reflecting on doctoral education in different contexts around the globe we also need to acknowledge the different terminology in different countries and regions. Therefore, we want to remind the readers, before immersing themselves in the chapters, about key different terminologies used across continents:

Synonyms

1   Postgraduate education (Europe, Australia, New Zealand, South Africa); graduate education (North America, India, Japan, China)

2   Doctoral candidates (Europe, Australia, New Zealand); doctoral students (North America, Japan, China, India, Latin America)

3   Supervisor; advisor

4   Academic department (China, India, Japan, North America); institute (Europe)

5   Faculty, Fakultät; college or school (North America)

6   Faculty (North America); professor, professors

7   Professional competencies; generic skills

8   Doctoral school; graduate school

Prologue
The thinking doctorate and the factory model of production: cautionary tales from the South

Jonathan D. Jansen and Cyrill A. Walters[1]

Across the world, the path of the doctorate in recent decades has been marked by exponential growth, design innovation and cross-border collaboration. In institutional terms, these trends have boosted revenues, improved rankings and created greater internal efficiencies within universities under pressure to strengthen the pipeline from baccalaureate and masters' degrees through to the achievement of the doctorate. Such record growth in doctoral graduates has inevitably raised questions about the preparedness of students, the rigour of training and ultimately the quality of the degree. The urge to accelerate doctorates is a worldwide phenomenon. In South Africa, the importance of the doctorate has increased primarily due to the country's *National Development Plan* which has prioritised the increase in doctoral output from 1,876 in 2012 to 5,000 by 2030. Universities in South Africa now require a PhD for almost all academic appointments.[2]

    The purpose of this chapter is to critically examine the simply quantitative or simply growth-oriented model of production with respect to the doctorate which we call provocatively the 'factory model of production' contrasted with what is called the 'thinking doctorate'. Using examples from developing countries, an argument will be set out that foregrounds the intellectual qualities of the doctoral graduate under threat from the mass production of students holding the highest qualification of the academy.

Trends in doctoral education
The explosion in doctoral enrolments worldwide signals an important moment for the global knowledge economy. In 2019 alone, China recorded graduate enrolments of 916,500 students, of which 105,200 were doctoral students and the rest (811,300) master's students. The US, on the other hand, recorded an increase of 34 per cent in doctoral degrees conferred between 1996–97 and 2009–2010; at the same time, there was a projected increase of 24 per cent in doctorates conferred between 2009–10 (about 120,000) and 2021–22 (approaching 200,000). In South Africa after apartheid, doctoral enrolments increased by 171 per cent between 1996 and 2012, an average growth rate of 6.4 per cent, which outstripped growth in undergraduate enrolments. Since 2012 (14,023) there has been a 75.4 per cent increase in doctoral enrolments through 2019 (24,594) and an 83.01 per cent increase in doctoral degrees awarded over the same period.[3]

What explains this massive growth in doctoral enrolments in the Global South? We draw on the South African experience not because it is exceptional among middle-income economies, but as a case in point. One of the key drivers of growth in South Africa is the pressure to increase institutional revenues in the face of real declines in state funding of the country's 26 public universities. The reliance on fees as second-stream income was always an unreliable source of income given the growth in numbers of poorer students and the historic revolt of 2015–16 against the unrelenting rise in tuition costs which movement came to be known as #FeesMustFall. Under pressure from intense and often violent student resistance to fees, the government would relent and offer free higher education to students whose family income was less than R350,000 per annum. This temporarily halted the protest movement but did not account for those who were not poor enough to qualify for free university education (that is, those incomes below or just above the threshold) and not wealthy enough to pay their own way; that group became known by the moniker 'the missing middle'.

If fees could not be relied on to 'make up' shortfalls in the revenue streams of public universities, and with South African universities not enjoying the kind of income opportunities from foundations and corporations as universities in North America and some European countries, the only option available was to optimise subsidy income from the government which came through a formula that counted student registrations and student graduations (as in Australia). More pertinently for this discussion, the higher the level of the degree, the higher the corresponding income from the state subsidy. In other words, a student graduating with a PhD in Chemistry would bring in eight times more subsidy (R764,495) to a university than a BA graduate in languages (R94,169).

There is also the perception and reality that the PhD matters in international rankings for a range of overlapping reasons. Reality: one ranking system includes in its performance indicators 'doctorate to bachelor's' ratio, 2.25 per cent' and 'doctorates awarded to academic staff ratio, 6 per cent'.[4] Perception, in that the status of a university in South Africa is measured against its senior degrees such as the doctorate. The doctoral candidate or fellow produces research and some universities in fact require that a condition for the award of the degree is a published article from the research submitted to or accepted by a scholarly journal. In the South African higher education sector, the pressure is on, not only for the generous subsidy income from publications of this kind but also for the academic reputation of a department or a faculty or a university based on its research outputs.

In South Africa, a large percentage of those doctorates awarded are to international students from other African universities who see their southern neighbour as having better universities which are also relatively more affordable than studies overseas. South African universities, on the other hand, welcome other African doctorates in part because of the revenue enhancement they allow for but also because another part of the ranking systems value 'proportion of international students, 2.5 per cent' but also 'proportion of international staff, 2.5 per cent' and 'international collaboration'.[5] In other words, the doctoral graduate carries enormous potential for reputation and ranking over and above the income generated in the government subsidy.

There is another element to the problem that is somewhat unique to the Global South and that is the comparatively smaller number of academic staff with PhDs. In South Africa, for example, for an academic to be appointed as a lecturer, a doctorate is not a requirement even if there is encouragement in the system to attain the same for promotion to senior lecturer and so on. In some ranking systems, the percentage of staff with PhDs matters, apart from the fact that doctorated staff are the ones who are more likely to produce research, supervise other doctorates and contribute to the academic reputation of the department or the university.

A third interest in increasing doctoral enrolments in South African universities is the managerial pressure for greater internal efficiencies in processing [sic] students from registration to graduation. For years, doctoral student numbers would remain stagnant in the system especially in the professional fields where older, working adults with families would progress slowly for lack of funds and time. In fact, the rates of completion for doctoral degrees are still the lowest in the higher education system at 13.5 per cent compared to other degrees (master's, 21.9 per cent; postgraduate below master's, 42.8 per cent; undergraduate degrees, 17.3 per cent; and undergraduate certificates and diplomas, 20 per cent).[6]

With new funding incentives, university managements were quick to put the pressure on department heads and deans for doctoral candidates to graduate more quickly. The faster students graduated, the more revenue was generated and the less the burden of supervision on academic staff. In other words, and to put it bluntly, the chain of efficiency brings in more students and more money.

Some universities in South Africa would deploy all kinds of innovative measures to manage internal inefficiencies with respect to the doctorate. One is to delay formal registration of a new PhD until a research proposal is completed, a measure that was not only anti-intellectual (how do you complete a proposal before you are trained?) but illogical (how do you access institutional resources, such as libraries, without a registration card?). But what this nonsensical arrangement allowed was for the non-penalisation of an institution for holding students within the system without marked progress towards completion of the degree. A more logical option exercised by other universities is to require doctoral students to complete a proposal within one year of registration at risk of being deregistered unless there was substantive progress towards completion of the research idea and plan after 12 months; that is, an arrangement similar to the candidacy option for US students though less the time-penalty phase.

The costs of the exponential growth of the doctorate

One of the difficult lessons learned in South Africa is that you cannot accelerate growth in the output of doctoral graduates when there is a weak pipeline from a highly dysfunctional school system. This pressure to generate more and more doctorates for funding, ranking and throughput comes at a very high cost for the quality of the highest degree qualification in a university.

Consider the following: of the 100 students who start school, only 60 write the terminal school examination (Grade 12, sometimes called the matric exam), of which a mere 14 gain a university entrance pass (called a bachelor's pass), from which group nine go to university immediately (three later), of whom only six get a university qualification within six years of writing the matric exam and only four get a degree within six years of writing that final school examination (Spaull, 2021).[7]

In such a highly inefficient school system, it is not surprising that very few South African students are available for continuing studies beyond the first degree (bachelor's) through an honours (a one-year full-time postgraduate qualification), a master's degree and the doctorate which follows. The situation is much worse when there is also pressure on the system to redress social injustices from the country's colonial and apartheid past reflected in the unequal outcomes of doctorates by race and gender. This trickle in the flow of graduates through higher education also explains the growing numbers of African doctorates from other countries on the continent, most of which have more functional school systems.

The pressure to perform with respect to doctoral outputs remains, and with heavily incentivised systems, the corruption of quality is almost inevitable. One university pays the full state subsidy directly into the bank accounts of its academics with the result that some of their lecturers have produced an unusually large number of doctoral graduates per annum. One of us, an experienced supervisor, noted elsewhere that:

> I find it more and more difficult to supervise doctoral students who cannot write with some measure of competence or reason with some level of depth. Many South African supervisors of doctoral candidates will complain about doing remedial work with students who had a poor master's, a poor baccalaureate degree and a poor school education but managed to get to the next level with the bare minimum requirements (Jansen, 2019).[8]

It is perhaps not surprising that there have been calls across the African continent to the effect that 'quality assurance of doctoral education is now urgent', while the Council on Higher Education in South Africa has commissioned a National PhD Review[9] that focuses, inter alia, on questions of doctoral quality and graduate attributes.

The 'factory model' for the production of doctoral graduates is not sustainable and raises the fundamental question about the purposes of the doctorate in the twenty-first century.

The case for the thinking doctorate

What does it mean to study for and gain a doctorate? It cannot simply mean the ability to do the basics – identify a good research question, conduct a competent literature review, devise an appropriate explanatory framework (theoretical or conceptual device), lay out research methods, collect and analyse data and represent the findings in the light of the original questions and the framing concepts for the study. Those, of course, are the necessary elements for execution of the doctorate. But is such mechanical production of the elements of a doctorate enough?

In the context of a competitive, global economy hinged on notions of a fourth industrial revolution, a doctorate should deliver much, much more. It should engender within these advanced postgraduate students a sense of themselves and of the intellect. Let us offer a descriptive list of a few of these attributes.

A thinking doctoral student should be able to give an articulate account of her/his thesis. We often remark on the differences across contexts and cultures when it comes to the level of articulateness of a doctoral candidate in giving a crisp, accessible and nontechnical account of their thesis (argument). The statement that 'I am curious about the socio-emotional effects of lockdown learning during the course of a pandemic' is the kind of statement that captures several admirable qualities. 'I am curious' points to an open-ended and non-dogmatic approach to an interesting subject. Being curious of course takes the question away from 'implementation' (what I am doing) to 'intellectualisation' (what I am thinking). Curiosity is and should be at the heart of a thinking doctorate. Why do things happen as they do? What would happen if X rather than Y were the explanation for observed outcomes? What would a different design allow me to see about this problem?

By focusing on the socio-emotional effects of lockdown learning, the doctoral candidate is shifting attention away from the already massive output of publications on the health dimensions of COVID-19 towards the social aspects of the pandemic. Such an articulation of a research idea recognises the complexity of learning under a specific set of constraint conditions, that is, a global pandemic. But importantly, the research is timely, topical and, in a sense, opportunistic. This is a once-in-a-lifetime pandemic and being able to map its effects on learning carries considerable significance intellectually and holds direct value practically in the global moment.

It is however the conciseness of the problem statement ('I am curious about the socio-emotional effects of lockdown learning during the course of a pandemic') that says everything that an uninitiated listener or reader would want to know. This level of articulateness is a skill. It takes time and can be acquired through good supervision and constant practice. Importantly, it is a disposition towards knowledge that cannot be cultivated in the factory model of doctoral production where the rush from research question to research results proceeds at great speed for reasons outlined earlier.

A thinking doctoral student should be able to make the case for significance

The intellectual bedrock of a thinking doctorate can be found in the claim to significance. There are three kinds: personal significance, practical significance and intellectual significance. A thinking student would be able to articulate the personal value of a particular piece of research. For example, 'As a teacher working with children during the pandemic lockdown, I found that my students were stressed by the long periods of isolation from their friends and teachers; the study therefore has personal significance for me as a teacher of these young people'.

Not only is the research personally meaningful to this teacher/doctoral student, but the findings could in fact provide her with the skills to better support the children in and outside of the classroom. This is the kind of practical significance that often comes from researching the profession within which a student works.

However, the highpoint of justification in a doctoral thesis is the intellectual significance of the proposed or completed research. A PhD is unlikely to change the world, but it *can, even in a modest way,* advance our understanding of a particular problem. To continue with the example used, a powerful statement of significance by a thinking student could look like this: 'Whereas the predominant lines of research on children's education in the pandemic has been concerned with their biomedical health, this study will examine the socio-emotional effects of lockdown learning on middle-school children in underserved communities'. These kinds of intellectual demand on the doctoral student require extensive reading and syntheses of existing research on the subject such that the graduate can eventually claim with some authority that a new insight has been gained from the study of a pressing problem.

Once again, to arrive at meaningful statements of significance requires an extraordinary amount of work and a competent command of the literature that can only be attained in a system that puts focus on learning and development for PhD students as future socially conscious scholars instead of churning out PhD graduates. A thinking doctoral student should be able to give a convincing justification for the choice of a particular theoretical or conceptual frame over competing explanations for a problem. The intellectual ability to weigh competing alternatives for explaining a complex problem is and should be a central attribute of the doctoral candidate. Too often, a chosen theory is used decoratively or in loyalty to a professor's preferred theoretical orientation with respect to the topic being studied. A theory, however, exists in relation to other theories and choosing the most appropriate explanation for the problem is a challenging intellectual task.

It is a particular shift in thinking that moves the doctoral student from the mere application of a theory to a frame of mind that is willing to test the theory, evaluate the theory and measure the efficacy of the theory among rival explanations. That kind of thinking makes theory both a guide to the investigation that is simultaneously open to being refined or even rejected should the data require a rethinking of theoretical postulates.

A particularly courageous doctoral student might not even feel the need for any obeisance to established theory and have intellectual grounds for allowing the data to speak for itself (this is complex philosophical terrain but hang in there for a minute). In other words, instead of moving mechanically from question to literature to theory to design, what if the doctoral students allowed for emergent explanations from 'thick data' as in ethnographic research? Grounded theory,[10] more demanding than most students think, would be an example of a particular method of explanation in qualitative inquiry.

Such an orientation to theory and its uses is certainly at odds with the reproduction of extant theory where routine application matters more than open-ended questioning of theory or its abandonment in favour of emerging explanations for complex problems. But the thinking doctorate demands much more than facility with techniques and methods; it also requires a social consciousness about ethics and politics in the research endeavour.

Ethics and politics in the thinking doctorate

The point made thus far is that the doctorate cannot simply produce someone who is narrowly competent in the techniques of research. We therefore make the case for new conceptions of the doctorate which grapple with the broader education of the graduate rather than simply the mechanical production of degreed students. And we illustrate the dangers of a lack of a social consciousness in research through a powerful example of how things can go dangerously wrong if students (and their supervisors) are unaware of the ethical and political pitfalls inherent in the conduct of inquiry involving human subjects.

In April 2019, a Stellenbosch University (SU) professor and four of her postgraduate students in a Sports Science department published a research report in which they claimed that 'coloured women in South Africa have an increased risk of low cognitive functioning, as they present with low education levels and unhealthy lifestyle behaviours.'[11] Read bluntly, coloured women are both unintelligent and unhealthy.

A group of university academics who discovered the publication started an online petition signed by more than 10,000 people to demand that the journal withdraw the article.[12] Shortly afterwards, the editors and publisher of the online journal, *Aging, Neuropsychology, and Cognition*, did in fact withdraw the article noting that 'assertions about 'coloured' South African women based on the data presented... cannot be supported by this study'.[13]

Across the campuses of this former white university, there was immediate outrage especially among black students and staff who objected to 'the use of stigmatising race-based categories in science and research'.[14] A number of symposia[15] were convened in response to the crisis in which senior academics addressed issues such as the legacy of historical racism in university, the role of various disciplines (like anthropology) complicit in racist science and the genetic refutation of the idea of separate races and the use of racial categories for marking out humanity.

In these public fora, questions were asked about ethical review – how did the protocols for the study escape scrutiny *within the institution*? The research was funded by a state agency, the National Research Foundation of South Africa, raising further questions about standards of external review. And how did the research pass peer review by an international journal?[16]

The university management showed an evolution of outrage that started with an appeal to 'rigorous discussion and critical debate' in the first reaction (24 April), to an 'unconditional apology' in the second response (30 April), concluding with emotive expressions that included words such as 'disbelief ', 'appalled', 'saddened', 'wrong', 'indefensible' and an invitation 'to reinvent Stellenbosch University' in the third and final statement (21 May). The senate of the university passed a unanimous motion condemning the article and committed the university to 'a module on anti-racism, democracy and critical citizenship to all first-year students'.[17] A common core curriculum was piloted, in which undergraduate students were exposed to 'big questions' about race, identity, fairness and the problem of change across the disciplines.

Taking a step back from the crude racism in this published research, there are much more complex issues of ethics and politics embedded in this cautionary tale. We argue in fact that there were five major problems with this research in which three of the five researchers were doctoral students and one other their supervisor.

First, the complete lack of *self-awareness* with respect to the identities of the researchers and the researched: five white researchers studying 60 coloured women in the shadow of apartheid. That lack of social consciousness in committing this kind of research in a context where white supremacy for centuries defined the white university researchers as racially superior and the coloured women as racially inferior did not occur to the team. There was not even a paragraph or footnote on what social scientists consciously call a statement of *positionality*, that is, a statement of self-awareness about where the researchers stand or come from in relation to the subjects under study.

Rather, the research team rushed into this study as if there were no past, no history of inequality and no consciousness about the relationship between knowledge and power in the ways the disciplines at their university constructed coloured people before and after apartheid. It is difficult to conceive of doctoral training that does not introduce doctoral students to a sense of their own identities in the conduct of research, whether the topic is drawn from the natural, social or biomedical sciences. What we call a social consciousness in the doctorate therefore extends beyond methods and theories, narrowly conceived, to invite the new researchers into thinking about themselves and others in the very conception of the problem under study.

A second problem worth pondering is the fact that this research passed through local, national and international peer-review processes without any part of that system raising fundamental concern about the focus and content of the proposed inquiry. Why not? A reasonable conclusion is the peers in the university, the national funding organisation and the overseas journal saw nothing wrong with the study as proposed and eventually as published. In other words, there was no social consciousness about the ethics and politics of the research on the part of those who are supposed to be concerned about the abuse of human subjects. Such an inability to 'see' the ethical and political dilemmas of research can only mean an *institutional* bias in the review and approval of research across contexts.

It would of course be tempting for international scholars outside South Africa to dismiss the case as exceptional, something unique to a country suffering from its apartheid hangovers. That kind of passing of responsibility on race and research would be disingenuous given the sheer volume of recent publications on the lingering effects of racism in scientific inquiry from fields like modern-day genetics, as one example. Here, the powerful new book by Angela Saini titled *Superior: The return of race science* offers a rich repository of the different kinds of socially unconscious or, in our terms, unthinking research which populates the pages of prestigious journals around the world. South Africa is no exception.

The problem is institutional, by which we mean bound up within the written and unwritten rules of peer review and approval that has made this kind of research normative with the academy – unless an alert scholar or association here or there raises the concerns in the public domain. Put differently, the dilemmas of unthinking research cannot be resolved on a case-by-case basis but must be addressed at its roots – the training of a new generation of doctoral students alert to the perils of ethics and politics of science in their foundational training before embarking on advanced research.

A third problem is the easy slippage into racial essentialism and racial determinism that threads through the research of our Stellenbosch colleagues but also global research, especially in the natural and biomedical sciences. The unshaken belief that *race* is real, even biological, rather than socially and politically determined, is fundamental to social science and humanities research around the world. And yet there is so much commitment to racial essences, as in the SU research, that there is a group of women called 'coloured' who are mixed-race and therefore distinctive from Africans, whites and Indians in South Africa's racial classification schemes from the apartheid past.

In this framework, not only is race taken as real, but the behaviours that flow from a particular racial identity correspond with the classification. Coloured women, in the generalisation in the article, are therefore of lesser intellectual and inferior hygiene to other people; for this position, there is an uninterrupted line of what we elsewhere called misery research on coloured people.[18] Here is the key point: apartheid as a legal and political system might have been dismantled, but the thinking that carried the ideology of racial separateness continues within institutions including those which carry responsibility for inducting doctoral students into higher education research. Once again, racial essentialism in research extends well beyond the borders of South Africa, whether it be *Making the Mexican diabetic*[19] or more broadly in the medicalisation of race.[20]

A fourth problem is the narrow disciplinary perspective (biomedical) applied to make social judgments (social sciences) about real people. There is a long tradition in the social sciences and humanities when it comes to dealing with race and racism in the construction of the disciplines. Such awareness of the pitfalls of race in the production of knowledge enjoys much less attention in the natural sciences, medicine and engineering. On the one hand, the hard sciences are more likely to labour under the idea that science is value neutral and not susceptible to politics in the design and conduct of inquiry. In a major study on the uptake of decolonisation in curricular knowledge, that sharp line of distinction was certainly evident among academic scientists in South African universities.

On the other hand, many natural scientists and engineers tend to think of the politics of knowledge as residing only in the (mis)application of knowledge for devious ends. In other words, the knowledge itself – its origins and constitution – are themselves devoid of social interests or ideological preferences; it is only when that knowledge is applied for destructive purposes, as in the case of nuclear energy, that its politics become evident. That sense of the innocence of the sciences was blown apart by the systematic work of feminists in the field of gender and science who demonstrated that in the very definition of a problem to be studied, social interests are in play. Foundational texts in this regard include Sandra Harding's *The science question in feminism*[21] and Evelyn Fox Keller's *Gender and science*.[22]

Clearly, a doctoral student in the physical or medical sciences would in most institutions be socialised into these established ways of thinking about the political neutrality of their disciplines. These students are therefore vulnerable to the kinds of choices and consequences that traumatised the graduate students in the Sports Sciences article, where there was a public backlash against the knowledge claims about objective, positive science.

That leads to the fifth problem, and that is the massive and multiple consequences of poor (unthinking) doctoral education. In the case of the Sports Science students, there was deep damage. An investigation was launched into the validity of the coming doctoral degrees on which this fraught knowledge was based. The public criticism was unrelenting and the personal health costs were very high. In this case, the doctoral students placed their trust in the guidance and supervision of their supervisor with respect to the choice of human samples to be studied, the research questions to be pursued and the emerging results that were validated.

The least of the problems of the students was the withdrawal of the article from publication, although this, too, would have implications for young careers. If a 90-year-old Nobel Laureate and DNA pioneer, James Watson, could be fired from his Cold Spring Harbor Laboratory in 2019 after repeating offensive, unfounded claims about race and intelligence, for these new doctoral graduates the future looked bleak.

What are the broader lessons to be learned from our thesis on the thinking doctorate and what can be done to prepare doctoral students within this proposed new frame?

How to prepare students for the thinking doctorate
Our example has demonstrated that a doctoral student's research can be technically competent but socially inept. It has also shown that the student's research claims can be peer-approved and still be dead-wrong, even dangerous. We hope to have shown that your research socialisation can be such that you cannot even 'see' the political dangers. How are these dilemmas to be resolved?

We propose that higher education institutions put a brake on speed when it comes to the doctoral-education *process*. Whatever the incentives of funding or other rewards, rushing through larger and larger numbers of doctoral graduates not only has questionable economic value in terms of labour market uptake, but compromises the depth, quality and meaningfulness of the apex qualification in a university.

We further propose a broadening of the education of the doctoral student that goes beyond toolboxes and techniques to deeper and broader engagements with knowledge. But we also propose a mandatory introduction to the social science foundations of knowledge and society for all students and especially those in the natural sciences. This of course requires taking a step back from the technical complexities of the discipline and engaging with pressing social questions involved in all research, such as knowledge, identity, power, agency, race, gender and the problem of change. Without such an orientation to knowledge, a doctoral student might be well trained but not well educated, and that is a crucial difference worth pondering.

And we propose prioritising the intellectual qualities of the doctoral graduate such as judgment, scepticism, originality, sensitivity, rationality and reflexivity. These qualities, sometimes called 'attributes', should not only be learned incidentally in the course of doctoral training but as a matter of explicit design in doctoral education. Nor should a focus on these qualities be limited to the discipline (for example, computational engineering) but become part of a general orientation to knowledge. For example, the Sports Science debacle could have been avoided if the researchers posed reflexive questions as a habit in doing research: How will my research affect those studied? Does the design protect those being studied? What if I were in the shoes of the researched? Are there other possible explanations for the education levels of the sampled subjects – such as white neglect of black education? And so on.

In a world that is becoming more polarised and more dangerous in a perfect storm of social, political and environmental upheaval, now more than ever we need doctorates and doctoral graduates who can think deeply within their disciplines, think broadly across disciplines, think carefully about small problems, think courageously about 'big problems', think consciously about choices and think boldly about change.

Notes

1. Adapted from the keynote speech by Jansen, J.D. and Walters, C.A., Stellenbosch University.
2. Cloete, N., Mouton, J. and Sheppard, C. (2016) *Doctoral Education in South Africa*. Cape Town: African Minds. Accessed 9 June 2022. http://www.africanminds.co.za/wp-content/uploads/2015/11/Doctoral-Education-in-South-Africa-WEB.pdf.
3. Cloete, N., Mouton, J. and Sheppard, C. (2016) *Doctoral Education in South Africa*. Cape Town: African Minds. Accessed 9 June 2022. http://www.africanminds.co.za/wp-content/uploads/2015/11/Doctoral-Education-in-South-Africa-WEB.pdf.
4. 'Methodology for overall and subject rankings for the *Times Higher Education* World University rankings 2021'. Accessed 9 June 2022. https://www.timeshighereducation.com/sites/default/files/breaking_news_files/the_2021_world_university_rankings_methodology_24082020final.pdf.
5. 'The World University Rankings 2021: methodology'. Accessed 9 June 2022. https://www.timeshighereducation.com/world-university-rankings/world-university-rankings-2021-methodology.
6. CRA (2021) *Macro Review: The education illusion*. Johannesburg: Centre for Risk Analysis. Accessed 9 June 2022. https://cra-sa.com/products/macro-review/2021/the-education-illusion.
7. Spaull, N. (2021) 'The race between expectations and realities'. National Student Financial Aid Scheme, Think Tank 2021:3 NSFAS and the funding of tertiary education: How do we balance free higher education with the challenges facing the South African economy?
8. Jansen, J.D. (2019) 'The thinking doctorate'. Hannover, Germany, Revisiting doctoral education worldwide, 5–6 September, Forces and Forms of Doctoral Education.
9. As of 1 July 2021, the National PhD Review has not been released.
10. Grounded theory comprises a systematic, inductive and comparative approach for conducting inquiry for the purpose of constructing theory. The method is designed to encourage the researcher's persistent interaction with their data while remaining constantly involved with their emerging analyses (Charmaz, K. (2006) *Constructing Grounded Theory: Practical guide through qualitative analysis*. London: SAGE).
11. Nieuwoudt, S., Dickie, K.E., Coetsee, C., Engelbrecht, L. and Terblanche, E. (2019) 'Retracted Article: Age- and education-related effects on cognitive functioning in Colored South African women'. *Aging, Neuropsychology and Cognition*, 27 (3), 321–37. Accessed 9 June 2022. https://doi.org/10.1080/13825585.2019.1598638
12. Boswell, B. (2019) 'Letter to the editorial board of *Aging, Neuropsychology and Cognition*'. Aging, Neuropsychology and Cognition. No longer available https://bit.ly/2UwthEh
13. 'Statement of retraction: Age- and education-related effects on cognitive functioning in Colored South African women'. *Aging, Neuropsychology and Cognition*, 27 (6), 963. Accessed 9 June 2022. https://www.tandfonline.com/doi/full/10.1080/13825585.2019.1614759?src=recsys
14. Motion for discussion at Senate submitted to Registrar of Stellenbosch University by 14 senior academics, 22 May 2019.
15. The first symposium was titled 'Race as a variable in scientific research – controversies and concerns', SU Tygerberg Campus, 13 May 2019; the second symposium (organized by three concerned University council members, Professors Amanda Gouws, Aslam Fataar and Usuf Chikte) was titled 'Restructuring science and research at SU', Library, SU Main Campus, 21 May 2019; the third symposium was hosted by the Department of Psychology at SU and titled 'Race, representation and psychological research', 7 June 2019.
16. Some of these questions were taken on in Wild, S. (2019) 'How long-discredited "race science" research got published from two South African universities'. Quartz Africa. Accessed 9 June 2022. https://qz.com/africa/1676892/race-science-published-from-stellenbosch-cape-town-universities/.
17. Motion for discussion at Senate, 22 May 2019.
18. Walters, C. and Jansen, J.D. (2022) 'A troubled body of knowledge: The duality of racial science in human anatomy research in South Africa'. *Comparative Education Review*, 6 (1)
19. Montoya, M. (2011) *Making the Mexican diabetic: Race, science and the genetics of inequality*.

Berkeley: University of California Press.
20 Duster, T. (2007) 'Medicalisation of race'. *Lancet*, 369 (9,562), 702–4. Accessed 9 June 2022. https://doi.org/10.1016/S0140-6736(07)60320-1
21 Harding, S. (1986) *The science question in feminism*. Ithaca: Cornell University Press.
22 Keller, E.F. (1985) *Reflections on gender and science: Origin, history and politics*. New Haven: Yale University Press.

PART I
Guiding principles and essential policy recommendations

1
The doctoral-education context in the twenty-first century: change at every level

Barbara Grant, Maresi Nerad, Corina Balaban, Rosemary Deem, Martin Grund, Chaya Herman, Aleksandra Kanjuo Mrčela, Susan Porter, Janet Rutledge, Richard Strugnell[1]

Doctoral education has become a key element of the higher education landscape everywhere. With the spread of higher education massification and the rise of the global knowledge economy that began in the late twentieth century and continues today, doctoral education has expanded tremendously. There have been significant changes in doctoral education worldwide in the twenty-first century. In many countries, the numbers of doctoral candidates and of doctoral-granting institutions have increased to help drive both national innovation and research performance of individual institutions. Worldwide, there is a greater focus on the diverse employment prospects and transferable skills of doctorate holders and postdocs. At the same time, the world is changing faster than ever, especially in the wake of the COVID-19 pandemic. There are adverse developments with yet unknown effects, namely digitalisation as a potential driver of progress and of more societal transparency, and simultaneously, the effects of the deterioration of democracies aligned with the rise of populist or fundamentalist movements. We have more research and knowledge about climate change, but also a seemingly greater denial of scientific evidence. We experience new nationalism and hate speeches, but also more awareness of the need for effective societal integration. In summary, at the beginning of the third decade of the twenty-first century, grave political, economic, media-related and cultural tensions challenge scientific work and the education of young scientists across the globe.

This chapter provides the larger contextual background of what motivated us to conduct this research project and how we arrived at the Hannover Policy Recommendations outlined in Chapter 3. We chose to place this overview chapter first to pique the reader's interest in the changes that have occurred since the turn of the twenty-first century and to help understand the 'social problematic' for the detailed analyses documented in this book. An overview of the subsequent chapters will follow in Chapter 2 which explains our approach to this interdisciplinary, international and intergenerational project.

Here we sketch trends and changes that have emerged on a range of fronts in the international scene of doctoral education over the past two decades and we discuss some of the accompanying tensions. In the later part of the chapter, we turn to two emerging concerns: challenges to doctoral candidates' mental health and the impact of COVID-19 on doctoral education. The final section of the chapter reminds us that explicit research on doctoral education has become a rapidly growing field.

Increasing participation in many countries

Since 2000, we have seen growing levels of participation in doctoral education in a number of countries, particularly in China, but also in Brazil, Chile, Malaysia, Mexico and South Africa. In most emerging economies, this growth was from a low base and mainly due to the pipeline effects from growth in universal access to education. For example, between 2005 and 2017, Chile increased the numbers of PhDs awarded by 213 per cent (from 232 to 725) and South Africa saw an increase during the same period by 157 per cent (from 1,189 to 3,057).[2] Such growth was and is also the result of governments' awareness of the role of doctoral education in the knowledge economy, an awareness prompted by policies from international agencies such as the OECD and the World Bank (for example, Kwon, 2009) and guided by economists, such as Nobel Laureate Paul Romer, among others. Many governments now link doctoral education to innovation, economic growth and global competitiveness. Some governments forget that for such a direct link to occur, many additional factors need to be in place, such as high-quality research and mentoring environments at universities, and collaboration with wider sectors of society and wider sectors of the labour market that hires PhDs, to name the most important links (Nerad, 2020a).

When we consider comparative data about doctoral participation, such as those from the OECD or the US National Science Foundation's *Science and Engineering Indicators*, caution is required as countries report their statistics differently. To give two examples: Germany includes the law and medical doctorates in their official statistics, whereas many other countries do not; Russia officially reports two different sets of data on doctorates, those who complete their PhD studies in three years (similar to what the US calls the 'all but dissertation' programme) and those who are actually awarded PhD degrees in a given year. Lastly, when looking at *any* statistics, we need to differentiate between an increase in enrolled doctoral students and an increase in doctoral degrees awarded: not all who enrol in doctoral studies complete with a doctorate. (Chapter 4 will discuss attrition as an indicator for quality assessment in doctoral education.)

Table 1.1 Increase in PhD Production 1991–2016

Country	1991	2004	2008	2012	2014	2016	2017
Australia	N/A	5,000	6,500	6,547	8,400	9,086	9,041
Brazil	N/A	N/A	10,700	13,912	16,745	20,605	
Canada (*2005)		5,600*			7,190	7,768	7,059
China	2,000	23,400	43,800	51,713	53,653	55,011	
Chile	232						725
Germany	22,000	23,100	25,600	26,807	28,147	29,303	28,404
India (*2011)	N/A	17,850	18,700	21,544*	21,830	25,095	
Japan (*2011)	10,000	16,900	17,300	15,911*	15,714	15,805	
Malaysia	750						4,556
Mexico							6,970
New Zealand							1,500
Russia	N/A	29,850	27,700	34,403	36,533	27,212	
South Africa						3,057	
South Korea	1,000	7,950	9,400	12,243	12,931	13,882	
United Kingdom	8,000	15,300	16,600	20,438	25,020	27,366	
United States	37,000	48,500	61,730	62,071	67,591	69,525	

Data sources: National Science Board, National Science Foundation. 2019. Higher Education in Science and Engineering. *Science and Engineering Indicators 2020*. NSB-2019–7. Table S2–16. Alexandria, VA. Available at https://ncses.nsf.gov/pubs/nsb20197/

Table 1.1 below uses *NSF Science and Engineering Indicators* data that have been reconciled with the various countries' peculiarities and provide full data definition.

In countries with a longer tradition of broad participation in higher education, growth in the number of doctoral enrolments is often associated with an increased number of international students, as in the case of Australia, New Zealand and the UK, where active recruitment of international students has occurred. North America has also benefited from an increase in international doctoral students, especially from Asian countries. Likewise, in South Africa, much growth flows from the increased number of international students from other African countries. Some growth in numbers is also a result of paying more attention to diversity. This is particularly evident, and fairly well established, with respect to the rise in the representation of women – for example, in Germany and the Czech Republic, but also in the US where women now constitute close to half of all doctorate recipients (NSF, SED 2020), as they do in Australia (Dobson, 2012), whereas in New Zealand they exceed the number of men (400 domestic women graduates in 2020 to 290 men[3]), albeit in an uneven pattern across disciplines/fields of study. In some countries, other underrepresented groups are also targeted for increased inclusion at doctoral level. For example, in New Zealand, a larger amount of government funding flows from the enrolment and successful completion by doctoral students from Māori/indigenous and Pacific Islands/migrant peoples, while in North America, national governmental funding agencies fund programmes targeted at increasing historically underrepresented race and ethnic groups. Alongside this common pattern of increase in doctoral enrolments, some countries are witnessing a decrease in the number of local doctoral graduates, which parallels a decrease in the overall population or in the 18-year-old cohort, for example in Japan.

A purpose under question

As the wider purposes of the university have changed over the past 50 years, the traditional purpose of the PhD has come under question. That purpose, dating back to the modern PhD's emergence in the German university system in the early nineteenth century (Clark, 2006), was to prepare male scholars who could teach authoritatively and research independently in their discipline. Their role was the transmission, conservation and advancement of largely disciplinary knowledge: thus, they would be '*stewards* of the discipline' (Golde and Walker, 2006, italics added) for the development and betterment of society and human life based on science. The late twentieth-century expansion of doctoral education led to a much more diverse population in terms of gender, age and culture. This increase occurred in the Global North, often accompanied by an absence in concomitant growth in academic positions. In the Global South countries, such as in China, India and South Africa professorial positions, especially qualified doctoral supervisors are in demand. Further, major changes in universities were followed by a closer collaboration of universities with their local communities and with industry to respond more directly to societies' needs and by expanding internationalisation and globalisation.

It is increasingly acknowledged that doctoral education should prepare graduates for a wider range of employment possibilities and that, indeed, such graduates are central to the business and public sectors of modern advanced knowledge economies (Maheu et al., 2014; Shin et al., 2018). As rationales for doctoral education have come to include a much wider range of economic and societal needs, so the putative roles of PhD students have shifted: from steward of the discipline, to thought leader in knowledge-intensive sectors beyond academia (Balaban, 2016), to individuals who can 'address the planet's and our society's most urgent needs with greater courage, imagination, humility and wisdom' (Porter, 2021). This has led to the creation of doctoral training programmes that include variously preparation for multi- and interdisciplinary research, cross-sectoral collaborations, entrepreneurship skills, internships or secondments and/or supervision in nonacademic organisations.

Different groups of stakeholders, such as universities, doctoral candidates, supervisors, and nonacademic employers, will likely have different opinions on what the purpose of doctoral education is or should be. With such a high-stakes credential, this means there can be plenty of opportunity for mis-matched motivations, expectations and outcomes. However, doctoral-education systems around the world are in operation and improving them is in the mind of many stakeholders.

New purposes also have implications for doctoral students. For example, Balaban (2018) looked at how the EU flagship doctoral programme – the ITN (Innovative Training Network) – embedded the concept of 'mobility' into its core. This was in line with the European

Commission's view of doctoral candidates as 'autonomous intellectual risk takers' (European Commission, 2011) able to work across countries, disciplines and sectors. While this mobility/flexibility is normally positively associated with transferable skills and adaptability, the study found that if mobility experiences are not accompanied by appropriate supervision and mentoring, some PhD candidates may associate geographical, disciplinary, cross-sectoral mobility with feelings of homelessness. The recent experiences with COVID-19 have already shown that some physical mobility can be substituted with online blended mobility that allows for international participation where supervisors have learned to support their doctoral candidates online, where mobility depends less on financial resources and so is available to a wider group of doctoral candidates.

Diversifying forms and outcomes

As the scope of the university and its doctoral education has steadily broadened to include new domains of knowledge, new varieties of doctorates and new kinds of doctoral outcomes have emerged over the past few decades.

New forms of doctoral degrees

Many more applied doctoral degrees have been established. Some of these new doctoral degrees, such as the doctor of fine or musical arts, are inextricably linked to artistic practice – for example, dance, musical composition, fine arts and film making – and produce a creative work in the field of practice plus a written exegesis (usually shorter than a full thesis). Others are linked to industries such as engineering or professions such as education (for example, the doctor of education), social work or psychology (for example, the doctor of clinical psychology), with coursework and a shorter dissertation related to advancing the domain of professional practice rather than disciplinary knowledge *per se*, although sometimes such theses will contribute to both domains. While professional doctorates have been offered in many systems since before the turn of the century, they have expanded in the past 20 years to incorporate new domains of professional practice. In the US, for example, there are now professional doctorates in audiology, acupuncture, art therapy, nursing and physical or occupational therapy. As can be seen, the majority of these degrees are in health-related fields. Their creation has been driven by professional associations and, while they do usually require some form of written thesis, they are not always research-based and, indeed, may be a year or so's extension of coursework produced for a master's degree (Zusman, 2017). Across the participating countries in this project, the establishment of the professional doctorate has taken place unevenly – much earlier in some countries and not yet at all in other countries, although generally expected.

New forms of dissertations

The traditional outcome of the PhD, like the purpose, has undergone change. Since the early nineteenth century, this outcome has most commonly been the candidate's thesis/dissertation, typically a sole-authored monograph making an original contribution to disciplinary knowledge (Clark, 2006). But in the past two decades, changes in the form of the outcomes have occurred.

In some disciplines, like economics or earth sciences, it has been instead a series of actual or presumptive journal papers. In parallel with new kinds of doctorates giving rise to new forms of examinable outcomes, the dominance of sole-authored monographs is being challenged even within the traditional disciplines and fields as an inappropriate 'preparation for the types of work that PhD graduates will do within and outside the academy' (Paré, 2017: 407). We are seeing collections of published papers or manuscripts intended for publication being submitted for examination with chapters by several authors (although the candidate needs to account for the contribution of any coauthors). Other forms of dissertations exist in which the research is primarily presented in non-traditional formats such as comic books or other creative art forms or in an indigenous language (allowed in New Zealand) or oral tradition (see Canadian Association for Graduate Studies, 2016 and 2018, for examples of these non-traditional formats).

Other changes swirl in contrasting directions. On the one hand, we see trenchant challenges arising from the global movement to decolonise the university, including doctoral education: indigenous doctoral students, especially, are pushing against the pedagogical and substantive constraints of knowledge-making prescribed by Western-style universities and disciplines (see, for example, Manathunga, 2020; McKinley, Grant et al., 2011). On the other hand, a trend travelling in an opposite direction is that towards more English-language doctorates being produced in non-English language institutions/nations, usually under the umbrella of internationalising graduates and increasing participation in global knowledge-making.

Joint and dual doctoral degrees

Another recent change in doctoral education is that of joint and dual doctoral degrees. Joint doctoral degrees are awarded by universities, that is by faculties and departments, which cooperate in national or transnational networks. Double degrees, also called cotutelle arrangements, require joint supervision and the fulfilment of the requirements of both universities' regulations. These new kinds of doctoral degrees often have physical mobility built into their programmes.

The dual 'outcome': the educated researcher and the dissertation

In recent decades, there has been a shift away from a singular focus on the dissertation and its peer-reviewed research publication to a dual focus on the thesis *and* the graduate as the main 'outcomes' of the PhD. This trend has emphasised 'transferable' skills and 'employability' while including the older emphasis on *Bildung*. This signifies the wider shift towards preparing PhD graduates for careers in nonacademic, knowledge-intensive sectors. For instance, flagship doctoral programmes like the EU-funded Innovative Training Network (ITN) and the US National Science Foundation-funded National Research Training Programs emphasise the traditional acquisition of research competencies alongside of training in leadership, teamwork and collaboration, as well as the ability to work across different disciplines, sectors and geographical boundaries.

Spreading responsibility

Alongside the changes to the purposes, forms and outcomes of the doctorate, the structure of doctoral supervision/advising as well as institutional structures are also under reform.

Reforming supervision

Most notable in some countries is the shift away from reliance on the single-supervisor model towards diverse multiple-supervisor models that spread supervisory responsibility more widely. Another notable reform in some countries is the emergence of oftentimes mandatory supervisor training and development (Taylor et al., 2020). Where training does take place, it is most commonly for new supervisors and/or newly appointed academics/faculty and often emphasises the institution's academic regulations. Refresher opportunities and expanded areas of emphasis, for example on pedagogy, student mental health or intercultural understanding are also common for experienced supervisors in some countries. (Chapter 5 provides detailed country vignettes with a synthesis of trends in supervision.) In some countries, supervision has become subject to codes or guidelines for practice (for example Australia, New Zealand and the UK) and increasingly part of the doctoral quality assurance process (Chapter 4 describes this in detail with country examples).

Reforming institutional structures

Spreading the responsibility for doctoral education more widely has gone well beyond reforming supervision. It has permeated institutional structures. The Bologna Process in Europe specified (in the 2005 Bergen communiqué) that member countries 'consider the need for structured doctoral programmes and the establishment of doctoral schools'.

Central Graduate Schools

In the past 20 years, we have seen internationally widespread reforms to institutional structures for doctoral education with the emergence of graduate schools as well as key senior academic and administrative leadership positions associated with these schools. A centralised structure allows for institutional oversight and greater opportunities for cross-campus innovation; it can also conduct research as a base for campus policies on doctoral education and facilitate the emergence of enhanced quality assurance (for more on quality assurance, see Chapter 4). These structures are a response to universities furthering their institutional responsibilities, despite reservations about possible increased bureaucracy or possible increases in time to degree.

A recent survey of 250 European universities from 36 countries (EUA-CDE, 2019) shows that the organisation of doctoral education in Europe has undergone a rapid transformation in the past decade. While the survey findings show the official central university administration responses to the European University Association, and thus tend to be more positive than what might actually be happening at the college/faculty/department level, nevertheless an overview of recent trends can be gleaned from the findings. As universities have increasingly assumed a more comprehensive approach towards the education, training and support of doctoral students and postdoctoral researchers, a wide diversity of practices, policies and structures has been implemented with doctoral programmes and schools becoming the dominant form of organisation in Europe. Doctoral programmes with specific elements such as taught courses, milestones, mobility options and so on are present in 73 per cent of responding universities, either 'to a great extent' (24 per cent) or 'always' (49 per cent). Doctoral schools in Europe are mostly field-specific units where the actual training takes place, for example, the Life Science Graduate School in Zürich or the Bremen International Doctoral School in Social Science. The schools oversee the development of programmes, ensure quality and develop regulations and guidelines. According to the EUA-CDE report, they exist in 62 per cent of responding universities, either 'to a great extent' (17 per cent) or 'always' (45 per cent). The emergence of field-specific doctoral programmes and schools as the predominant organisational form of doctoral education does not take away from the central role of doctoral supervisors, but the survey results indicate that, nowadays, the latter only rarely work without institutional oversight.

In North America, while a central, campus-wide graduate school (sometimes called a graduate division) has commonly existed since the early 1900s, its remit in most universities has expanded greatly in recent decades.[4] Graduate schools now tend to work collaboratively with programmes and have a critical role in leadership and innovation in the graduate and often postdoctoral realm. They are generally led by a graduate dean, who is a senior faculty member and this position tends to be on a par with other deans at the university. This centralised graduate school typically has several comprehensive roles and functions: (1) It is the executive body of the academic senate responsible for the development and oversight of high-level policies for master's and doctoral education across the entire university, such as minimum admission requirements, programme academic requirements and supervision policies (with individual programmes often having additional requirements). (2) It is the central body responsible for quality assurance in master's and doctoral education. (3) It provides administrative services related to admissions, registrations and most aspects of academic progress. (4) It oversees most graduate funding administration and policy and is the primary liaison with external funding agencies. (5) It provides a number of supportive services and programmes for students, faculty and graduate programmes. These may include professional development offerings for students (usually in collaboration with other campus units), community-building opportunities (for example, celebration of milestones) orientation, support to students and faculty for complex academic or supervisory problems and professional development for faculty and programme staff, for example around graduate supervision or administration. (6) It is the institutional 'hub' for all graduate matters and is responsible for data collection and analysis (including time-to-degree and attrition information, student experience and outcome analyses) and internal and external advocacy and representation (Nerad and Bai, 2021).

Graduate schools have spread beyond North America. In the UK, for example, graduate schools for taught master's degrees, as well as doctorates, first emerged in the early 1990s. Recently, they have become more common in New Zealand and Australia and there, too, they are gradually expanding their roles beyond those of policy and administrative oversight and often provide developmental activities for students.

Preparing for work: steering the content of doctoral education and professional development training for students

Under the influence of knowledge-economy and market-driven discourses, governments, for example, in Canada, New Zealand and the US, and national research funding agencies have steered an increase in applied STEM research. Sometimes this comes with a concomitant reduction in national funding available for humanities, social sciences and the arts. National governments tend to align their national needs with research funding priorities of certain research areas, for example bioengineering, cybersecurity and STEM learning in the US or nuclear science research and biotechnology in India.

Another current trend is the expansion in offering diverse forms of professional development training for students by central university units (often by graduate schools), a shift away from reliance on supervision/ mentorship as the sole mode of instilling general professional skills and competencies. These offerings are intended to prepare students for all kinds of careers through non-mandatory workshops and career advising and through internship programmes or other placements. Moreover, with the flow of non-English-speaking international students and the still existing dominance of anglophone journals and books in the academic publishing market, more substantial English language training is offered within the professional development courses and workshops. Increasingly, individual university and national surveys assess the existence and usefulness of the professional development training for doctoral students in light of the career path of PhD holders (examples exist in Australia, Slovenia, the UK and the US).

The pressure for efficiency: a squeezing of time-to-degree

Another widely reported trend has been towards fixed timeframes under which doctoral candidates must complete their degree. This reform (in which quality assurance has sometimes come to play a policing role) has been going on for much longer in some jurisdictions than others. It is largely driven by changes in government funding regimes, usually through mediating agencies in which academics play active roles such as research councils or national research audit exercises but also by long-standing institutional concerns about attrition for those whose study extends to many years. Commonly, governments and other scholarship-awarding bodies restrict doctoral funding to three or four years (mainly European countries) for doctoral candidates who study full time. Some countries (for example, Canada, Japan and the US) target for an ideal time of five years. Part-time doctoral study is permitted in most countries around the world, accordingly with longer completion times.

Tensions arising from recent trends and reforms: a discussion

Most of the reforms and changes of the two past decades have been a response to problems, as well as the drive for innovation and the wish for a highly educated and well-trained researcher labour force. Sometimes the wish by governments and university leaders to position high in the international rankings of world-class universities steers doctoral education to increase outputs in the form of more PhDs awarded or more articles published, without considering the context in which a quality doctoral education and research results are possible. Doctoral career-path surveys that include retrospective views of the PhD graduates on their recent doctoral education (for example, European Science Foundation Doctoral Career Tracking 2017, UK Vitae 2016, the German-based National Academic Panel Study 2018 or the comprehensive US-based CIRGE *PhD 10 Years Later*, *Social Science PhD 5 Years Out* survey, see Aanerud et al., 2006; Nerad et al., 2007) find that a good number of the changes have had positive impacts, but they also had some unexpected side-effects. We identified several questions for discussion, some of which come in cycles and so are not necessarily new.

Pressures on the supervisor–candidate relationship

The earlier-mentioned changes in the dominant model of supervision towards being more transparent and team-based has a positive impact on the doctoral candidate (empowering, emancipating, stimulating) and for supervisors and research communities, leading to enhanced mobility, innovation and the surpassing of comfort zones. At the same time, in connection with fixed time limits for the doctorates, this has sometimes meant that the practice of supervision has become more loaded with bureaucratic work as well as entailing more complex relational work between supervisors (Australia is an example – Manathunga, 2012) and between supervisor and student. The prologue of this book also describes the negative effects of pressures on time and alludes to more complex relationships of supervisor with student but also that of supervisor to the university administration.

Massification of doctoral education or not

In considering the evidence of doctoral reforms since 2000, particularly the significant increases in doctoral degrees awarded, we discussed whether this participation increase can be called a massification of doctoral education. As a consequence of considerable discussion, we decided we could not call this trend 'massification'. Available data (including OECD and NSF Science Indicators) show that neither the increase in total PhD graduates nor their numbers as a function of population size are uniform across countries. Less than 2 per cent worldwide have a PhD. The share of 24- to 65-year-olds with a doctorate range from 4 per cent to 0.1 per cent (OECD, 2019). In many ways, doctoral education is still limited and selective: to reach the stage where an individual has the opportunity to participate requires a huge amount of economic, academic and, perhaps, social capital.

In relation to this, we discussed the increased flow of international students in many countries that drive up PhD 'production'. Some countries with new strong levels of participation at the undergraduate level remain reliant for growth at the doctoral level on incoming flows of international students. In middle-income countries, where faculty at universities generally lack a PhD, there is enormous potential demand for doctoral graduates. In these cases, an increase in doctoral degrees by local and international PhD holders is highly desirable to fill the ranks of much-needed university academic staff (for example, in Chile, India and South Africa). However, the future of this flow is unclear as the countries of origin build stronger higher-education systems of their own and as the COVID-19 pandemic and climate change start to limit international travel.

Widening the field of employment

Limited employment prospects in academia for doctoral graduates come up again and again, with concerns about the dearth of academic employment opportunities in countries producing large numbers of PhDs. Public media contribute to the myth of the unemployed PhD focusing solely on the academic sector and ignoring other labour market sectors such as government, industry, business and non-profits. In China, with a rapidly growing higher education sector, there are reports of a shortage of opportunities for academic positions in the urban universities, which is where most doctoral holders want to be employed, focusing on a restricted geographical and labour market area. But considering the entire labour market and not solely the academic sector, PhDs have the lowest unemployment rate in a nation's population.

In the US, a country with a steady increase of PhD production between 2000 and 2019 (from 41,369 to 55,703, not including medicine and law doctorates (NSF, 2020; SED, 2019)), the unemployment rate of PhDs is 2.5 per cent for people 25 years and over (Bureau of Labour Statistics, current population survey 2020).[5] Societies need people who can do research in all sectors of employment. Societies also need people who can operate in complex situations, provide evidence and understand causal connections and relations. Nevertheless, we must not shy away from a discussion of the employment possibilities of doctorates, nor postpone the discussion by creating more postdoctoral ('holding') positions without a career path available.

Education at home or abroad

A related tension is experienced by countries where doctoral education is newer and less well established. These countries have tended to rely substantially on scholarship programmes for doctoral studies abroad. Today, these countries experience tension between continuing to invest in such scholarships, hiring international PhD holders or investing instead in the development of local capabilities for doctoral education that may eventually reduce the need to send people abroad: examples are Brazil, albeit formerly and Chile.

Concerns

Tensions and major concerns have arisen in all countries and most doctoral programmes alike. Recent studies of the worsening wellbeing of doctoral candidates and the shock of COVID-19 have dominated the field of doctoral education since 2020.

Worsening mental health?

Current discussions about postgraduate researchers' mental health in many Western countries suggests the incidence of worsening mental health appears greater for this group than for the general population, including other highly educated adults. These discussions predate COVID-19. For example, a major study of well-paid doctoral researchers in Belgium (Levecque et al., 2017) confirmed a high incidence of mental health problems. A 2019 German survey of some 2,500 doctoral researchers found around 18 per cent showed moderate to severe depression symptoms and almost 63 per cent showed a moderate to high state of anxiety (PhDnet Survey Group, 2020). Likewise, an analysis of over 1,000 responses from a 2019 *Nature* PhD student survey and a 2020 Wellcome Trust research culture survey found that 37 per cent had sought help for anxiety or depression (Cornell, 2020). A similar picture is found in the US, both pre-pandemic (Flaherty, 2018) and post-pandemic (Soria et al., 2021). We noted that these studies are relatively small in scale with a limited literature review (Mackie and Bates, 2018; Schmidt and Hansson, 2018).

  A 2020 study by the US GradSERU consortium at the University of California Berkeley[6] that surveyed 8,500 doctoral students across nine public US research universities found doctoral students experienced major depressive disorders stress at an only slightly higher level (38 per cent) than undergraduates (35 per cent). Similarly, a longitudinal research project carried out in New Zealand, involving both undergraduates and those transitioning to doctoral study, has found that the incidence of mental health problems is only marginally higher for doctoral researchers than undergraduates (Winter et al., 2020).

Many remedies for improving doctoral mental health and wellbeing have been suggested (Metcalfe et al., 2020; Waight and Giordano, 2018). A good number emphasise the dispositions of those who have taken up doctoral study, for example, taking steps to build individual resilience is one common approach. Others propose that supervisors receive training to recognise mental health problems and know where to refer students to access adequate support. A study found that through peer support, most students learned to take responsibility for their progress by owning their research programme and meeting milestones, with supervisors helping in the process of developing self-agency and in supporting reasonable on-time thesis submission (Dowle, 2020).

Relatively few strategies for assisting doctoral wellbeing have emphasised the need to change the academic and social environment in which doctoral education exists, although Levecque et al. (2017) and Mackie and Bates (2018), respectively, emphasise the significance of organisational factors and the ecosystem of doctoral education and point to a competitive, even bullying nature, including sexual harassment of women (see UK Wellcome Trust report, Moran and Wild, 2019). Also suggested is that doctoral researchers forge a sense of agency and value by using their deep expert knowledge to contribute to the wider public good through activities such as getting involved in lifelong learning, helping disadvantaged school students to improve their achievement levels, promoting public understanding of science or acting as public intellectuals (Deem, 2020). This approach can encourage community-related and 'public good' activity for doctoral researchers as something positive and worthwhile, boosting wellbeing alongside enhancing thesis work.

The shock of COVID-19

We decided to include the most significant, post-Hannover conference, event, which is the effects of the COVID-19 pandemic for doctoral programmes and candidates. Many impacts are common to a wide range of countries and higher education systems (European University

Association Council for Doctoral Education, 2020; Herman and Pillay, 2021; Hume and Soar, 2020; Levine et al., 2021; Soria et al., 2021). These include impacts from campus closures, cancelled fieldwork and in-person conferences, abandoned or curtailed laboratory work, through to financial hardship due to loss of temporary teaching university jobs and the loss of paid fees and stipends before thesis completion. In addition, there were impacts to mental and physical illness with a worse overall experience for those from disadvantaged backgrounds, women and people of colour, and equally in non-Western countries. There were the tribulations of working from home with poor connectivity in cramped spaces and reduced access to non-electronic library or archive resources. As many countries went into lockdown in early to mid 2020, training, supervision and oral thesis examinations were rapidly moved online and physical mobility of doctoral researchers between countries has become almost impossible. The long-term effects of all these factors will not be evident for several years, especially delayed doctoral thesis submissions, which in turn may affect candidates' employment prospects. Mixed in with these common impacts, some countries faced distinctive challenges from the pandemic's disruption to doctoral education as the following country and region vignettes illustrate.

Australia

In Australia, from early 2020, as COVID-19 started spreading worldwide, conflicting messages were sent out to doctoral candidates as governments, institutions and individuals struggled to deal with the implications of such an unforeseen event. Given the abrupt onset of the pandemic and with little time to prepare, the procedures for getting extensions to study time were inevitably bureaucratic and blanket extensions were rare; sick leave beyond short periods was difficult to obtain. The mental health effects of COVID-19 on PhD training in Australia were keenly felt by laboratory-based students who, with laboratories closed and experiments curtailed, also experienced extended working in isolation for the first time. Humanities and social science doctoral candidates, in turn, missed being able to work in university libraries, study spaces and archives. Many international students believed that they did not get the same financial help offered to 'home' students, with a knock-on effect in consequences for basic needs like rent and food. At the same time, there was evidence of both 'kindness and duty of care shown through countless support programmes for international students and others in need initiated by state governments, local institutions and communities' (Le, 2021: 134).

Subsequent to the pandemic and because of its impact on university finances and government decisions to make universities specifically ineligible for federal 'furlough' support (that is, the 'Jobkeeper' programme), a number of Australian universities have been making academic staff redundant, so both the supervision of and future jobs for doctoral candidates have been affected. An overall impression is that Australia's prosperous higher-education system, despite its many international students and its high emphasis on market competitiveness, has not provided as much support for pandemic-affected doctoral candidates in general and international doctoral researchers in particular as might be expected.

Europe

In Europe, a report on a series of online debates held with staff from member universities explored the implications of the coronavirus crisis for doctoral education (European University Association Council for Doctoral Education, 2020). While European universities were able to swiftly transition many activities to online training for doctoral candidates, many others could not so easily be transferred. Many cotutelle supervision agreements were postponed, activities requiring international mobility through the Erasmus programme became 'blended' and all forms of doctoral-education collaboration were significantly hampered by lockdowns. Many institutions tried to enhance a sense of community for doctoral researchers through setting up blogs, social media activities, newsletters and guidelines offering tips on how to, for example, do academic work remotely, manage anxiety and deal with sleep disorders. European universities also introduced flexibility for the submission of theses. This was easier where universities could decide about deadlines unilaterally, but not where broader regulations needed to be changed. In some countries, national funding agencies granted funding extensions to doctoral researchers while, in contrast, those on EU-funded Marie Skłodowska-Curie Actions (MSCA) schemes received deadline extensions without additional funding. The report's conclusion was that the current situation will have a long-term influence on doctoral education, probably leading to more 'blended' doctoral education (2020: 5) and that the move towards online training and assessment makes it easier to have examiners and supervisors from different parts of the world with the effect of making the European doctorate more global.

South Africa

In South Africa, a study of the effects of COVID-19 on STEM doctoral students in both historically disadvantaged institutions (HDIs) and historically advantaged institutions (HAIs) found that doctoral candidates in the former suffered much more from COVID-19-related challenges than those in the latter (Herman and Pillay, 2021). Students from HDIs, mostly from rural areas, were less likely to have access to personal laptops, had smaller data allowances on their mobiles and struggled with connectivity. They were also more likely to suffer from the absence of a learning community than students in HAIs. In contrast, HAIs were better able to adapt quickly to online teaching modes and to supporting their students during the lockdown. Some home-working supervisors themselves struggled with technology and finding time for supervision amidst childcare. In some contexts, doctoral candidates reverted to 'vanilla research', which meant that the doctoral theses were not of very high quality.

United Kingdom

In the UK, university closures led to some students in university residences being corralled into compulsory isolation, sometimes with inadequate food provision. Doctoral students with temporary teaching contracts found their employment terminated. A major funder of doctoral researchers, UK Research and Innovation (UKRI), struggled with extending funding even to final-year award holders and ruled out blanket extensions (Grove, 2021). The expectation was that mitigation of thesis projects would be the norm for all other candidates. Pressure from doctoral researchers and institutions saw more funding appear, but it was still insufficient to meet all demands. There has also been concern about the criteria for doctoral awards in relation to reduced thesis data or content and how to ensure fairness for all (Houston and Halliday, 2021). However, a meeting of doctoral school heads run by the UK Council for Graduate Education in early 2021 suggested there have not yet been any changes to awarding criteria and no increase to date in thesis resubmissions.

United States

The situation in the US was not much different from elsewhere. A mid-2020 study carried out by the American Educational Research Association and the Spencer Foundation, using focus groups with doctoral students and early-career researchers concentrated especially on women and people of colour to explore the effects of COVID-19 disruption (Levine et al., 2021). Closure of the nation's schools had impacted respondents in multiple ways, from affecting working at home while trying to home-school children (common everywhere) to losing access to valuable research data from schools which had been part of research projects (a discipline-specific concern). Scholars of colour felt torn between getting on with their academic research and being asked to use their specialist expertise by the media or wanting to take part in political activism. They also noted that microaggressions and systemic bias had not waned during the pandemic.

This overview from several countries and regions shows many common experiences but also some contextual specificities. Though higher-education institutions have often tried to support doctoral candidates academically and pastorally, financial support has been more limited. In addition, with the rise of COVID infections and uneven vaccinations in some countries, travel is still limited, so even in mid 2022, international fieldwork, cotutelle arrangements, international mobility and face-to-face conferences are still limited and/or hybrid. Some developments like online training, supervision and thesis defences have positive features and may lead to longer-term changes in the norms and practices of doctoral education. However, for candidates, their concern at getting awarded a 'COVID-19 PhD' months or even years after initially expected remains a source of anxiety. Also, the labour markets they hoped to enter have been hard hit by pandemic expenditures on public health, supporting shrinking economies and supplementing workers' declining incomes, as well as by a collapse in charitable giving to many non-governmental organisations currently funding university research. The doctorate will survive COVID-19, but it may retain some of the pandemic scars for a good few years and universities will need to carefully assess the lessons they learned from the pandemic and steer towards structural and pedagogical changes where needed.

Trends in researching doctoral education

As a field of academic scholarship and research, doctoral-education studies have proliferated since the early 1990s and the disciplinary background of researchers investigating this topic has become more varied. For example, in the US (Nerad 2020b), economists wrote in the 1950s and 60s on doctoral education in the context of labour market projections. Then, in the 1970s and 80s, sociologists and economists focused on doctoral education because they wanted to understand the growth of US higher education and its international standing. In the 1990s, in the move to accountability, the Mellon Foundation, a private foundation focusing on the humanities and social sciences, funded studies to examine the most effective way to allocate money for graduate education and to reduce institutional and human costs created by long time-to-degree and doctoral attrition (Bowen and Rudenstein, 1992). Then also humanities scholars undertook research into doctoral education (Weisbuch and Cassuto, 2016). Today, scholars writing on doctoral education span the entire scope of disciplines and fields (including physics, chemistry, engineering and geography) with the commissioning of research by professional disciplinary associations and public and private research funders.

The study of doctoral education has a steadily growing academic infrastructure. Leading international higher-education journals have featured special issues dedicated to research on doctoral education. Further, specialist international journals have emerged – *Studies in Postgraduate and Doctoral Education* (previously *International Journal for Researcher Development*) and the online *International Journal of Doctoral Studies*. Research into doctoral education at regional, national and institutional levels is also generated by specialist organisations, such as the European University Association Council for Doctoral Education (EUA-CDE); dedicated research centres of higher education, such as the Center for Innovation and Research in Graduate Education (CIRGE) at the University of Washington; and by various national professional associations of graduate deans. In addition, the International Doctoral Education Research Network (IDERN), established in 2010, provides a forum for the growing community of researchers of doctoral education across the globe.

Doctoral-education research has used a variety of methodologies influenced by its diverse disciplinary underpinnings from large-scale quantitative, sometimes comparative, studies to much smaller, often qualitative, case studies. A wide range of topics has been addressed, including student retention and completion times, supervision/advising and mentoring, doctoral writing and publishing, student progress and aspirations, experiences of diverse students (for example, women, indigenous, black, working class or internationals), funding, the organisation and quality of doctoral education, internationalisation and globalisation, interdisciplinarity and transferable skills, doctoral careers and the labour market, (international) collaboration, history and ideas about doctoral education. Nearing the end of the twenty-first century's first quarter, almost no aspect of doctoral education has been left untouched by researchers and yet many more studies and exploring the specific local context by considering the national histories of higher education need to be undertaken.

References

Aanerud, R., Homer L., Nerad, M. and Cerny, C. (2006) 'Paths and perceptions: Assessing doctoral education using career path analysis'. In P.L. Maki and N. Borkowski (eds), *The Assessment of Doctoral Education: Emerging criteria and new models for improving outcomes*. Sterling, Virginia: Stylus, 109–41.

Balaban, C. (2016) 'From steward to leader: A decade of shifting roles for the PhD student' (review article). *Learning and Teaching: The International Journal of Higher Education in the Social Sciences*, 9 (1), 90–100.

Balaban, C. (2018) 'Mobility as homelessness: The uprooted lives of early-career researchers'. *Learning and Teaching: The International Journal of Higher Education in the Social Sciences*, 11 (2), 30–50.

Bowen, W.G. and Rudenstine, N. (1992) *In Pursuit of the PhD*. Princeton, NJ: Princeton University Press.

Canadian Association for Graduate Studies. (2016) 'Consultation document: The doctoral dissertation: Purpose, content, structure, assessment'. No longer available. https://secureservercdn.net/45.40.150.136/bba.0c2.myftpupload.com/wp-content/uploads/2018/09/The-dissertation-consultation-document-FINAL-ENG2.pdf.

Canadian Association for Graduate Studies. (2018) 'Report of the task force on the dissertation'. Accessed 9 June 2022. No longer available. https://secureservercdn.net/45.40.148.221/bba.0c2.myftpupload.com/wp-content/uploads/2018/09/CAGS-Dissertation-Task-Force-Report-1.pdf.

Chirikov, I., Krista, S. and Horgos, B. (2020) 'Undergraduate and graduate students' mental health during the COVID-19 pandemic'. *SERU Consortium Report*. Accessed 9 June 2022. https://escholarship.org/uc/item/80k5d5hw

Clark, W. (2006) *Academic Charisma and the Origins of the Research University*. Chicago: University of Chicago Press.

Cornell, B. (2020) *PhD Life: The UK student experience*. Oxford: Higher Education Policy Institute.

Deem, R. (2020) 'Rethinking doctoral education: University purposes, academic cultures, mental health and the public good'. In S. Cardoso, O. Tavares, C. Sin and T. Carvalho (eds), *Structural and Institutional Transformations in Doctoral Education: Social, political and student expectations*. Cham, Switzerland: Palgrave Macmillan/Springer, 13–42.

Dobson, I. (2012) 'PhDs in Australia, from the beginning'. *Australian Universities Review*, 54 (1), 94–101.

Dowle, S. (2020) 'Retheorising doctoral completions: Exploring the role of critical events, structure and agency'. Royal Holloway: Unpublished PhD thesis.

European Commission. (2011) 'Principles for innovative doctoral training'. Brussels.

European University Association Council for Doctoral Education. (2020) *The New Balance: Insights from EUA-CDE online sessions on doctoral education and the coronavirus crisis*. Geneva: EUA-CDE.

European Science Foundation. (2015) 'Career Tracking of Doctorate Holders'. A pilot Project Report. Accessed 11 September 2021. Accessed 9 June 2022. http://archives.esf.org/fileadmin/Public_documents/Publications/Career_Tracking.pdf.

Flaherty, C. (2018) 'Mental health crisis for grad students'. *Inside Higher Ed*. No longer available. https://www.insidehighered.com/news/2018/03/06/new-study-says-graduate-students-mental-health-crisis.

German Centre for Higher Education Research and Science Studies (DZHW) 'National Academics Panel Study (Nacaps)'. (2018) Accessed 9 June 2022. https://metadata.fdz.dzhw.eu/en/data-packages/stu-nac2018.

Golde, C.M. and Walker, G.E. (2006) *Envisioning the Future of Doctoral Education: Preparing stewards of the discipline*. San Francisco: Jossey-Bass.

Grove, J. (2021) 'More funding but no blanket extensions for English PhD students'. *Times Higher Education*. Accessed 9 June 2022. https://www.timeshighereducation.com/news/more-funding-no-blanket-extensions-english-phd-students.

Hasgall, A., Saenen, B. and Borrell-Damian, L. with coauthors Van Deynze, F., Seeber, M. and Huisman, J. (2019) 'Doctoral education in Europe today: Approaches and institutional structures'. European University Association Council for Doctoral Education. Accessed 9 June 2022. https://www.eua.eu/resources/publications/809:doctoral-education-in-europe-today-approaches-and-institutional-structures.html.

Herman, C. and Pillay, V. (2021) *Investigating the Potential for the Expansion of Science, Technology, Engineering and Mathematics (STEM) Research Capacity in South Africa: The case of African South Africans'*. (ASA) PhD outputs. Pretoria: National Advisory Council on Innovation (NACI) at the Department of Science and Innovation.

Houston, G. and Halliday, D. (2021) *Covid-19 Impact on Assessment of Research Degrees*. Lichfield: UK Council for Graduate Education.

Hume, E. and Soar, M. (2020). *Impact of the COVID-19 Pandemic on Research Students in Aotearoa New Zealand*. The University of Auckland: Te Punaha Matatini.

Jacobs, P.A. and Newstead, S.E. (2000) 'The nature and development of student motivation.' *British Journal of Educational Psychology*, 70, 243–54.

Kwon, D-B. (2009) *Human Capital and its Measurement*. Korea: OECD World Forum.

Le, A.T. (2021) 'Support for doctoral candidates in Australia during the pandemic: The case of the University of Melbourne'. *Studies in Higher Education*, 43 (1), 133–45.

Levecque, K., Anseela, F., De Beuckelaerd, A., Van der Heyden, J. and Gislef, L. (2017) 'Work organization and mental health problems in PhD students'. *Research Policy*, 46, 868–79.

Levine, F.J., Nasir, N.S., Rios-Aguilar, C., Gildersleeve, R.E., Rosich, K.J., Bang, M., Bell, N.E. and Holsapple, M.A. (2021) 'Voices from the field: The impact of COVID-19 on early-career scholars and doctoral students'. American Educational Research Association and the Spencer Foundation. Accessed 9 June 2022. https://www.aera.net/Education-Research/Voices-from-the-Field-The-Impact-of-COVID-19-on-Early-Career-Scholars-and-Doctoral-Students.

Mackie, S.A. and Bates, G.W. (2018) 'Contribution of the doctoral education environment to PhD candidates' mental health problems: A scoping review.' *Higher Education Research & Development*, 38 (3), 565–78.

Maheu, L., Scholz, B., Balan, J., Graybill, J. and Strugnell, R. (2014) 'Doctoral education as an element of cultural and economic prosperity: National building in the era of globalization'. In Nerad and Evans (eds), *Globalization and Its Impacts on the Quality of PhD Education Worldwide: Forces and forms of doctoral education worldwide*. Rotterdam, Netherlands: Sense Publishers, 161–206.

Manathunga, C. (2012) 'Supervisors watching supervisors: The deconstructive possibilities and tensions of team supervision'. *Australian Universities Review*, 54 (1), 29–37.

Manathunga, C. (2020) 'Decolonising higher education: Creating space for Southern knowledge systems'. *Scholarship of Teaching and Learning in the South*, 4 (1), 4–25.

McKinley, E., Grant, B.M., Middleton, S., Irwin, K. and Williams, L.T. (2011) 'Working at the interface: Indigenous students' experience of undertaking doctoral studies in Aotearoa New Zealand'. *Equity & Excellence in Education*, 44 (1), 115–32.

Metcalfe, J., Day, E., de Pury, J. and Dicks, A. (2020) *Catalyst Fund: Supporting the mental health & wellbeing of postgraduate research students: Programme Evaluation*. Cambridge: VITAE.

Moran, H. and Wild, L. (2019) *Research Culture | Opinions Research | Qualitative Report Wellcome Trust*. London: Shift Learning for Wellcome Trust.

National Science Foundation. (2020) 'Doctorate recipients from U.S. universities: 2019. Executive summary and Table 16'. Accessed 9 June 2022. https://ncses.nsf.gov/pubs/nsf21308/report/executive-summary.

Nerad, M., Rudd, E., Morrison, E., Picciano, J. (2007). 'Social Science PhDs– Five+ Years Out. A National Survey of PhDs in Six Fields. HIGHLIGHTS REPORT, CIRGE: Seattle, WA'. Accessed 11 September 2021. No longer available. https://www.education.uw.edu/cirge/phd-career-path-tracking/2261-2/.

Nerad, M. (2020a) 'Governmental innovation policies, globalization and change in doctoral education worldwide: Are doctoral programs converging? Trends and tensions'. In S. Cardoso, O. Tavares, C. Sin, and T. Carvalho, (eds), *Structural and Institutional Transformations in Doctoral Education: Social, political and student expectations*. Cham, Switzerland: Palgrave Macmillan/Springer, 43–84.

Nerad, M. (2020b) 'Doctoral education worldwide: Three decades of change'. In M. Yudkevich, P. Altbach and H. de Wit (eds), *Trends and Issues in Doctoral Education: A global perspective*. Thousand Oaks, CA: SAGE, 33–50.

Nerad, M. and Bai, Z. (2021) 'Is it time for a central campus office to ensure quality in doctoral education in the 21st century?'. In A. Lee and R. Bongaardt (eds), *The Future of Doctoral Research: challenges and opportunities*. London: Routledge.

OECD. 2019. 'Education at a Glance 2019: OECD Indicators'. OECD Publishing. Accessed 9 June 2022. https://doi.org/10.1787/f8d7880d-en. Accessed 9 June 2022.

Paré, A. (2017) 'Re-thinking the dissertation and doctoral supervision'. *Journal for the Study of Education and Development*, 40 (3), 407–28.

PhDnet Survey Group. (2020) 'PhDNet Report 2019', Max Planck Society. Accessed 9 June 2022. No longer available. https://pure.mpg.de/pubman/faces/ViewItemOverviewPage.jsp?itemId=item_3243876 and http://hdl.handle.net/21.11116/0000-0006-B81B-D.

Porter, S. (2021) 'Postformal learning for postnormal times'. In R. Barnacle and D. Cuthbert (eds), *The PhD at the End of the World: Provocations for the doctorate and a future contested*. Dordrecht: Springer, 67–81.

Schmidt, M. and Hansson, E. (2018) 'Doctoral students' well-being: A literature review'. *International Journal of Qualitative Studies on Health and Well-being*, 13 (1), 1–14.

Shin, J.C., Kehm, B.M. and Jones, G.A. (2018) *Doctoral Education for the Knowledge Society*. Dordrecht: Springer.

Sonn, R. (2017) 'The challenge for a historically disadvantaged South African university to produce more postgraduate students.' *South African Journal of Higher Education*, 30 (2), 226–41.

Soria, K., Horgos, B. and McAndrew, M. (2021) *Obstacles that May Result in Delayed Degrees for Graduate and Professional Students during the COVID-19 Pandemic: SERU Covid 19 survey*. Berkeley: UC Berkeley, Center for Studies in Higher Education.

Taylor, S., Kiley, M. and Holley, K.A. (eds). (2020) *The Making of Doctoral Supervisors: International case studies of practice*. Abingdon, Oxon: Routledge.

Turley, J. (2019) 'Ending the second-year blues: A systematic literature review of strategies and interventions implemented to support the second-year experience and increase student motivation, engagement and retention.' Australian Association for Research in Education 2019 conference paper. Brisbane: Queensland University of Technology.

Vitae. (2016) 'What do researcher staff do next? Report 2016'. Accessed 9 June 2022. https://www.vitae.ac.uk/vitae-publications/reports/vitae-what-do-research-staff-do-next-2016.pdf.

Waight, E. and Giordano, A. (2018) 'Doctoral students' access to non-academic support for mental health'. *Journal of Higher Education Policy and Management*, 40 (4), 390–412.

Weisbuch, R. and Cassuto L. (2016) 'Reforming doctoral education, 1990 to 2015: Recent initiatives and future prospects'. A Report Submitted to the Andrew W. Mellon Foundation.

Winfield, G. (1987) *The Social Science PhD: The ESRC inquiry on submission rates (The Winfield report)*. UK: Economic and Social Research Council.

Winter, T., Riordan, B.C., Hunter, J.A., Tustin, K., Gollop, M., Taylor, N., Kokaua, J., Poulton, R. and Scarf, D. (2020) 'A longitudinal study of mental wellbeing in students that transition into PhD study'. Accessed 9 June 2022. PsyArXiv PrePrints, https://psyarxiv.com/eq6xg/.

Zusman, A. (2017) 'Changing degrees: Creation and growth of new kinds of professional doctorates'. *The Journal of Higher Education*, 88 (1) 33–61

Notes

1. We want to thank two more workshop contributors: Andrés Bernasconi and Markéta Lopatková.
2. The data were provided by workshop country participants from their national data statistics.
3. Source: https://www.educationcounts.govt.nz/statistics/retention_and_achievement Accessed 9 June 2022.
4. The original purpose of the North American graduate school was centred primarily on quality assurance and administrative oversight for graduate education across the university; it was often seen as having mainly a 'gatekeeper' role in ensuring adherence to policy.
5. https://www.bls.gov/emp/documentation/education-training-system.html Accessed 7 June 2021. No longer available.
6. https://escholarship.org/uc/item/80k5d5hw Accessed: 9 June 2022.

2
Guiding principles

*Maresi Nerad, David Bogle, Ulrike Kohl,
Conor O'Carroll, Christian Peters, Beate Scholz*

Training doctoral candidates to become the next generation of creative, critical, autonomous and responsible intellectual risk takers[1] is more essential than ever in these times of epochal and unsettling changes. The editors of this book are colleagues who have worked together on many challenges in doctoral education from funding to the development of the collection of relevant decision-making data, to supporting the design and implementation of institutional policies in the US, Europe, Australia, the Middle East, South Africa and Asia. In the process we have learned to respect our diverse views and trust each other. Similarly, during the compilation of this book manuscript, we respectfully explained to each other our underlying concepts of, for example, the word 'norm' and 'normative', and at the end came to a collective conclusion on the meaning of these terms.[2]

With years of active engagement in doctoral education and a passionate commitment to preparing our next generation of doctoral graduates, we became convinced that it was time to review the changes in doctoral education, their successes and failures, and to explore ways forward for training new generations of researchers to become future leaders in both developing and developed societies.

Goals and scope of the book

We applied to the Volkswagen Foundation, a private German foundation which has allocated substantial resources to doctoral education since the end of the twentieth century, for grant funding for an international workshop and conference on doctoral education in September 2019. We invited international experts and early-career researchers (ECRs)[3] to: (1) bring together and assess reforms and changes in doctoral education during the last two decades across all continents and in various fields; (2) critically evaluate these changes for success and failures and their impact on researchers, institutions, the economy and on society more broadly; (3) explore ways of training and preparing new generations of doctorate holders for a future in testing times and (4), based on the outcomes of (1)–(3), develop meta-level policy recommendations across our diverse continents, diverse doctoral systems and disciplinary cultures. We hope to contribute to a more just and inclusive world through leadership of critical inquiry that helps expose actions that are not supported by evidence and reason. It is our hope that the readers of this book engage in translating these recommendations into their countries and local institutions, just as the authors of the following chapters have done.

We want to remind the reader that in times when nationalistic agendas are prevalent and the funding of doctoral students is more uncertain due to a global pandemic, doctoral education is a space that is not only in charge of educating the next generation of scholars and leaders, but is also a place where different types of knowledge are discovered in systematic ways, are passed on and are re-interpreted. These roles of a university, of preserving knowledge, passing on knowledge and creating new knowledge, give doctoral education unique access to individuals and institutions that are or will be in positions of authority in different political environments. Consequently, doctoral education has an extra responsibility to work towards implementation of democratic values, inclusion, diversity and equity, in short, for social justice worldwide.

The scope of this book is limited to doctoral education. It is not a book towards 'a collaboratively reimagined higher education system'. Our explicit long-term goal is to support the next generation of doctoral candidates, regardless of whether they are from Africa, Asia, Australasia, Latin America, Europe or North America and regardless of their backgrounds; whether they are considering research in engineering, natural sciences or the humanities and social sciences; and whether they study in structured doctoral programmes, individually with a doctoral supervisor/advisor or in a cotutelle, joint or dual programme. Consequently, we have emphasised that all along, ECRs were included in the planning and implementing process. It is this generation of current ECRs who need to solve future problems and move our societies forward to a more just, inclusive and humane world.

Approach

Our wish to contribute to the preparation of the next generation inspired us to plan for two events, the results of which are documented in this book. First, we called for a three-day workshop of 30 international experts and 11 ECRs from all six continents to work together to assess, evaluate and conceive possible recommendations for a way forward. Second, following this workshop, we planned and designed a 1.5-day open international conference in September 2019 for a much larger audience of relevant actors in doctoral education, including of course ECRs. Its goal was to present the assessments, the evaluations and the possible recommendations from the 41 intergenerational and interdisciplinary workshop team and receive feedback and more recommendations from the larger circle of conference participants (180). Employing a new communication technology tool,[4] we designed a highly participatory conference. The resulting final seven recommendations presented in Chapter 3 were widely vetted by all.

These seven recommendations are the core themes around which Chapters 4 to 9 of this book are organised. They are the common topical framework for the subsequent chapters.

The seven foci of the recommendations emerged from the critical evaluation of the changes and reforms of doctoral education during the last two decades and the forward thinking of experts together with ECRs both from the Global North and the Global South. The Hannover Recommendations in the next chapter tried not to homogenise our differences but are guidelines to actively learn from each other as how to act courageously within a complex context.

Conceptual framework

The preparation of an international workshop and subsequent public conference and our post-event reflection eliminated any earlier idea of a benefit of a global PhD (see title of 2008 book: *Towards a Global PhD?*).[5] In contrast, we are conceptualising a *joint core value system*, existing in different shapes and forms of doctoral systems around the world, as Recommendation 7 states: 'The pivotal goal of doctoral education must be and remain the development of original, responsible, and ethical thinkers, and the generation of new and original ideas and knowledge.'

We believe that doctoral education can become more socially just, if the hurdles, processes and requirements for doctoral education become transparent. We are convinced that having clear admissions criteria, a process of more than one person being the evaluator of student admission, written doctoral programme requirements, a well-laid-out mechanism for monitoring of the doctoral process within a supportive peer community, and a multiple-supervisor model that encourages and provides professional development training for doctoral students, lead towards a more open, fair and inclusive doctoral education.

Such a view sees doctoral education both as a process of training to undertake research by encouraging curiosity-driven, creative, doctoral research and as a passport into better employment prospects within and beyond academia. Our view does not juxtapose 'efficiency' versus 'worthwhileness'. After all, higher education and doctoral research is supported mostly by public taxpayers' money and a certain amount of efficiency in time-to-doctoral degree and in departmental doctoral completion rates is already in place. We consider a balanced efficiency model as one that questions a 12-year-long doctoral study but allows certainly more than three or four years to complete a doctorate.

Recognising the enormous diversity of different academic cultures and institutional systems, this book advocates for a core value system based on an ecology of knowledges which recognises and seeks to overcome existing inequalities in the access to doctoral education and the provision of knowledge. With the concept 'ecology of knowledges' we wanted to stress the need for the coexistence of different knowledge systems which are shaped by different knowledge cultures around the globe.

Structure of book chapters

The core value system described above underlies all of the following chapters. Equally, the chapters use the same structure to address their specific topic: (a) assessing what has changed by providing examples of various geographical regions of the world and countries; (b) critically evaluating the positive and negative effects of the changes; (c) providing recommendations and examples of how moving forward might look, given the expressed core values. In short, this book goes beyond collecting and describing what has been going on in doctoral education around the world – recently two such books[6] have been published to which authors of this book have contributed – but steers doctoral education into a responsible, *Bildung*[7] educational path. The chapters are linked by an introductory bridge paragraph reminding the reader of the 'golden thread' through the storyline of the book.

The chapters of this book were initially drafted by a team of selected experts and ECRs in preparation for the three-day workshop. The 41 workshop participants from all parts of the world, chose one of five topical working groups aiming to: (1) provide an overview of forces, structure and quality assurance of doctoral education from a systemic level; (2) focus on supervision and funding assessed from an institutional level; (3) zero in on doctoral education as capacity building in the era of globalisation; (4) discuss global labour market developments through doctoral education with an economic lens; and (5) rethink the ethical and political role of the researcher and in particular the doctoral graduate from a systems view. In preparation for the collective work of assessing, evaluating and developing recommendations either from an institutional, a political, an economic or across a social/political/transcultural view, each member completed a survey of basic facts on doctoral education in their country. These data were then frequently consulted during the conception of the working papers.

During bimonthly videoconferences (well before COVID-19) the groups came together to formulate their thinking and analysis. Their working papers were distributed before the in-person three-day workshop in September 2019. The workshop followed the format of an international workshop series developed by the Centre of Innovation and Research in Doctoral Education (CIRGE) at the University of Washington from 2005 until 2011. These workshops always included experts from all six continents, graduate deans, funders of doctoral education, top university administrators and, of course, doctoral candidates. The meetings were vehicles for stimulating cross-national research and for establishing international networks for information exchange and collaborations. During this three-day workshop meeting, the preparatory papers were presented and the subsequent discussion was stimulated by an expert commentator. The papers were then presented and further developed at the 1.5-day conference resulting in the formulation of the Hannover Recommendations. The core chapters of this book reflect the collective thinking of the working groups, the expert commentator responses and the entire group of conference participants. The workshop as well as the conference were hosted by the Volkswagen Foundation in its Herrenhausen conference centre, a renovated palace, which provided a most congenial working environment.

From the beginning of the workshop, the 11 ECRS were asked to prepare for each workshop day their views, comments and concerns relating to what they had heard and experienced during the previous day. This special role and space for daily feedback by the ECRs not only enlivened the workshop and made sure that their voices were heard, but it also provided confidence and camaraderie among the ECRs during the three days which carried over into the open public conference following the workshop.

This book began with a prologue presenting an example of research that was technically competent but socially inept, and of research that claimed to be peer reviewed and was still wrong. Building on this example, Professor Jonathan D. Jansen[8] and Dr Cyrill Walters, both from Stellenbosch University, South Africa call for broadening doctoral education and prioritising the intellectual qualities of the doctoral graduate: 'We need doctoral graduates who think deeply within their disciplines, broadly across disciplines, carefully about small problems, courageously about big problems, consciously about choices and broadly about change.' Chapter 1 presented the contextual background; Chapter 3 presents the full text of the Hannover Recommendations 2019. Each of the following six chapters in Part II, 'Contentious issues in doctoral education', focus on a particular aspect for current doctoral education referring to the Hannover Recommendations. The beginning of each of these chapters helps the reader retain the storyline of the book and bridges the contents from chapter to chapter.

Chapter 4 details the mechanisms of quality assurance, explains underlying common principles and spotlights the diversity in quality assessment approaches within their various national governance structures of higher education by presenting several country cases, the European region and a number of smaller single university cases. Chapter 5 focuses on changes in doctoral supervision and illustrates four vignettes from different world regions, taking these as examples to analyse common trends and differences in supervision across the globe. Chapter 6 examines dynamics in the global funding landscapes of doctoral education and research and expresses major concerns in funding trends and their particular consequences for doctoral candidates. Chapter 7 investigates the various dynamics of mobility (international, intersectoral, interdisciplinary and virtual) that influence capacity building for doctoral education in the context of mobility. Chapter 8 concentrates on the changing role of doctoral education in the labour market beyond academic research and teaching roles. It considers the changes made over the last decade and whether these are meeting the needs of the doctoral graduates and those who employ them. Chapter 9 reminds us that science, meaning *Wissenschaft*, and research do not function in an independent sphere within the academic 'ivory tower' but, on the contrary, are closely linked to the social, cultural and political systems they reside in. The opportunities and great tensions that these interlinked domains create will be explored and answers are sought as to what are the future roles and responsibilities of doctoral graduates vis-à-vis society at large.

In Part III, 'the way forward', Chapter 10, the early-career researchers assess their experience and lessons learned from participating in the week's immersion in doctoral-education issues and the exploration of a system of core values for doctoral-education around the world. Chapter 11 concludes with reflections by the editors and encourages the reader to leave behind the idea of a global PhD, but to implement the seven Hannover Recommendations in their countries and their local universities based on a system of core values. These recommendations and reflections are meant as encouragement and thus invitation to reflect on the framing and conditionality of doctoral education. In this sense, our recommendations may be exploited for creating a catalogue of concrete measures.

Towards a global core value system in doctoral education

Our discussions, which recognised the need for a number of different kinds of change in doctoral education, maintain a strong commitment to the value of developing an autonomous scholar-researcher with the capacity for making critical and original contributions to knowledge. The more general academic competencies that we value are critical thinking, knowing and applying research methods and design, undertaking competent data analysis, academic writing and publishing within the rules of ethical and responsible research. These traditional capacities are more and more complemented by the development of professional competencies, such as intercultural communication and skills such as grant writing, presenting complicated scientific concepts and results to a diverse audience, working effectively in teams, managing people and budgets and working effectively with people from different classes, races/ethnicities, cultures, religions and perspectives. We would like to see the capacities and attributes associated with doctoral-level work more explicitly articulated by institutions, supervisors and students alike, especially in relation to the strengths they furnish doctoral students for future employment in a wide range of fields.

We suggest finding a balance between the 'holistic' education of the person, *Bildung*, and the training for basic and applied research, as well as workforce preparedness. We are concerned by the decline in the financing of humanities and social-sciences research in many countries around the world. We are delighted that humanities and social sciences have become more than accessories in interdisciplinary research on important topics such as environmental issues, use of new energies and technological development – they have become integral to many natural science studies. We are extremely concerned that in countries like Hungary, Poland and Brazil, and in parts of the former Trump administration in the US, the social sciences are being attacked by right-wing political parties for being 'ideological' and not scientific.

The Hannover Recommendations 2019 in the next chapter emerged by reflecting in detail on the trends that this chapter sketched. Recommendation 5, to 'support more research on doctoral education for evidence-based decision-making on doctoral education around the globe', accepts that change at every level is occurring, which necessitates new research. What we have in common between the Global South and Global North is an agreement of working toward a core value system in doctoral education regardless of different programme shapes and forms around the world.

Notes

1   LERU (League of European Research Universities) (2010) 'Doctoral degrees beyond 2010: Training talented researchers for society'. Accessed 9 June 2022. https://www.leru.org/publications/doctoral-degrees-beyond-2010-training-talented-researchers-for-society.
2   The differentiation on normative/norms reveals a dilemma that has continuously accompanied the collaboration at the Hannover conference: The framework for scientific knowledge production as we know it is deeply rooted in rationalist, Western traditions of thought. Scientific objectivity and neutral value judgement go hand in hand. Normative orientation and an open knowledge process seem to stand in each other's way and the history of the twentieth century shows many examples of how the intervention of one side into the domain of the other has restricted free thought.
3   Early-career researchers (ECRs) are advanced doctoral candidates, postdoctoral fellows and professionals with a doctorate in their early years of career.
4   Slido is a Q&A and polling platform for meetings. Accessed 9 June 2022. https://www.sli.do
5   Nerad, N. and Heggelund, M. (2008) *Towards a Global PhD? Forces and forms in doctoral education worldwide*. Seattle: University of Washington Press. In the wave of effects of globalisation at this time forms and structures of doctoral education seemed to be moving towards converging. Note Nerad (2020) has identified that a convergence has happened among the forms and structure of national or regional doctoral flagship programs.
6   Yudkevich, M., Altbach, P.G., de Wit, H. (eds) (2020) *Trends and Issues in Doctoral Education Worldwide: A global perspective*. New Delhi: SAGE. Cardoso, S., Tavares, O., Sin, C. and Carvalho, T. (eds) (2020) *Structural and institutional transformations in doctoral education*. London: Palgrave.
7   *Bildung* refers to the German tradition of self-cultivation, wherein philosophy and education are linked in a manner that refers to a process of both personal and cultural maturation. Wikipedia.
8   Professor Jansen was the keynote speaker of the conference.

3
The Hannover Recommendations

1. **Establish a global joint value system for doctoral education based on an ecology of knowledges which recognises and seeks to overcome existing inequalities in the access to doctoral education and the provision of knowledge.**

We recommend:

a. establish a joint value system rooted in the universal principles of the United Nations Human Rights Charter, which should be based on respect for the individual and aim for an equilibrium of knowledges from South, North, East and West including indigenous knowledge systems in an 'ecology of knowledges';
b. realise a broader concept of education in the sense of *Bildung* by including political, social and ethical dimensions to prepare engaged and wise global citizens working to extend and translate knowledge for the public good;
c. consider as knowledge that which is defined and assessed by international and intercultural peer communities;
d. promote open science where research data and other research results are freely available in such a way that others can collaborate and contribute, with just access to data, research resources and ownership of intellectual property.

2. Foster diverse ways of operating – embracing diversity of cultures, people and universities.

We recommend:

a. support translations between cultures, acknowledging their diversity and respecting their varied ways of addressing research challenges;
b. embrace the full spectrum of people and be open to and for all on equal terms, giving those with suitable creative, critical and intellectual potential the opportunity to participate in doctoral education, including protecting those who are at risk in countries where they are striving for freedom of thought and creativity;
c. respect that different universities have their own distinctive missions and priorities that relate to their particular societal context;
d. recognise that there are diverse ways of achieving excellent doctoral education and that maintaining this diversity is an asset and guarantor for mutual learning worldwide.

3. Encourage diverse forms of mobility to develop multiple careers and ensure a more balanced distribution of talent around the globe.

We recommend:

a. provide international, intersectoral and interdisciplinary as well as virtual mobility opportunities in doctoral education in order to support exposure to new fields and to empower deep and diverse questioning leading to new ideas, assembling evidence to support these ideas and defending them to peers and to society;
b. ensure that funding balances existing inequalities between research systems by helping to address unequal flows of talent and by challenging traditional mobility patterns.

4. Ensure that the key contribution of the arts, humanities and social-sciences research and doctoral education gets strong support.

We recommend:

a. recognise the pivotal role of the arts, humanities and social sciences in critical questioning and in reflecting on basic human and social questions and technological developments;
b. review the balance of funding between disciplines continuously, particularly to ensure that the arts, humanities and social sciences are not disadvantaged in comparison to STEM fields.

5. Support more research on doctoral education for evidence-based decision-making on doctoral education around the globe.

We recommend:

a. identify attributes that are sought and needed in doctoral graduates and the ways that they are best attained;
b. support research on skills development, considering that attributes are not entirely clear or consistent and may change over time given the very diverse careers that doctoral graduates may follow;
c. track careers transparently and comprehensively to establish an evidence base for change in doctoral education, to encourage and involve alumni as agents of change and to illustrate the value of doctoral education to society at large, especially in the face of recent political curbs on higher education and research;
d. work towards standardised and shared data on doctoral education across countries in addition to national data collection.

6. Advance the institutional environment for doctoral education continuously.

We recommend:

a. continually review and enhance the way doctoral candidates are educated to ensure that they meet the needs of our times, especially in view of the increasingly complex and urgent problems, the rapidly changing digital environment and the need for understanding and interaction across cultures and disciplines;
b. address issues of lack of diversity in admissions and of high attrition rates in some disciplines;
c. allow for more flexibility in doctoral completion timeframes;
d. foster transparent processes which can be judged by clear and credible quality assurance processes for accountability to and transparency for all stakeholders;
e. provide individual fellowships alongside project funding at sufficient rates to cover adequate living costs, particularly in order to support intellectual risk taking and the full spectrum of research topics;
f. ensure that all doctoral candidates, regardless of funding source, have equal access to continuous professional development and education opportunities;
g. raise the awareness of employers around the world of the changes in doctoral education in recent decades and the value of doctoral graduates in the workforce.

7. The pivotal goal of doctoral education must be and remain the development of original, responsible and ethical thinkers and the generation of new and original ideas and knowledge.

We recommend:

a. instil social and ethical responsibility in doctoral candidates and as well a desire to stand up for their own ideas and take them forward for the benefit of society;
b. foster a culture where doctoral candidates undertake research with integrity, recognise the issues of reproducibility and the importance

of negative results and see beyond bibliometric and other quantitative parameters as a means to value success;

c. develop responsible and resilient researchers who are entrusted with defending the freedom of research and thought, limited only by ethical boundaries.

PART II
Contentious issues in doctoral education

4
On quality assurance in doctoral education

Maresi Nerad, Janet Rutledge, Richard Strugnell, Hongjie Chen, Martin Grund, Aleksandra Kanjuo Mrčela[1]

Over the last two decades, quality assurance in doctoral education has become increasingly important for governmental higher education agencies, research councils and universities. It is an arena where many competing interests are converging to affect policy and to set standards. The 'Cautionary tale from South Africa' of this book's prologue is an excellent reminder of the complexity of the many dimensions involved in assuring the quality of doctoral education.

Chapter 4 is particularly relevant for those who are involved in any dimension of assessing doctoral programmes and who want to understand the process for the purpose of improving the value of doctoral education and research training to the individual, their institution and country/region in an ever-changing complex world and with changing actors. This chapter points to the two dominant approaches of the quality assurance process, one based on the value of regulatory assurance focusing on compliance and sanctions, the other emphasises the use of formative feedback to bring improvement. It presents three detailed and several brief region and country case examples of quality assurance practices.

This chapter expands on Hannover Recommendation 6 and specifically 6d:
6. Advance the institutional environment for doctoral education continuously.
6. d) foster transparent processes which can be judged by clear and

credible quality assurance processes for accountability to and transparency for all stakeholders.

Importance of quality assurance and its stakeholders

Over the last two decades, national governments and supranational agencies (among others the European Union and UNESCO) are seeing academic research as a source of activities and discoveries that are indispensable to the achievement of vital national goals (see also Chapters 1, 6, 7 and 8). Accordingly, national higher education agencies have encouraged and, in several cases, even pressured universities to produce high-quality, socially relevant, economically useful researchers. In light of globalisation and the internationalisation of higher education governments are eager to demonstrate not only that their countries offer outstanding research preparation, but also that they can and do support world-class research efforts as well as the development of nationally based universities that offer quality doctoral education (Nerad, 2014). This intense interest in the production of qualified researchers in the context of university-based research has motivated the authors to present examples from their countries and universities that make it possible to extract good practices and to point to practices that improve the quality of doctoral education, and not simply increase the numbers of PhDs graduated but to consider the quality of the outcome and the quality of the experience of getting a doctorate.

Quality assurance in doctoral education spans from professors assessing the work of doctoral candidates within and among universities to external units and organisations that assess the quality of the entire doctoral training process with various approaches and tools. Today, the stakeholders in the process are the doctoral students who want a consistent quality of doctoral education/research training; the supervisors who want creative, analytical thinkers, who are able to perform responsible ethical research; the universities which want to be proud for offering quality doctoral education and contributing to the wellbeing of societies; the employers who want well-trained professionals; the governments who want an innovative workforce; and the public and private funders who want assurance that their financial investment resulted in a quality training of the next generation of researchers. This said, quality assurance of doctoral education sits at the intersection of governmental policies, interests of future employers, university management, supervisors and doctoral candidates as actors in the process.

In 2020, many countries, national or supranational agencies have developed documents with guidelines and standards for assuring the quality of their higher-education systems, including doctoral education. (See various country reports on the topic: US National Research Council (2003) on the methodology of doctoral programme assessment; the Group of Eight leading Australian research-intensive universities 2013; China 2011; EC, 2011; LERU 2016, South Africa 2019, India 2020).

There is no single model for quality assurance that will work for all countries, universities and programmes as the processes for selecting students, funding their candidature and co-responsibilities such as teaching assistant (TA) roles, vary considerably. Because of the complexity of the quality assurance, this chapter: (1) Lays out two basic concepts underlying the quality assurance approaches and explains key elements involved in any quality assurance process. (2) Presents three detailed country examples (Australia, the US and China) of how doctoral quality assurance plays out at the national and institutional level by walking us through the entire journey of getting a doctoral degree in these countries. (3) Further illustrates the diverse nature of doctoral quality assurance around the world, and presents results from a European survey (Hasgall et al., 2019) on the existence of doctoral quality assurance systems in 311 universities and additional, short single-university cases mostly by heads of central graduate schools. (4) Concludes with a summary of dos and don'ts from authors and participants of the Hannover conference in the form of detailed recommendations of good practices.

Basic concepts and elements

There are basic concepts and process elements that run across all national and institutional quality-assurance processes in higher education. Two dominant approaches to quality review have emerged in higher education over the past decades. One approach emphasises the value of regulatory assurance, measurement and control of institutional processes and outcomes (Krause, 2021). This approach tends to use regular audits that focus on compliance and sanctions for institutions failing to deliver required minimal standards. In contrast, the other quality enhancement approach emphasises the use of formative feedback to bring about improvement.

The quality assurance process in doctoral education involves three levels. The LERU advice paper of 2016, *Maintaining a Quality Culture in Doctoral Education*, explains these levels: (a) The first level addresses quality assurance of the structural and administrative aspects of doctoral education as implemented within a programme, department, institute or school/college/faculty, such as admission and examination. (b) The second level involves the quality of each doctoral research training programme, which may be either an individual or a structured programme within a cohort. This focuses on curriculum and progress steps in a structured program or a training plan for individual candidates. (c) A third level involves assessing and enhancing the quality of the output, that is the well-prepared independent new researchers and their research products, the dissertation and/or peer-reviewed publications.

Another way of conceptualising the quality-assurance approach is to focus on what quality resources and people are necessary for doctoral education to take place. This leads to thinking in terms of input, throughput, output and outcome. The *input* is people and resources. People at the input level are the applicants who have had prior education and are eager to begin research training, the professors who have the capability to be good advisors and teachers and an excellent research infrastructure both in the programme and in the wider university environment. The second component in the quality-assurance process, the *throughput*, pays attention to the progression of the education in transforming the doctoral candidate into an independent, critical and ethical researcher who has the skills to work collaboratively in various environments. At this stage, advising and supervision are important together with an up-to-date training programme and specific professional development activities (see Chapter 1). This stage is similar to the concept of the second level in quality assurance as defined earlier. The last step or third level is a focus on *outputs* and *outcomes*. Outputs are both the successful doctoral holders and their dissertations and/or publications. At this level, quantifiable output measures are in place, such as numbers of PhD graduates, time to doctoral degree, completion rates per cohort, external peer assessment of the dissertation and blind review of research publications. However, neither short a time to degree nor high degree-completion rates are in themselves guarantees of the quality of the person nor the dissertation. Both are efficiency measures. *Outcomes* and *outputs* are not the same thing. The *outcomes* of doctoral education are the impact doctoral holders make to the field of study, the new knowledge created and on society in their career path. Career tracking is therefore valuable information to help examine the longer-term outcomes of doctoral education.

Combining the three levels of the quality assurance process with the concepts of the regulatory and the enhancement approach, we arrive at a

series of logical steps to implement a doctoral quality assurance process as proposed by the 2016 LERU advice paper page 3:
1. Defining of expectations.
2. Setting up assessment/scrutiny processes to explore whether expectations are met.
3. Measuring key quality indicators.
4. Providing feedback mechanisms to facilitate both correction and enhancement of the system.

Keeping these steps in mind will be useful when analysing the following country cases. These elements will also allow for comparison in a heterogenous world of national and regional systems of doctoral quality-assurance approaches. Of course, we also need to understand that the development of a quality-assurance system is necessary but not sufficient. The implementation of these standards at all universities and programmes is necessary. This takes time as well as the willingness to learn, an open mind and an agreement on core values by diverse stakeholders. Open communication and an open learning culture are key in the success of such a system.

Country examples of doctoral quality-assurance processes

In the following, we present the Australian, United States and Chinese quality-assurance systems by describing the entire journey of a doctoral student/candidate from admission to degree completion with a focus on the existing quality-assurance mechanism along the way. The US and Australia have relatively seasoned and comprehensive quality-assurance systems. The key distinction between the Australian and US arrangements is that the Australian system is centrally managed by the national government and pressured by a retrospective and binary national funding system for research training. At the institutional level, the Australian system focuses on the individual doctoral candidate and their supervisor(s). The US doctoral quality-assurance system in contrast is nationally decentralised, but institutionally centralised. It focuses on the department or programme level as well as on the progress of the individual student. The Chinese quality-assurance system is very young and evolving. It started out being completely centrally steered by the government. In recent years, the government has allowed for the very top universities to define more of their own policies.

The authors of the country sections understand that the governance, accreditation and assessment arrangements in these countries and regions differ, and that these differences impact what can be imposed at a national level and what is left to individual institutions to determine. However, the purpose of reviewing the degree journey of doctoral candidates at the national level is to highlight potentially transnational elements of good practice and to allow some benchmarking among diverse systems that are all focusing on improving the value of doctoral education and research training to the individual, their institution and country/region.

Australia

Australia has a national regulatory and quality assurance agency for higher education called the Tertiary Education Quality and Standards Agency (TEQSA, https://www.teqsa.gov.au/) which was established by the government in 2008. TEQSA regularly audits universities to standards; the standards for doctoral education are defined by the Australian Council of Graduate Research (ACGR, https://www.acgr.edu.au/), which is an association of the deans of graduate research of Australian universities. The rights of international students are further protected by the Education Services for Overseas Students (ESOS) Act, specific legislation to protect their interests which impacts on various research-training process parameters, including supervisor qualifications. The responsibility for doctoral education, which inclusive of the research master's is termed 'research training', is typically managed at the departmental, school, faculty and university levels by identified staff, for example the associate dean of research training. Dissertation advisors are termed 'supervisors'. There is also a national rubric for all post-secondary qualifications in Australia called the *Australian Qualifications Framework*, a national policy which covers the requirements for doctoral education. Many Australian doctorates have limited or no coursework, though some institutions have introduced courses to better align the qualifications with those outside Australia. There will be 'soft skill training', called elsewhere 'professional competency workshops', (for example, academic writing and publishing, grant proposal writing, working effectively in teams, cultural competencies) in most institutions and an assumption that areas like ethics and integrity and intellectual property will be addressed by supervisors.

The Australian Council of Graduate Research has described six Good Practice Principles (each supported by several sub-principles) that provide the minimum Australian university compliance requirements for key components of the doctoral-training process from admission to examination. Each university has the freedom to set requirements above these minimal national criteria. These six principles are:

1. Admission requirements and processes are transparent and clearly documented.
2. Support for candidates focuses on facilitating a successful completion within a reasonable timeframe.
3. Candidates are supported to undertake original research and scholarly activities whilst developing key research and employability skills for academic and nonacademic careers.
4. Candidates have access to information on the resources available to help facilitate the timely completion of a quality research project and have an opportunity to engage with scholarly communities both within the university and globally.
5. Supervisors must provide guidance to graduate research candidates in the design, conduct and timely completion of the research project, support in publication and dissemination of research findings, and advise on the acquisition of a range of research and other skills as appropriate to the discipline and the background of the candidate. Supervisors also play a critical role in the development of both research and transferable skills to equip candidates with graduate attributes relevant to the breadth of employability opportunities open to postdoctoral candidates as well.
6. Thesis examination is conducted by at least two experts of international standing in the discipline who are external to the enrolling institution, independent of the conduct of the research, and without any real or perceived conflict of interest in reaching their decision.

Each of these key principles is supported by several sub-principles.

Admission to doctoral education in Australia will usually require the prospective identification of a dissertation supervisor before the candidate commences. At least two supervisors are typically appointed, a primary supervisor and co-supervisor(s). Supervisors are usually required to hold a qualification equal to, or higher than, that sought by the candidate, have employment tenure of at least three to four years and have usually co-supervised a successful candidate prior to being appointed as the primary supervisor. Supervisors are required to keep within supervisory load limits and supervision is seen as a right of faculty appointed into tenured positions or into long-dated employment contracts (see extensive covering of supervision in Chapter 5).

Government funding for research training is driven by a formula that includes recent completions. This component is retrospective and binary, meaning completion or not completion. Under the federal funding arrangements in Australia, only limited financial support is provided to the university for students who fail to complete their research qualifications. Hence there is pressure on universities, candidates and supervisors alike for a completion.

At the university level, most candidatures in Australia are managed and monitored by specific university committees and supported by IT systems. It is typical that the candidature is probationary until the end of the first year when a review process, known as 'confirmation', occurs. Candidates on entry into the institution agree to abide by the various university policies that relate to all aspects of candidature from academic integrity to intellectual property, to regular reporting and to maintain appropriate workplace behaviours. The confirmation process usually requires some form of public or private presentation of the research question, the research conducted to date and any outcomes. The purpose of the confirmation process is to provide the institution with a level of quality assurance over the research problem, candidate, supervisory and infrastructure support. Termination of candidature through the confirmation process is an expected outcome for a minority of candidates. In such circumstances, it is often a failure of due diligence in the scrutiny prior to enrolment and/or the subsequent fit of candidate, project and supervisor.

Beyond confirmation, the required annual report by the candidate is an opportunity for them to impress the assembled academic staff committee as to their progress, for the committee to provide assistance with additional resources and for the candidate and the supervisor to report on additional training needs. The sanctions available to committees responsible for monitoring performance can include placing the candidate under closer scrutiny through setting specific tasks or to recommend candidature termination. The annual reporting process involves a formal meeting of the candidate and supervisors with notes taken. This meeting provides a touchpoint for self-reflection on skills development, exit strategies and general acquisition of the doctoral attributes – areas such as independent research planning, execution and reporting.

As the candidate nears completion, the committee overseeing the candidature in a final meeting uses the opportunity to work through a publication strategy and to ask questions about career plans. There will be opportunities for the candidate to seek career-planning advice from the members of the committee, who may also act as referees. In most Australian universities, central career advice for doctoral candidates is usually limited. In submitting the dissertation, candidates must assert to the institution that the dissertation is their own work, and most universities also offer use of plagiarism testing software as a test of the candidate's integrity. In some institutions, candidates can submit a dissertation without sign-off from the supervisor. Usually however, the primary supervisor is required to sign-off on the dissertation as an original work that meets the standard for the qualification for which the thesis is offered.

Australia has evolved a means of assessing the quality of the dissertation that is different from many other countries. It was argued when the original PhDs were submitted to Australian universities in the 1940s and 1950s that the thesis examination would be external and independent. The physical distance between Australia and other countries where the Humboldt traditions of the modern PhD were well entrenched meant that Australian PhDs were, and are, examined externally to the enrolling institution. International examiners read the dissertation as they would a monograph or large paper and make comments that are sent back to the examination board. Doctorate examiners are usually selected from external academics, often from overseas, who have at least the same qualification along with experience in supervising and examining doctoral candidates. The examiner reports are usually vetted by the chair of examiners and the supervisor before being passed on to the candidate. The candidate can be asked to make amendments or, less commonly, to rewrite the dissertation. Even more rarely, the examiners may deem that the thesis failed outright.

Where is the oral examination in this atypical examination process? Up until recently, Australian universities did not conduct oral exams (using a *viva voce*) as part of the examination of the doctorate in Australia. Increasingly, Australian universities that have introduced oral defence examinations are using technical solutions to overcome the problems created by the necessity to travel to Australia to meet with the candidate. These solutions for virtual oral exams allow the Australian universities to maintain the core elements of the Australian doctoral examination – independent and external – while adding the inclusion of an oral defence examination.

There is no central requirement to publish as a component of the doctoral examination in Australia at many Australian universities, though there are provisions for examination of published works through a thesis with publications or thesis by publication. The rise of 'vanity' publishers where authors pay for the full publication costs in for-profit journals of dubious quality has created issues around the quality of publications when they are used in this regard, and most academics recognise that the strict use of impact factors and other metrics to determine publication quality is fraught.

The other output that can quality-assure the research-training process is an assessment of the level to which the doctoral-education process prepares the candidate for employment. Australia, like most other countries (New Zealand aside), has a poor tracking capability for doctoral graduates. Some Australian universities have joined the US Council of Graduate Schools study ('Closing Gaps in our Knowledge of PhD Career Pathways') in an attempt to learn more about the career outcome of doctoral education, but definitive results will not be available for several years.

The United States

In 2018, according to the Carnegie Classification of Institutions of Higher Education, there were 418 doctoral-granting universities in the US.[2] The US Council of Graduate Schools, the professional association of graduate deans, has been a leading voice in the discussions on quality standards for doctoral education.

Many research universities around the world have internal quality- assurance processes that include doctoral programmes, generally titled 'academic programme review', that proceed in a similar way as in the US. We include a short description here, as this has not been covered in other chapters nor in the other country case examples. The academic programme reviews are typically administered from a central office within academic affairs and may be done at a department level, including undergraduate and graduate programmes within that department or on an individual programme basis that considers undergraduate and graduate programmes separately. These reviews most often require the unit being evaluated to prepare a self-study report that will be reviewed by external visitors and internal committees. These reviews drive future planning strategies and can drive changes in programming, budgets and space for doctoral programmes as well.

Quality assurance in the admission to doctoral studies is similar at most universities in the United States. The information required from applicants to a doctoral programme needs to contain a statement of purpose, transcripts from all post-secondary coursework completed and letters of recommendation. Until recently, most doctoral programmes also required scores from the Graduate Record Examination (GRE) (https://www.ets.org/gre/) and some disciplines required scores for GRE subject tests. The GRE is a general, standardised test that was designed to measure overall academic readiness for master's and doctoral programmes. Some universities require the use of a third-party transcript evaluation service such as World Education Services (https://www.wes.org/). In most cases, doctoral admissions are reviewed by the faculty in each individual graduate programme. It is rare that these faculty are given formal training on how to conduct admissions. The prevailing assumption is that faculty will recognise quality when they see it. Often, faculty are reviewing applicants to determine which students they want to work with directly and are willing to fund on their research grants.

Over the last decade there has been much more focus on the racial, ethnic and socioeconomic diversity of applicants and students who enrol in doctoral programmes. The graduate community has engaged in exploration of how to review application materials in a more holistic way to understand the applicants as more than just numerical scores such as coursework grade point average and GRE standardised test scores.[3] Some universities have introduced preadmissions interviews with applicants, and sometimes with those who write reference letters, or have added additional materials to the application packets in exchange for the loss of the test scores. Studies have shown that the top-ranked private universities have higher average grade point averages than lower-ranked public universities for their undergraduate programmes, giving applicants from the top-ranked universities a real advantage in admissions.

Doctoral programmes are structured and typically admit once a year. They all have some set of courses with a comprehensive exam, either oral or written, or a comprehensive portfolio that measures the student's mastery of the core material in the programme and readiness to move on to the research stage of the programme. The dissertation consists of both a written document and an oral defence. In most cases the defence includes a presentation that is open to the public and a closed session with the dissertation committee. Most universities require dissertation committee members to undergo some level of review to determine that they are qualified to teach and mentor doctoral students. This is referred to as 'graduate faculty' membership. At some universities there are additional requirements for a faculty member/professor to chair a dissertation committee, such as first serving on another committee all the way through to completion, so that they have knowledge and experience of the process (see also Chapter 5).

In the United States, the completion rate of doctoral students is estimated to be a little over 50 per cent. After several studies into reasons for attrition (Lovitts 2001; Nerad 1991, 1997; Tinto 1997), the current national efforts such as the PhD Completion Project sponsored by the

Council of Graduate Schools (CGS) have helped draw attention to the experiences that students have in their programmes. This project and other national initiatives have focused attention on programme milestones, including keeping track of student progression and providing support for students to meet programme milestones in a timely manner. Conducting formal annual reviews with each student in the programme, plus monitoring time to each milestone by the graduate school, has proven to result in significant positive input on student retention, success and graduation.

Doctoral education in the US has not changed much over the past decades. The changes that have happened are relatively minor when looking at the bigger picture, but they may have had a profound impact on individual students. For example, some programmes in science and engineering are moving away from the comprehensive exams that usually come near the end of the coursework phase. Some graduate programmes have adopted more holistic portfolios that include performance in courses and early research with at least one faculty member. A recent and evolving change is that more graduate programmes are adopting student learning outcomes (SLOs) that explain what they expect their graduates to know or be able to do.[4]

Time to doctoral degree, student satisfaction/engagement and demographic information that allows comparison along these metrics by gender, race/ethnicity, age and family income (at a basic level) are provided in aggregate by the National Science Foundation (NSF) for doctoral recipients in the Survey of Earned Doctorates (SED), and each university assesses and collects their own information. The SED includes all fields of studies, not only science and engineering fields.

At the national level, the National Academies of Science, Engineering and Medicine used to conduct a multi-year data collection effort every 10 years to assess and compare doctoral programmes. The last one occurred in 2010 and produced the report 'A Data-Based Assessment of Research-Doctorate Programs in the United States'.[5] While many members of the doctoral-education community found it useful, there was no agreement that the methods used led to a best approach in assessing programmes and leading to improvement. It is likely that this approach will not be used in future.

Further, at the national level, the Association of American Universities is the group of US universities that produce the most PhD graduates. They are working on a common data set that all member universities will use to report enrolment, graduation data including time to degree and completion rates and, increasingly, career information of their PhDs in order to provide benchmarking information for the purpose of collective improvement. Similarly, the Coalition for Next Generation Life Science is another group of universities that have agreed to report data for PhD students and graduates as well as postdocs in the life science disciplines.

Information on the employment of doctorates after degree completion has become a much-valued criterion to assess doctoral-education outcome and societal impact. Twenty years ago, many people in the US assumed that most doctoral graduates pursued careers in academia. That was not true then for physical sciences and engineering and it is not true today for most disciplines. However, many employers have found value in the education provided at the doctoral level. But since many people who decide to pursue the PhD do so planning a career in academia some have started to question whether the degree is worth pursuing given the number of years needed to complete the degree. Articles abound in newspapers, magazines and blogs aimed at both higher education and general audiences that quote the low number of doctorate graduates in academic careers to suggest failure in doctoral education. Rarely will they mention that PhD degree holders have had the lowest level of unemployment, even during the great recession that started a decade ago.

China

Since the implementation of a new degree system in China in 1981, doctoral education has developed rapidly. At the beginning of reform and opening up, China drew on the experiences of the US and European countries to inform the development of their doctoral-education systems. In addition to colleges and universities, there are three other major systems that are engaged in doctoral education: research institutes, military establishments and party schools. However, colleges and universities are the central bodies of doctoral education in China. From the development of doctoral education in colleges and universities, the spread of doctoral education experienced three stages: initial development (late 1970s to the early 1990s); rapid expansion (early 1990s to 2003); and now controlled growth and improving quality. In 1995, in order to ensure equivalence with developed countries, the Academic Degrees Committee of the State Council decided to conduct a degree authorisation review every four years. In 1998, the doctoral supervisor's examination and approval authority were delegated to research training units rather than overseen by the central government.

At present, China has a doctoral-education model with predominantly academic doctorates supplemented with professional doctorates. Academic doctors are mainly trained in the following 13 fields: science, engineering, agriculture, medicine, law, management, education, economics, philosophy, literature, art, history and military. Professional doctorates exist in engineering, clinical medicine, veterinary medicine, stomatology (dental medicine) and education. In 1982, the first six Chinese-trained students were awarded doctoral degrees. By 1999, the number of doctoral degree holders exceeded 10,000 for the first time. In 2019, approximately 60,000 doctoral degrees were awarded annually. According to the Ministry of Education, as of 2019, there are total of 2,663 institutions of higher education, of which 344 are authorised to award doctoral degrees. The State Council Degree Committee is responsible for leading the national degree review system, which implements a centralised and unified evaluation.

A successful doctoral journey in China generally requires that students (1) complete compulsory courses, (2) pass a comprehensive qualification examination, (3) pass their thesis-proposal defence, (4) pass thesis pre-examination and (5) successfully master the final defence. For the final defence, doctoral students usually need to give a presentation to an examination panel that will include two to three external examiners, the supervisor and a professor who chairs the final defence. In most cases, external examiners have reviewed the dissertation before the final defence. The formal requirements and progress assessment stages of the doctoral student are relatively similar to the steps that students move through in their doctoral programme in the US, except that the review process of the thesis is also double blinded, meaning the dissertation is reviewed by an external person unknown to the doctoral candidate and the supervisor.

Most institutions require students to publish several publications in a specified, rated journal as a necessary condition for receiving the doctoral degree. However, the system has begun to change slowly in some institutions. For example, in 2019, Tsinghua University (considered one of the leading universities in China) issued a new standard which eliminated the traditional requirement that doctoral students must publish in academic journals to graduate. The policy aims to reduce the pressure on doctoral students during their studies and at the same time to give doctoral students full freedom to conduct academic exploration rather than to meet rigid publication requirements.

Another important strategy to enhance the quality assurance is a doctoral dissertation (and master's) thesis sampling recheck mechanism.

Each year, the State Council Academic Degrees Office organises a national-level assessment where a random inspection of the doctoral theses awarded in the previous academic year is undertaken through peer review. If a university has been found to have problematic theses for two consecutive years, the university may lose permission to admit doctoral candidates until certain changes are made.

There has been a long-standing argument over the quality and scale of doctoral education in China. At present, there is no conclusion. While there is some improvement of the quality of doctoral education, a 'China Doctoral Quality Survey' by Professor Zhou Guangli of Huazhong University of Science and Technology administered in 2008 and published in 2010 found that the quality of doctoral training in China has not progressed significantly in the 10 years prior to 2010, and there may even be a downward trend. To enhance the quality, government and universities still need to develop new strategies for the development of doctoral education. Specifically, it is important to enhance the quality of doctoral degrees in terms of the demand and requirement of society and the employment market within and beyond academia. For doctoral education, it is essential to enhance creativity and originality rather than focusing heavily on publications.

A recent report from August 2021[6] by the US Centre for Security and Emerging Technology found that the quality of doctoral education in China has risen in recent years and that much of China's current PhD growth comes from high-quality universities. According to the findings, approximately 45 per cent of Chinese STEM field PhDs graduate from the country's most elite educational institutions and about 80 per cent of PhD graduates come from universities administered by the central government.

The diverse nature of quality assurance

In this section of the chapter, we offer a series of brief country cases to further illustrate the diverse nature of doctoral-education quality-assurance systems and mechanisms around the world and varying levels of implementation, from the national to the institutional.

Europe

The organisation of doctoral studies in Europe is diverse as each European country has its own system of doctoral education and its own legal framework. As of 2019, there exist 1,361 doctorate-awarding universities across 32 European countries (EUA Survey, 2019). However, some convergence of doctoral education has developed due to the 'Salzburg Principles' published 15 years ago. This process was instantiated in three central documents between 2005 and 2015 (see EUA-CDE publications). In 2016, guidelines for the continued implementation of reforms were issued via 'Doctoral education: Taking Salzburg forward: Implementation and new challenges' (Salzburg Report, 2016).[7] These guidelines proposed the following: 'Institutions must be able to develop their systems for quality assurance and enhancement independently within their national frameworks. They must have the freedom to develop their own indicators for quality that correspond with the standards of the individual disciplines as well as with the overall institutional strategy.' (Salzburg Summary 2016, see 3.3). This includes that universities are to set up their own applications and admissions criteria which typically focus on the research potential of doctoral candidates. Simultaneously, in 2016, the League of European Research Universities, a group of 23 research-intensive universities, published a report 'Maintaining a quality culture in doctoral education'. This report showed how within a quality assurance cycle (setting expectations, scrutiny informed by measurements, and feedback leading to enhancement), there is room for a diversity of practices.

In 2018, the European University Association (EUA) conducted an extensive survey assessing the impacts of the 'Salzburg Process' (EUA Survey, 2019).[8] This report provides an overview of the state of the implementation of quality assurance recommendations of the 311 participating European universities as recommended by the Salzburg summary of 2016. The responses covered 21 per cent of doctoral-awarding institutions and 40 per cent of doctoral candidates in the 32 countries. The EUA survey found that 83 per cent of institutions declared that they had established an internal quality assurance system for all their PhD programmes. In addition, a majority of doctoral programmes are evaluated by some external body such as funding agencies or external quality assurance agencies at 59 per cent of the surveyed institutions (see EUA Survey 2019, Figure 21).

Furthermore, the EUA Survey 2019 showed that at more than half of the participating universities doctoral education is managed through an organisational unit, the doctoral school, which oversees the development of programmes, ensures quality, and develops regulations and guidelines in a major field of studies, for example in oceanography or materials. Many European doctoral schools oversee doctoral training in a specific field under a specific topic, often under general national standards (for example, Luxembourg and Ireland have guidelines for good practice in PhD training).

This is in contrast to the US, Canadian, Australian and Chinese graduate schools model, which is a centralised administrative unit that oversees all of doctoral education at a university (see also Chapter 1).

European universities report that doctoral education is still more likely to be organised at a disciplinary rather than institutional level (64 per cent vs. 52 per cent). Most universities reported that at least half of their doctoral programmes or doctoral schools offer required courses. The training mainly focuses on specific research competencies, professional competencies and on teaching by the doctoral candidates. Management of labs or leadership skills are less often included in the training process.

Admission procedures in the Czech Republic[9]

In the Czech Republic, the following doctoral admission process ensures high-quality doctoral students. Each doctoral applicant submits either a short dissertation project proposal prepared together with a potential supervisor or a more detailed proposal prepared on their own (prior approval of a potential supervisor is highly recommended as well). One or two letters of recommendation are also required. The application packages are reviewed by *Fakuläten* or, in US terms, by a field-specific college in cooperation with subject-area boards which are responsible for doctoral programmes. All applicants must write an entrance exam and all applicants must already have acquired a master's degree.

According to Czech law and accreditation standards, each professor or associate professor can supervise doctoral students. Other academic researchers must be approved as a supervisor by the scientific board of the university. Members of the Czech Academy of Sciences or other external experts can also supervise doctoral candidates if approved by a faculty of the university.

A national code for quality assurance in the UK[10]

In the UK, quality assurance is an example of a system where an external non-governmental body, contracted by the government, sets a quality code of high-level statements, expectations and core conditions according to which the quality of doctoral education at universities are assessed. It is up to the individual institution how it provides evidence of the existence of high quality in doctoral education. Providing high-level statements allows for considerable flexibility within each university.

The UK Quality Assurance Agency (QAA) is an independent body under contract to the government to report on standards and quality including doctoral education. In its Quality Code, the QAA sets out expectations and core practices that are required for providers of doctoral degrees. The UK Quality Assurance Agency (QAA) is an independent body under contract to the government to report on standards and quality including doctoral education. In its Quality Code (https://www.qaa.ac.uk/en/quality-code/advice-and-guidance/research-degree) and the Doctoral Degree Characteristics Statement (https://www.qaa.ac.uk/quality-code/characteristics-statements), the QAA sets out expectations and core practices that are required for providers of doctoral degrees. The Quality Code gives a set of descriptors for the doctorate, setting out what doctoral graduates need to have demonstrated. The core practices are high-level statements where, for example, 'where the provider offers research degrees, it delivers these in appropriate and supportive research environments' allowing universities to evidence how they are achieving this during the five-yearly review cycle. This is supplemented by a 'Characteristics Statement' for doctoral degrees, recently reissued in 2020, which describes the distinctive features of the doctorate in the UK. The Code allows considerable scope for innovation while still meeting the requirements: for example, programmes with 'rotations' giving experience on a range of related research topics; incorporating more formal courses and training, sometimes with internships; and new forms of professional doctorate. This creates quite a heterogeneous provision across the country, where the quality of doctoral education is judged alongside other educational levels and is not seen as overly bureaucratic because of its flexibility.

In addition, a biannual national survey, the Postgraduate Research Experience Survey (PRES), is conducted by universities across the UK. It solicits students' opinions on such items as supervision, resources, research culture, progress and assessment, responsibilities, support, research skills, professional development, overall experience and, in 2021, questions on the COVID-19 pandemic. The information in the PRES reports is used to benchmark and inform individual institutions on what works and what needs improvement.[11]

Doctoral candidate voices in quality assurance in Germany

In Germany, quality of the doctorate is assured internally at the level of each individual *Fakultät* (in US terms, at the college level) for each major field of study. For example, engineering has somewhat different quality-assurance mechanisms than the social sciences or the physical sciences. In this internally decentralised system, the voices of the doctoral candidates are becoming a force in the country's quality-assessment mechanism through the Max Planck institutes. These research centres are among the most prestigious German research institutes. However, the doctoral degrees of these students are still conferred by the university where a Max Planck Institute is located.

Due to the decentralised governance of German universities and a powerful professoriate, every discipline has its own dissertation regulations. The adherence to the *Promotions Prüfungsordnung* (doctoral examination policies) is usually monitored via the faculties/colleges within the universities.

By 1990, a small number of structured doctoral programmes had already been established at German universities, initiated and funded by the German Research Council (DFG). In 2006, the Excellence Initiative funded theme-oriented graduate schools with structured doctoral programmes. Since 2020, every university has had at least one theme-based graduate school that provides courses and services. However, still only a small fraction of doctoral candidates undertakes their doctoral studies in structured programmes (in 2017, circa 20 per cent).[12]

In 2011, the *Wissenschaftsrat*, an independent advisory body to the national government, published recommendations for the quality assessment of the doctoral degree. Since each of the 16 states of the German Federal Republic has its own educational authority, and each college/*Fakultät* decides independently about dissertation rules and regulations, these recommendations have not been widely implemented. One driving national force for reform of doctoral quality assurance is the Technical University of Munich, which has implemented a comprehensive quality-management scheme for its doctoral education.[13] This quality-assurance system includes mentors, supervision agreement and good scientific practices. It includes organisational processes like internal and external evaluation and personnel development by doctoral candidates and supervisors alike.[14]

The Max Planck PhDnet, a national Max Planck doctoral-candidate network which established its own quality assessment of doctoral education, has conducted annual surveys of doctoral students since 2012. In 2019, the survey was completed by more than 2,500 doctoral candidates (a participation rate of 50 per cent). These surveys, similar to UK's PRES but under the control of students, include questions about mental health, supervision, training offers and access to the new type of German graduate schools. As a consequence of data gathered, in 2018, Max Planch PhDnet published a position paper on power abuse and recommended the establishment of mandatory thesis advisory committees and the breakup of structural dependencies by separating the payment for research undertaken by doctoral candidates from the supervising responsibility of the same professors.[15]

Single university cases

The following individual university cases, written by graduate deans or heads of central graduate school offices, are their opinions. They bring another view to our understanding of the variety of doctoral assurance systems and their impact on the local level.

University of Otago, New Zealand[16]

The eight New Zealand universities are all public – partially government funded – and regularly audited to ensure good practices are in effect for students and other stakeholders. The audit is carried out by the national Academic Quality Agency for New Zealand Universities, which was established in 1993 by the New Zealand Vice-Chancellors' Committee. The audit cycles focus on one university at a time and involve panels of external academics (from NZ and overseas) and usually include a focus on graduate programmes. The audit system is underpinned by regular self-review by the universities, which ensures ongoing internal quality assurance. Consequently, universities have to strive for best practice, and this helps ensure a quality experience for doctoral candidates. For doctoral programmes, this means striving to admit students who are likely to succeed, a probationary period after enrolment, close monitoring throughout candidature, holistic support services, training of supervisors, using external examiners and routinely gaining feedback on the doctoral experience. A key benefit of the system is programmes with high completion rates (see Spronken-Smith et al., 2018), who report an institution-wide PhD thesis submission average over 13 years of 83 per cent, with a median time to submission of 3.4 years for full-time candidates). But, more importantly, candidates report high levels of satisfaction with their doctoral experience and supervision is overall highly rated. The inevitable downside of an audit culture is the perception amongst academics that the bureaucracy is time-consuming and unnecessary, failing to realise that the administrative processes are necessary to support candidates and help ensure an equitable and satisfying experience.

Universiti Sains Islam Malaysia, Malaysia[17]

The Malaysian Qualifications Agency (MQA) is the body entrusted to ensure that quality-assurance standards and processes in both public and private higher-education institutions are in keeping with current practices in higher education internationally. It has brought about greater accountability and raised the bar among private education providers, which mushroomed when the Private Higher Education Institution Act (PHEI Act) 1996 democratised the country's higher-education system.

A significant milestone is the levelling up on the quality of education in private higher-education institutions to that of the more established public institutions, contributing in part towards the transformation of Malaysian higher education to what it is today, a global education hub. However, being essentially process-centric, some consequences of zealous implementation of quality assurance are overregulation, too much homogeneity and infringement of the University Senate prerogatives on academic matters, compromising educational creativity and innovation.

An example is the adoption of the UNESCO International Standard Classification of Education *in toto* for all levels of studies. This coding system silos disciplines and contradicts the current momentum towards the convergence of knowledge, especially of the sciences and humanities, and can impinge on the development of knowledge, especially in doctoral-level research and studies. If the government would provide more leeway for universities in applying the UNESCO standards in doctoral research, this would leave more room for research and innovation creativity in the education and training of the next generation of researchers.

University of British Columbia, Canada[18]

Universities in Canada have historically had, and the vast majority continue to have, centralised graduate schools with a core mandate of quality assurance. So does the University of British Columbia at Vancouver. Quality assurance occurs at all levels of the university, however central oversight enables consistent standards and expectations across the campus. The arms-length relationship of the graduate school with the supervisors and programmes is an essential element in assuring quality in individual issues and decisions. A downside of having university-wide standards is that they are not always seen as appropriate for different disciplines, programme types or individual situations, and it is crucial that a spirit of wisdom and collaboration is inherent in all interventions and is supported by the graduate school and all other stakeholders involved.

Goethe University of Frankfurt am Main, Germany[19]

German scientific culture strongly emphasises the individual scientific achievement of the candidate as the core of a doctorate. Thus, the debate on quality assurance focuses largely on the quality of the results of doctoral research and related defects like plagiarism. At the same time, the systematic management of doctoral study programmes receives less attention than in some other countries. Still, a number of German universities, such as the Goethe University Frankfurt, actively support and monitor the quality of doctoral research and education.

At the Goethe, quality standards for doctoral research and education are established in the Guidelines for Doctoral Supervision at Goethe University and spelled out in the individual supervision agreements between candidates and supervisors. Regarding the implementation of quality standards, the faculties (schools or colleges) hold the primary responsibility. Hence, doctoral education plays a significant role in the regular strategy-review process between the university management and the faculties. Large doctoral study programmes are generally based on funding from the German Research Foundation (DFG). Thus, they are subject to regular external evaluation by the DFG. Finally, Goethe University participates in the Germany-wide National Academic Panel Study (Nacaps), a longitudinal career-path study of doctoral candidates and doctoral holders, in order to generate and benchmark data on the quality of doctoral education. Overall, then, while there is no integrated, university-wide quality assurance system for doctoral education at the Goethe University, quality assurance is achieved by the interaction of the several interrelated policies and measures.

Lessons learned

What do we take away from these examples? Despite the diversity of higher-education systems in the sampled countries, the direct responsibility for doctoral quality assurance usually lies with the universities themselves, although, typically, they are overseen by some form of external authority. The degree of *direct* involvement by governmental agencies varies greatly.

Who defines quality-assurance standards? Government agencies, disciplinary and professional societies and higher-education organisations are all generating, promoting and enforcing standards to varying degrees. The examples we have presented in this chapter illustrate this diversity: a national state council (China), an inter-country (regional) agreement

(European University Association), a national-level professional body (Australian Council of Graduate Research) and a distributed system with high institutional autonomy (US and Canada).

What have we learned did not work so well or were hurdles on the way? Quality monitoring of doctoral progress is uneven among universities and, in some countries, does not yet exist at all. In principle, at all stages of quality assuring during the degree process, it is best to involve more than one academic evaluator. This applies to the admission process, to annual progress reporting and, particularly, to the final defence where external independent evaluators should always play a role. Generally, too, the collection of institutional data on doctoral education is uneven, which makes aspects of quality assurance more difficult (see Chapter 1). While most universities collect time-to-degree and degree-awarded data, doctoral degree completion rates and career path information of doctoral graduates are often missing.

In all, the comparison across countries allows the reader to recognise that any quality assurance system and its implementation needs to pay attention to the steps outlined earlier: (1) defining of expectations, (2) setting up assessment processes to explore whether expectations are met, (3) measuring key quality indicators and (4) providing feedback mechanisms to facilitate both correction and enhancement of the system. Further to this, the Hannover Recommendations under Recommendation 6, 'advance the institutional environment for doctoral education continuously' and its six specifications, suggest several core values to be considered in each step of a quality-assurance process:

1. continually review and enhance the way doctoral candidates are educated to ensure that they meet the needs of our times, especially in view of the increasingly complex and urgent problems, the rapidly changing digital environment, and the need for understanding and interaction across cultures and disciplines;
2. address issues of a lack of diversity in admissions and of high attrition rates in some disciplines;
3. allow for more flexibility in doctoral completion timeframes;
4. foster transparent processes which can be judged by clear and credible quality-assurance processes for accountability to and transparency for all stakeholders;
5. provide individual fellowships alongside project funding at sufficient rates to cover adequate living costs, particularly in order to support intellectual risk-taking and the full spectrum of research topics;

6. ensure that all doctoral candidates, regardless of funding source, have equal access to continual professional development and education opportunities.

Adhering to these basic values allows each country, university and programme to cement their approach to the quality assurance of doctoral education so that it fits their system, environment and background and provides a strong basis for constantly improving the quality of our diverse doctoral systems.

References

Australian Council of Graduate Research (ACGR). Accessed 9 June 2022. https://www.acgr.edu.au/.

Hasgall, A., Saenen, B. and Borrell-Damian, L. (coauthors: van Deynze, F., Seeber, M. and Huisman, J.). (2019) 'Doctoral education in Europe today: approaches and institutional structures'. European University Association. Accessed 9 June 2022. http://www.eua.eu/resources/publications/809:doctoral-education-in-europe-today-approaches-and-institutional-structures.html.

Krause, K. (2012) 'Addressing the wicked problem of quality in higher education: theoretical approaches and implications.' *Higher education research and development*, 31(3), 285–97.

League of European Research Universities (LERU). 'The LERU Advice paper of 2016: Maintaining a quality culture in doctoral education'. No 19, March 2016. Accessed 9 June 2022. https://www.leru.org/files/Maintaining-a-Quality-Culture-in-Doctoral-Education-Full-paper.pdf

Lovitts, B. (2001) *Leaving the Ivory Tower: The causes and consequences of departure from doctoral study*. New York: Rowman & Littlefield Publishers.

National Research Council. (2003) 'Assessing research-doctorate programs: A methodology study'. Washington, DC: The National Academies Press. Accessed 9 June 2022. https://doi.org/10.17226/10859.

Nerad, M. and Cerny, J. (1991) 'From Facts to Action: Expanding the Graduate Division's Educational Role'. In *Communicator*, Special Edition, Council of Graduate Schools. And (1993) In L. Baird, 'Increasing Graduate Student Retention and Degree Attainment'. *New Directions for Institutional Research*, 80.

Nerad, M. and Miller, D. (1997) 'The institution cares: Berkeley's efforts to support doctoral students in the humanities and social sciences with their dissertations'. In L. Goodchild, K. Green, E. Katz and R. Kluever (eds), 'Dissertation Players and Process: Factors Affecting Completion'. *New Direction for Higher Education*, 99.

Tertiary Education Quality and Standards Agency (TEQSA). Accessed 9 June 2022. https://www.teqsa.gov.au/.

Tinto, V. (1997) 'Towards a theory of doctoral persistence'. In M. Nerad, P.G. Altbach, R. June and D. Sands-Miller. (eds), *Graduate Education in the United States*. New York: Garland Publishing.

Spronken-Smith, R., Cameron, C. and Quigg, R. (2018) 'Factors contributing to high PhD completion rates: a case study in a research-intensive university in New Zealand'. *Assessment & Evaluation in Higher Education*, 43, 94–109.

Notes

1. We would like to thank David Bogle and Barbara Grant for gracious editorial support and comments.
2. From the Carnegie Classification of Institutions of Higher Education '2018 Facts and Figures Report'. Accessed 11 September 2021. No longer available. http://carnegieclassifications.iu.edu/index.php.
3. https://cgsnet.org/holistic-review-graduate-admissions-report-council-graduate-schools. (Accessed 11 September 2021 No longer available.).
4. https://cgsnet.org/publication-pdf/4923/ArticulatingLearningOutcomesinDoctoralEducationWeb.pdf. (Accessed 11 September 2021 No longer available.)
5. https://www.nationalacademies.org/our-work/an-assessment-of-research-doctorate-programs. (Accessed 11 September 2021 No longer available.)
6. Zwetsloot, R., Corrigan, J., Weinstein, E., Peterson, D., Gehlhaus, D. and Fedasiuk, R. (2021) 'China is fast outpacing U.S. STEM PhD growth'. Center for Security and Emerging Technology. Accessed 9 June 2022. https://doi.org/10.51593/20210018.
7. https://www.eua.eu/resources/publications/354:doctoral-education-taking-salzburg-forward-implementation-and-new-challenges.html. (Accessed 9 June 2022)
8. https://www.eua.eu/resources/publications/809:doctoral-education-in-europe-today-approaches-and- institutional-structures/. (Accessed 9 June 2022).
9. We thank Markéta Lopatková for this information.
10. Special thanks to David Bogle and Rosemary Deem for this information on the UK.
11. PRES post graduate research experience surveys show that satisfaction with doctoral study in the UK is high.
12. 2021 Institut für Innovation und Technik (iit) Accessed 9 June 2022. www.buwin.de
13. https://www.gs.tum.de/en/tum-graduate-school/quality-management/. (Accessed 9 June 2022).
14. https://www.gs.tum.de/en/tum-graduate-school/quality-management/organizational-processes-at-tum-graduate-school/. (Accessed 9 June 2022)
15. https://www.phdnet.mpg.de/news/2018/power-abuse-statement?c=3839. (Accessed 9 June 2022).
16. We thank Rachel Spronken-Smith for this case example of her university.
17. We thank Roshada Hashim for providing this case example.
18. We thank Susan Porter for illustrating this case example.
19. We thank Matthias Koehler, Goethe Research Academy for Early Career Researchers (GRADE), for providing this case example.

5
Supervision in context around the world

Ronel Steyn, Liezel Frick, Reinhard Jahn, Ulrike Kohl, William M. Mahoney, Jr, Maresi Nerad, Aya Yoshida

The earlier parts of this publication provided a broad picture of the changes in doctoral education around the world over the past decades. This chapter narrows the focus and highlights doctoral education and supervision practices within a variety of specific local contexts. It contains critical, evidence-based reflections and suggestions around the topic of supervision that emerged from the participatory process at the Hannover conference described in the introduction and the discussions with early-career researchers at the conference.

The chapter aims to share some of the variety, changes and innovations in doctoral supervision that we found and attempts to situate them within their historical and current local contexts. It is structured around four *vignettes* written by contributors who are involved in supervision in four different countries (Japan, South Africa, Germany and the US) on four continents and includes perspectives from natural sciences and humanities and social sciences (HSS). We asked each contributor to explicitly focus on aspects of their chosen example that they thought might be *different* compared to the supervision that occurs in other contexts or *new* compared to traditional supervision practices in their contexts. We also asked them to reflect on what changes they have seen and would like to see in supervision within their contexts. In choosing these vignettes as vehicles for sharing the reflections of our working group, we hope to give the reader a taste of what we experienced during the Hannover workshop and conference, namely the sheer diversity of doctoral-education contexts, the varieties of practices, the range of interest holders with a stake in doctoral education, the unique personal perspectives of the participants and yet, the remarkable number of commonalities and connections. In doing so we intend to remind our readers that doctoral education is a complex social practice that emerges within the constraints and possibilities structured by a variety of unique contexts – be they national, institutional, disciplinary or even project-specific. This means that enhancing doctoral education will always have to involve more than sharing 'best practices'. Such an understanding is expressed in the second Hannover Recommendation to 'foster diverse ways of operating… to respect that different universities have their own distinctive missions and priorities that relate to their particular societal context; and recognise that there are diverse ways of achieving excellent doctoral education'. An important caveat here is that none of these vignettes claims to be representative of a particular discipline, research field, institution or country. Also, they are certainly not exhaustive of the variety of contexts and practices across the globe. Rather, we hope that they illustrate the opposite – specificity and locality, both temporal and spatial – while also highlighting generic aspects of supervision beyond the local context.

While we insist on the structural embeddedness of doctoral-education practices, we do not claim that there is a linear or unmediated causal link between structure and outcome. We need to look towards the future, thinking collectively about how doctoral supervision might evolve alongside programmatic, disciplinary, institutional, national and international trends shaping doctoral education. The examples shared here are testament to the creative powers of individuals and groups who have strengthened and renewed doctoral education by finding innovative ways to exploit the opportunities within, and work around the limits of, their contexts.

Introducing the vignettes

Many changes in doctoral-education practices have occurred ever since the emergence of the modern doctorate in nineteenth-century Europe when disciplines became the bases for organising knowledge and the production of knowledge. Disciplinary scholars and researchers were responsible for maintaining and developing disciplinary knowledge and PhD candidature was a period of apprenticeship through which successive scholars were developed to become the next stewards of the discipline

(Boud and Lee, 2009). The research output was evaluated by other disciplinary peers based on the level of scholarship reflected in it and on its contribution to the field of knowledge.

As this model of doctorate spread over time to the rest of Europe, the US and further afield, considerable variations developed according to national systems and in different fields of study. These differences have typically had to do with the degree of structure in the programme, the methods of education and training and the relative weighting of the research dissertation (Boud and Lee, 2009). Very crudely speaking, doctoral degrees could traditionally be grouped into two categories:

1. those that follow a structured curriculum with specific learning outcomes, typically consisting of a period of coursework followed by a research project under the supervision of a dissertation committee; and
2. degrees that are awarded to researchers who have completed a research apprenticeship under the supervision of an established researcher or scholar in a particular field, with the apprenticeship coming to an end once the apprentice had succeeded in producing an original piece of research to the satisfaction of academic peers in that field.

The former type is often referred to as the North American model and is associated with more institutional oversight of the doctoral experience and outcomes. This model is contrasted with the typical European models, which are normally associated with reliance on a single supervisor who acts both as gatekeeper and guide to the disciplinary standards and practices. Within these broad categories, there has always been considerable variation, and in recent decades there has been such a proliferation of new practices, new role players and new doctoral-education settings, that these categories might have become less helpful than they used to be.

Vignettes 1–3 (Japan, South Africa, Germany) share doctoral-education forms that are atypical or distinctive within their broader contexts or that represent innovations of their traditional practices. All three of these vignettes highlight more *collective and collaborative forms of research supervision*, despite a strong tradition within their broader contexts of institutional hierarchy and single supervisor-student dyads. They are also characterised by *increased structuring of the doctoral experience* through the introduction of programmatic elements. Such elements include the selection of a cohort of doctoral students by a collective decision-making body; the use of more explicit selection criteria and more formal, standardised application processes; the introduction of coursework and other prescribed activities with defined learning outcomes; evaluation (again by committee) of key milestones; and upper time limits for thesis completion. As Vignette 4 (US) illustrates, many of these features have been standard in the US for many years.

The US case in Vignette 4 in turn highlights the equal importance of a *rich and supportive institutional environment* that is critically *responsive* to societal and students' needs. It shows the variety of people involved in creating such an educational and nurturing environment – individual supervisors, mentors and support staff – and the novel ways in which they help doctoral students navigate their way through it and into environments beyond.

We discuss these themes in more detail after presenting the four vignettes below. The chapter ends with some final reflections on potentially worrying trends in the broader doctoral-education sector and a reminder that as key role players in doctoral education, researchers and scholars do have an opportunity to direct these trends.

Vignette 1: innovation in engineering: Waseda University, Japan

This vignette was compiled by Professor Aya Yoshida, School of Education, Waseda University, in conversation with Professor Yasuhiro Hayashi in the School of Advanced Science and Engineering and head of PEP (power, energy and professions) programme at Waseda University. The latter is also Dean of the Advanced Collaborative Research Organisation for a Smart Society at Waseda University and has been involved in industry–academia alliances for education and research for many years.

Over the past three decades, the Japanese government has embarked on efforts to expand and reform graduate education. Since the early 2000s, the government has used competitive project-based funding to develop key research fields and to direct and focus funding towards select research centres and graduate schools that are able to compete or lead internationally. There has also been a growing emphasis on more applied and interdisciplinary research.

Despite the success of these funding schemes in expanding and improving the research environment of Japanese universities and an initial increase in doctoral enrolments, the number of doctoral enrolments has been declining since 2003. This is not only the effect of a shrinking population: *Hakasebanare*, roughly translated as 'PhD flight', refers to the unwillingness of bright young graduates in Japan to pursue postgraduate studies, whether at home or abroad (Ministry of Education, Culture, Sports, Science and Technology (MEXT), 2021: 3). Japanese companies do not tend to recognise and reward PhD qualifications in their salary and career structures in a way that makes higher degrees an attractive choice for young graduates. In a context in which research jobs in academia are decreasing and many posts for young academics have become fixed-term jobs, the cost of PhD study outweighs the benefits for many Japanese graduates.

One of the challenges faced by Japan is a relatively stagnant economy. The Japanese economy heavily depends on its technological industries. Rapid and large-scale changes in global industrial structures mean that entire industry supply chains have been disrupted (MEXT, 2021: 4). An example, illustrated in this vignette, is the need to transform and reconstruct national energy networks in response to the rise of small-scale distributed energy supply made possible through renewable energy sources (MEXT, 2021: 40). Such changes cannot be achieved through individual companies but require collective and coordinated action across the industry supply chain as well as the country's knowledge and innovation system. What is needed is not only innovation *within* existing industries, but the creation of *new* industries altogether.

National WISE scheme and PEP doctoral programme at Waseda University

In 2018, the government introduced the WISE (World-leading Innovative and Smart Education) doctoral-funding scheme to create better alignment and collaboration between universities and industry. This scheme goes beyond supplying new knowledge and innovations to existing industries or preparing doctoral graduates for industry careers at individual companies. Through harnessing knowledge and innovation to *create* new industries, the government hopes to revitalise the Japanese economy, create new career paths for PhD graduates, as well as rejuvenate the shrinking university sector. Graduate schools can apply for funding to create and offer an integrated five-year master's-doctoral programme in an existing area of strength through collaborations with other universities, research institutions and corporations in and outside Japan. One of the programme objectives is to create cross-disciplinary collaborations. A further explicit aim is that these selected programmes will also initiate reforms within their universities' entire graduate programme.

To date, 30 WISE projects have been selected from a total of 140 applications from research and higher-education institutes across Japan.

One of these is the PEP doctoral programme in the School of Advanced Science and Engineering at Waseda University. Waseda University is a private research university located in Tokyo. The PEP programme is situated within the narrower discipline of power engineering, energy materials science and engineering, but in line with programme objectives, it includes a cross-disciplinary element, in this case with the HSS.

New doctoral-education practices in science and engineering in Japan

The Waseda PEP programme introduces a doctoral experience and a supervising system that is unique in the Japanese context. In the field of science and engineering, a graduate student traditionally affiliates with one laboratory with a single professor acting as supervisor. Research normally focuses on aspects of the supervisor's own research project and some coursework is involved (30 credits for master's and 10 credits for PhD). The master's and PhD degree programmes are separate, with a duration of two and three years, respectively. A thesis review committee, consisting of the supervisor and a number of other professors, often from other universities, examines the thesis.

In contrast, the Waseda PEP programme is an integrated five-year programme covering both the master's and doctoral level. It is offered through a collaboration of 13 universities throughout Japan, six overseas universities (three in the US and one each in China, Thailand and Germany) and five energy companies in Japan. The programme is open to graduate students from any of the alliance members. Most of the students are selected for the programme after undergraduate studies at one of the partner universities, but there are also a smaller number of master's degree holders already employed in one of the partner research companies. These students join the programme from the third year. Scholarships for graduate students in Japan are usually small and it is not uncommon for graduate students to work part-time while studying. In comparison, students on the PEP programme are well-supported financially, through research assistantships, industry donations, tuition waivers for compulsory coursework and travel bursaries. In being able to focus solely on their research for five years, they are in a relatively privileged position.

Each graduate student is supervised by a team of professors and researchers (both academic and industry-based). The main supervisor is a professor at the participating university where the student is enrolled; the rest of the team consists of a co-supervisor from a different university in the alliance, a researcher in a company and a professor in HSS at Waseda University. Supervising team members who are researchers in the partner companies, are called consulting professors and they specifically assess the business viability and social significance of students' research. In addition, six overseas professors are on hand to give advice to students on request and to accept those that wish as collaborative research members or interns in their own institutions. Graduate students are strongly encouraged to explore these opportunities, especially to travel abroad.

The coursework over the five years consists of three sets: (1) a set of seven mandatory courses for all students, including courses in HSS, such as business creation or social science for energy innovation – these courses are provided by Waseda University; (2) a range of specialised courses developed through collaboration among the 13 universities; (3) a range of practical courses such as collaborative research in overseas universities, internship in companies or laboratory rotations in alliance institutions. Most of the courses, apart from the last set of practical courses, are provided online for the convenience of students in different places.

The programme is structured around four milestones, each involving an examination by the entire supervising team. Students are selected onto the programme through the selection examination, which consists of written applications and oral examinations. At the end of the second year, students who have completed at least 30 coursework credits and have submitted one academic paper, are allowed to take the qualifying examination (QE). This is an hour-plus-long oral exam. The most important evaluation point at this milestone is the social significance and business potential of their research. Here the consulting professors (supervising team members from the alliance companies) play an important role in guiding students from an industry perspective. At the end of five years, there is a thesis defence called the final exam 1 (FE1). A PhD degree is conferred to successful students from the university with which the candidate was affiliated. Final exam 2 (FE2) is the final milestone and occurs around the same time or shortly after FE1. To qualify for the exam, students must have completed 45 credits of coursework and published at least one coauthored paper with collaborative universities and institutions in an international journal. FE2 involves an oral exam in front of the entire supervising team. Again, the consulting professors are key in assessing the business viability and social significance of students' research. After successful completion of FE2, students receive a certification of completion from the PEP programme. There are stamps from all 13 cooperating universities on the certificate.

In addition to these milestones, students complete a self and peer evaluation at the end of every year. For this purpose, a rubric is used that visualises the students' learning outcomes in six key areas, including topics such as whether the research contributes to the creation of new industries, the extent of international cooperative research and whether the student has a holistic overview of the research problem. The completed rubrics make up part of the evaluation discussions in both the QE and the FE2.

Members of the supervising team individually advise students in their daily research, both formally and informally throughout the doctoral journey, but the four milestone evaluations offer a number of additional benefits to both students and the programme. First, the collective examination by the supervising team plays an important role in evaluating students' progress fairly. Second, the milestones allow for visualising students' progress longitudinally over the five years. Finally, each examination provides an opportunity to reflect on the PEP programme itself in the context of students' development.

Vignette 2: international collaboration, South Africa/ United Kingdom

This vignette was compiled by Professor Liezel Frick, Associate Professor in the Department of Curriculum Studies and Director of the Centre for Higher and Adult Education within the Faculty of Education at Stellenbosch University (SU). She is the Stellenbosch University lead on the project described here, in collaboration with Ferdie Gerber (Walter Sisulu University – WSU) in South Africa and Katherine Wimpenny (Coventry University – CU) in the UK.

As highlighted in the prologue of this book, South Africa is seeing a very strong growth in doctoral enrolments, with increasing numbers of doctoral students from other African countries. But the country is also still experiencing high doctoral dropout and non-completion rates. Supervisory capacity to support the growing number of doctoral students is limited and a number of scholars have raised concerns about the ageing professoriate, which will soon leave an even greater gap in this regard. Supervisory capacity is furthermore not equally distributed amongst universities. The apartheid legacy of a racially segregated and unequal higher-education system has led to lasting and persistent inequalities. Older, historically advantaged and better resourced universities have a greater capacity to supervise doctoral candidates, while historically disadvantaged institutions tend to have a low percentage of academic staff who hold PhD degrees. A key rationale behind the government's drive to increase PhD numbers is to enlarge and enhance research capacity and scholarship within all public higher-education institutions. Thus the South African PhD degree is primarily focused on advancing an academic career. There have also been concerted efforts to encourage existing academic staff to work towards a doctoral degree. Almost half of South African doctoral candidates and an even larger proportion of those in HSS study part-time. That is, they are in full-time employment during their doctoral studies, both within and outside of the higher-education sector.

Doctoral programmes in South Africa are traditionally research focused and shaped around a candidate's research activity and output only. In other words, it is not a taught or structured programme. Coursework is not a standard feature and if it is included, it is not credit bearing. Supervision normally follows the traditional UK PhD model of a single supervisor guiding the research of an individual doctoral candidate. Even where a number of students have the same supervisor, they will not necessarily form a cohort, as they all follow their individual research journeys at their own pace, especially in the HSS fields. In the laboratory sciences, research groups working on a common research project tend to develop naturally into small teams, although an individual supervisor typically remains ultimately responsible for each candidate's doctoral experience and the output of the group.

Doctoral education and supervision in South Africa are deeply embedded within disciplinary structures, including the selection of candidates and the monitoring of the doctoral process, both of which are often left to individual supervisors themselves. There is a growing number of doctoral schools that serve to support students, but these schools are usually situated within departments or disciplines. Central support and oversight of the doctoral experience from institution-wide units are often limited in their influence, as they can be perceived as a form of administrative encroachment on disciplinary autonomy.

In South Africa, examination occurs through peer review in the broader disciplinary community, but supervisors are never examiners themselves. The process consists of an evaluation and approval of the completed thesis by two or three disciplinary experts. The use of external examiners from different institutions – including international examiners – are key elements of quality assurance in the South African system. At some South African universities, an oral defence in front of the same examiners who evaluated the thesis is also required.

Cross-university and cross-country collaboration in doctoral education

Recent national and institutional drives towards internationalisation have unlocked funding opportunities for joint and dual doctoral degrees in collaboration with universities abroad. However, these programmes remain small and linked to specific funding regimes. This vignette describes the supervision involved in a project supported by one such funding scheme. Utilising both national and institutional funds, the scheme is specifically aimed at building academic capacity within universities. The goals are to increase the number of staff who hold doctoral qualifications and to develop the supervisory capacity within the participating institutions.

The specific project described here is situated within the HSS field and more specifically within the broader discipline of education. The project is unusual in this context, as it has moved away from the traditional mode of individual supervision to a more cohort-based approach within a structured joint doctoral degree programme that contains scaffolded coursework. It involves a cotutelle arrangement between two degree-granting universities, with students and supervisors from three universities: Walter Sisulu University (WSU) and Stellenbosch University (SU) in South Africa and Coventry University (CU) in the United Kingdom. SU is a research-intensive university that places an emphasis on research output, including that at the postgraduate level. WSU is a comprehensive university (covering a range of qualifications from vocational diplomas to research degrees). WSU resulted from the merger in 2005 of three separate institutions and is still facing severe restrictions in resources, research and supervision capacity. SU and CU are the two degree-awarding institutions.

The students and supervisors involved in this project are all permanent staff members at one of the three partner institutions. The doctoral candidates are early to mid-career academics and professional staff permanently employed at one of the three participating universities. Since candidates would be continuing with their academic work at their home institutions, prospective students had to show that their participation would be supported by their line managers, before being accepted into the programme. This was to ensure that all participants had the necessary study leave to attend compulsory support programmes and regular meetings scheduled at specific points during the overall project. Without these measures, it would not be possible to create a structured cohort-based programme. Participating students have master's degrees (a requirement for admission into the doctoral programme), but their academic backgrounds and foci vary widely. However, they all have a keen interest in teaching and learning within higher education, which is the focus of the overall project. The candidates' doctoral studies need to align explicitly to one of three themes identified within this broad focus, while pushing the boundaries of the existing knowledge in the particular area.

Candidates were selected onto the programme through a rigorous application process and by completing a structured predoctoral programme offered by the two degree-granting institutions (SU and CU). The project team assessed the applications in terms of the funder criteria and the alignment of the respective applications in terms of the project's academic focus. As part of the predoctoral programme, prospective students explored what doctoral studies entailed and what would be expected of them over the duration of the project. They were also introduced to the central themes of the project and started drafting their own research ideas in alignment to these themes. A total of 20 candidates were initially selected to participate in the predoctoral phase. Candidates were informed that the predoctoral phase was to be followed by a secondary filtering process prior to the selection of the final group of PhD students to Year 1 of the programme. A total of 14 candidates were invited to join the project, of which 12 ultimately accepted positions in the programme.

A new approach of doctoral education in the HSS in South Africa

The approach followed in this project has a number of features that differ from the typical doctoral-education practice in the HSS fields in South Africa. First, instead of the traditional single supervisor-student dyad commonly found in HSS, it introduces a cohort of students who follow the same structured programme over the same time period. Second, the programme includes coursework which, although non-credit-bearing, is compulsory for all candidates. Coursework is made up of already existing support programmes within each institution, as well as bespoke offerings developed by the project team. Third, each candidate's individual research project is supervised by a small team of supervisors from all three partnering universities. Each candidate has primary supervisors allocated from both SU and CU, to ensure they comply with the programme requirements of both degree-awarding institutions. Co-supervisors from WSU are appointed from a cohort of staff members who indicated an interest in acting as supervisors in the project, who had the necessary subject and/or methodological expertise and who held doctoral qualifications themselves. Supervisor allocation only happened after initial research ideas were formulated to ensure expertise and interests were properly aligned. A final unique feature in this project is a supervisor capacity-building programme for the entire group of supervisors involved in the project, running parallel to the student development programme.

This structured approach offers more input and support to the candidates and supervisors than would normally be the case in individual one-to-one supervision arrangements, as both students and supervisors regularly meet and take part in capacity-building initiatives. Candidates' learning and progress is much more closely tracked and monitored than would be the case otherwise (also because the funding is limited to four years from registration to completion). There are also increased opportunities for interaction and peer learning amongst candidates who are working within specific thematic groupings, through journal clubs and a buddy system. The focused emphasis and commitment to supervisor capacity building within the overall project is different to what is common practice elsewhere within the broader context, as supervisory expertise and experience varies considerably within the supervisor cohort. This project also differs from many other institutional collaborations in its emphasis on equal participation, commitment and investment of all the participating institutions, with representation on the project team from all the partner institutions.

In this model, doctoral education requires careful planning and regular communication and involves cooperation between academic and nonacademic staff in the three institutions. A small project team was established consisting of a project lead in each of the partner institutions, existing support and administrative staff within the partner institutions and an independent evaluator overseeing the overall project. Some aspects of the project management are highly regulated and in general fall outside the control of supervisors and student; because they are aspects governed by either the project specifications (such as the scope and focus of the project overall and monetary spending) or by the cotutelle arrangements (such as how degrees get awarded, the required levels of expertise in supervisory team compositions and the progress requirements for students). Other aspects are more flexible and open to interpretation by the team itself, such as individual project foci, matching specific students to the available supervisors and how supervision, and more generic capacity building, happens within the overall project.

Vignette 3: structured programme MPI-University of Göttingen, Germany

This vignette was compiled by Professor Reinhard Jahn, recently retired as Director of the Department of Neurobiology at the Max Planck Institute for Biophysical Chemistry, where he is currently Leader of an Emeritus group. He was one of the founders of the International Max Planck Research School in Molecular Biology in 1997. He served as Dean of the University of Göttingen Graduate School for Neurosciences, Biophysics and Molecular Biosciences (2007–15) and President of the University of Göttingen (2019–20).

Until about 20 years ago, most universities in Germany did not have structured doctoral programmes. Students who completed the diploma degree – comparable to the master's degree – were free to choose a topic of interest, a supervisor, a research group or even an industry lab to work in for their PhD thesis. No enrolment was required and no additional training or curricular activities were needed. The only formalised supervision was provided by the *Doktorvater or Doktormutter* – a professor at the respective university. In theoretical disciplines or in the HSS, it was acceptable to disappear from the radar screen of the academic institution for years and then resurface with a written and completed thesis at a later date. In fact, all that was needed to obtain a PhD was a diploma or equivalent degree, a completed PhD thesis, a university professor serving as supervisor who grades and signs off on the submission of the thesis, and a formal graduation procedure, usually consisting of a public defence and the thesis publication.

Despite considerable reform efforts, there are still many German university professors who do not see the need for changing this system of what may be regarded as benevolent patriarchical. Clearly, there are advantages for both students and professors: the students are free to choose a PhD project independent of university affiliations – in principle anywhere in the world – as long as a professor agrees to represent the thesis in the faculty (school). The focus is exclusively on thesis research. Any additional activities such as courses, conferences and seminars are voluntary and are negotiated between the student and supervisor.

However, the complete dependence of the student on the supervisor can backfire in cases of conflict. Then, the student is in a weak position, particularly when the doctoral student's stipend is controlled by the supervisor. Moreover, there is no oversight to ensure regular progress is made towards completion. Additional training is often discouraged, as it means time away from research, and there is generally no education in non-disciplinary skills.

A further idiosyncrasy of the German system that is potentially problematic is that only in the past several years, researchers who are not full professors (for example, assistant professors or junior professors) can serve as the formal supervisor for the degree. Supervision in the German system is still limited to a small and select group of academic staff, since professorship is typically reached at a later career stage, with an average age well over 40 years, and other faculty with supervision rights still constitutes a minority – although a growing one. The limitation in the number of supervisors creates problems, especially in the laboratory or experimental sciences. Young researchers, as they build their own research groups, are highly dependent on doctoral students, but their status as junior faculty members means they are not necessarily allowed to supervise their trainees' doctoral work. Similarly, scientists and laboratory heads in non-university research institutes are not allowed to be formal supervisors, even though such institutes are important sites for PhD research, unless they have a dual affiliation with a university. In these situations, a disconnect develops between the daily supervision by the lab head – in the case that they have no supervision rights – and the distant formal supervisor, whose oversight of large numbers of students can become increasingly perfunctory.

Development of a new approach of international doctoral education in Göttingen

The University of Göttingen is one of the major research-oriented universities in Germany. Göttingen is also home to five major institutes of the Max Planck Society. Max Planck institutes are independent research entities separate from the university. They do not have the rights to confer the doctorate, although many graduate students pursue their thesis projects within them. Research lab heads within these institutes normally do not hold university professorships.

Twenty years ago, the University of Göttingen and three Max Planck institutes collaborated to create two international graduate programmes that constituted a radical departure from the conventional doctorate in Germany. The two doctoral programmes are in the fields of neuroscience and molecular biology. These programmes adopted concepts from US graduate programmes and their success contributed to the development of the Göttingen Graduate School for Neurosciences, Biophysics and Molecular Biosciences of the University of Göttingen, a large graduate school with approximately 400 doctoral students.

Features of the programmes

Changes to supervisor requirements: Supervisors on these two doctoral programmes are no longer confined to professors or assistant professors (or junior professors). They are selected solely based on their scientific credentials and whether they have principal investigator status. Thus, both junior faculty and scientists from Max Planck institutes could join and formally supervise their own students, including those who just started their own laboratory after a successful postdoctoral fellowship.

It was not easy to convince the senior faculty in the biology, chemistry and physics departments of the university to accept this change. It required adjustments in the bylaws and new contracts between the Max Planck institutes and the University of Göttingen.

Selection: Students are recruited internationally. Selection consists of three phases: (1) a standardised online application; (2) suitably qualified applicants then complete a multiple-choice test (similar to the US Graduate Record Examination), complemented with basic disciplinary questions; (3) based on the test results, prospective students are invited for personal interviews conducted by two faculty members. Admission of the students by an admission board instead of individual selection by the supervising professors means that students join the programme without knowing who will supervise their work. Although common in the US, this was unheard of in Germany when these two programmes started. Supervisors are responsible for funding the students' salaries and were accustomed to choosing a student of their preference. However, the matching between student and supervisor rarely created difficulties because the first year of the programme includes ample opportunity for interactions between students and potential supervisors. Moreover, the programmes are well funded, granting an opportunity to distribute programme-based fellowships to research groups with insufficient funding.

The first-year curriculum: The first year involves an intense theoretical and practical training programme that aims to harmonise the different backgrounds of the students, familiarise them with modern concepts of the respective discipline and introduce them to the local research laboratories. It involves lectures and tutorials throughout the year and a set of mandatory practical courses in laboratory work and basic research methods. In addition, students participate in three seven-week lab rotations, focusing on a small research project in each. Students give presentations about their rotation projects in a seminar series supervised by an experienced faculty member. The introduction of laboratory rotations allows students to choose between the participating research labs for their main project, and they are not limited to the professors at a particular school or department. Occasionally, this has even resulted in the competition of several faculty members for attracting a particular student for a thesis project.

First-year examinations: At the end of the first year, there is an exam consisting of a written and an oral component. Based on the result of the exam, the students can either opt for entering the fast track, that is, begin directly with their PhD thesis in a research group of their choice, or they may need to do a master's thesis, the result of which decides whether they will be admitted to the PhD phase of the programme.

The PhD phase of the programme: The thesis itself is supervised by a Thesis Advisory Committee (TAC) that includes the direct supervisor of the work and two additional members. Committee members must be approved by the Programme Committee to ensure suitability and independence. Meetings must be held at least once a year (enforced), and the TACs also decide whether progress is sufficient for thesis completion. TACs were completely new in Germany and thus were initially met with major mistrust. However, they quickly turned out to be beneficial not only for the student, but also for the participating scientists – quite a few unanticipated and highly successful collaborations have originated from animated scientific discussions in the TACs. The move away from reliance on a single supervisor has certainly been one of the most positive changes introduced by these programmes. However, there are quite a few colleagues who resent the time commitment a TAC requires, especially for those serving on multiple TACs. Unless a programme has the means and resources to enforce regular TAC meetings, they can quickly degenerate; meetings are cancelled or rushed, resulting in a short written report, signed off by the TAC members without a meeting.

Additional coursework: The course workload in the PhD phase is minor, with only one mandatory course – 'Good Scientific Practice'. Students can choose from a variety of other short courses both in specific science methods (hosted in participating labs) and in professional skills (offered by outside trainers). These latter courses were initially developed for students in the two doctoral programmes discussed here, but they have since been made available to all graduate students at Göttingen University and are jointly organised with other graduate programmes.

Evaluation: The TACs are responsible for grading the thesis and, together with additional programme faculty, for overseeing the thesis defence. The duration of the thesis work is limited to three years. There are limited opportunities for extending this. The enforced time limit constituted a rather harsh infringement of the authority of the professor to control the completion of the thesis. It is still only grudgingly accepted by quite a few senior faculty members. However, it has proven to be very effective and is supported by the majority of the faculty and almost all students.

An unanticipated benefit of the programme has been the strong cohesion that the student cohort, who come from many different countries, develop in the first year. Lasting friendships are made and the student network is fast and effective. Students often know better than supervisors where to obtain a missing item of equipment or who to ask for advice on a particular method or technique. There is also a growing alumni network.

Twenty years on

After 20 years, both programmes are thriving and are heavily oversubscribed. The introduction of these programmes was one of the early attempts to introduce structured doctoral training in Germany, besides the DFG's Research Training Groups (RTG) that were created in 1990 and were indeed the first structured doctoral programmes in Germany. In particular, what was different compared to the DFG RTG, the Max Planck institutes' doctoral programmes described here were targeting a broader embedding in an institutional approach right from the start and thus had a stronger structural impact.

In the meantime, many universities have created formalised graduate programmes, in which doctoral students must be enrolled. However, there is enormous diversity between these programmes in terms of how many of the above-described features they include. Also, according to current estimates, the majority of all doctoral students in Germany still graduate outside such programmes. After a boost in the last decade, mainly driven by competitive funding for graduate schools during the German Excellence Initiative, a subtle 'roll-back' towards the old system can be observed after funding has expired. It will require commitment and persuasion by university leadership to stop this trend and to ensure that the achievements of the past two decades are maintained and further developed. In the case of Göttingen University, the university was willing to commit funds to maintain the graduate school. The collaboration with the Max Planck institutes helped in that some of the initiatives funded there could be shared with the broader graduate community (for example, professional skills training, career advice, postdoc advice officer and so on). It is hoped that the proven benefits and advantages of structured graduate education will become increasingly acceptable and will receive even more support from major funding organisations and university leadership.

Vignette 4: PhD programmes at University of Washington, Seattle, US

This vignette was compiled by Professor Maresi Nerad and Professor William (Bill) M. Mahoney, Jr, both from the University of Washington. Professor Nerad is Director of CIRGE, Professor of Higher Education and Policy Studies at UW and Affiliate Faculty of the University of California, Berkeley Center for Studies in Higher Education. Professor Mahoney is Associate Dean of Student and Postdoctoral Affairs at the UW Graduate School and Associate Professor of Laboratory Medicine & Pathology in the UW School of Medicine, where he directs the Molecular Medicine & Mechanisms of Disease (M3D) PhD programme, an interdepartmental and interinstitutional PhD programme.

Doctoral education in the US at the University of Washington, Seattle

Doctoral education in the US is a structured, cohort-based process of five to seven years. Graduate students may pursue a master's degree followed by a PhD; alternatively, they may enrol directly in a PhD programme following their undergraduate degree. In some cases, a master's degree might be awarded along the way (see Figure 5.1). Some may choose short-term employment prior to returning to their graduate studies. In the US, only about 20 per cent of PhD holders continue on to tenure-track faculty positions, although this number varies by discipline.

The examples of doctoral education described in this vignette are situated at the University of Washington (UW), Seattle, Washington. The UW is located in the Northwest of the US. It is the major public research university of the state of Washington and one of the highest ranked public research universities in the US. At UW, completion of PhD programmes takes five to eight years, on average. UW has around 15,000 graduate students (master's and doctoral students combined) and 1,100 postdoctoral fellows.

The two specific examples illustrated here are the doctoral programmes in higher education and policy studies in the College of Education and the biomedical PhD programmes in the School of Medicine. The features of the former are generally typical of programmes

Basic Structure of US PhD Programs including Master's Degree on the Way

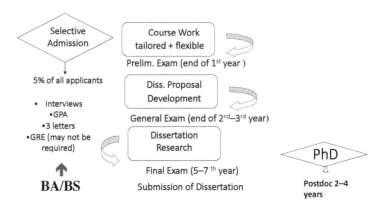

Figure 5.1: From admission to PhD completion: Basic requirement and program structure of US PhD Programmes (Source: CIRGE, University of Washington)

in HSS, education and public policy studies. The latter is generally representative of science, technology, engineering and mathematics (STEM) programmes.

Admission is selective and performed by either a dedicated admissions committee or the entire programme faculty. As an example, figures by UW for the academic year 2020/21 indicate an overall admission rate for PhD (=research doctorate) at UW of 5 per cent from a total of 16,000 applications with huge varieties across disciplines (for example, School of Medicine PhD programmes: 3 per cent from 2,000 applications; College of Education PhD programmes: 12 per cent from 200 applications). Enrolment is followed by several official orientations provided by various institutional structures and levels, for example the programme, college, graduate school and the international student office.

During the first two years, the emphasis of the structured programme is on understanding the scope and limits of one's own and other disciplines or fields of studies. This includes courses on various research methodologies or undertaking practical experiences to choose a relevant doctoral research project and to pass major programmatic and disciplinary milestones.

In humanities and social sciences programmes, the successive milestones include a pilot research project design presented in front of the entire college or department; the forming of a five-member dissertation committee at the end of year two; a two-part general or qualifying exam (the written part consists of essays addressing three questions focusing on theory, methods and a research design in the broad areas of the doctoral student's dissertation interest; the oral part involves questioning of the candidate by the dissertation committee, focusing on the essays but also broader issues related to the dissertation topic); the submission and approval of the dissertation proposal by year three at the latest; conducting the research, being a teaching assistant or teaching their own class, writing and submission of the dissertation to the committee; a public oral defence of the dissertation and a closed-door questioning by the committee; six weeks' time for revision of the dissertation after the passed defence; and finally, the formal approval and submission of the thesis to the university's general campus graduate school.

In the biomedical sciences, in addition to the dedicated coursework of the first two years, the programme also typically involves the following elements: students rotate through two to three research laboratories in their first year to identify both an interesting research area as well as a supportive mentor/advisor and a welcoming research group. During the second year, students develop their research question and produce preliminary data and prepare for the general exam. The general exam may consist of one or two parts; many programmes have eliminated the comprehensive written exam, but most continue to include presentation of the student's hypothesis, any collected preliminary experimental data and the plan for their research and data analysis. This presentation is to a committee of from four to six faculty and/or industry experts. Following successful completion of this exam, students continue their research, while also assisting on research or independent fellowship grant applications and various teaching and mentoring opportunities (for example, teaching of undergraduates and/or peer graduate students). Once a unique observation and study has been completed, usually highlighted by the submission as a primary literature article to a biomedical journal, students will defend their dissertation in a public oral defence and a closed-door question and answer session with their PhD committee. The final step is the same as described for the HSS programmes above.

Supervision – by primary advisor and other role players

In the US, all departmental professors are involved in overseeing the many issues facing doctoral students, such as admission decisions, allocation of fellowships and assistantships, awards for exceptional graduate students' teaching, initiation of programme revisions and the overall monitoring of student progress. Every department or programme has one administrative assistant dedicated to master's and doctoral student matters. This person holds a permanent staff position to offer continuity to the graduate students and to the programme.

Supervision of doctoral students by the primary advisor occurs within this structured context of influences of many other learning communities and professors from various disciplines. The main advisor is also chair of the dissertation committee. New advisors are initiated into their roles during their first years as assistant professors by serving as members of the doctoral committees of senior professors. They may become a dissertation committee chair after two to three years of observation and mentorship by senior faculty.

In the HSS fields, students are initially assigned an advisor for the first phases of the programme. The main advisor and additional dissertation committee members are chosen at the time they begin working on their dissertations. Generally, it is recommended that the main advisor may not mentor more than five to seven doctoral candidates at the same time, allowing each trainee to receive adequate mentorship. In the biomedical sciences, doctoral students chose their main advisor upon completion of their laboratory rotations, at the end of the first year. Once their research project is more fully designed, but well in advance of the general exam, additional faculty and/or industry experts are recruited to the committee to provide additional expertise, evaluation capacity and mentorship.

The main advisor is available for the day-to-day guidance of the doctoral candidate according to their particular needs and phase of the doctoral programme through in-person advice and feedback (for example, refining the research topic, choosing a dissertation committee, field work, data analysis, writing of chapters, publishing and defence). Advisors are also valuable mentors in areas outside of the dissertation focus. No single advisor has all the necessary experience or expertise to mentor all students equally and according to their unique needs. Therefore, there is a growing recognition that doctoral students need to develop a mentoring team, either formally or informally, that includes other professors and role players.

Personal reflections by the vignette authors

This vignette ends with reflections by the authors of the vignette, adding a personal note to the picture outlined above.

"In addition to weekly office hours, I offer a weekly doctoral seminar in the late afternoon, as most of our students have half or full-time professional jobs. These seminars do not carry any credit. I invite doctoral students beyond my own advisees who are to undertake their dissertations in the higher-education domain, as well as visiting non-US doctoral or postdoctoral visitors to CIRGE. The purpose of this seminar is to create a learning community that extends ideally beyond the time spent in graduate school. These seminar sessions begin with a five-minute personal check-in, discussion of each other's written work, practice presentations for any exams, conferences and ample practice of giving professional feedback. With permission from journal editors, we review together journal articles that I receive for review. We inform each other of conferences and encourage paper submissions. We attend talks together on campus and at conferences and meet at least once a term socially." (Maresi Nerad)

"I meet with my direct mentees and graduate students from across the UW community to provide educational, career and professional development advice. These sessions are offered as both one-on-one counselling sessions and as group sessions to different cohorts of graduate students (based on time of admission or advancement to PhD candidacy). These sessions may be formal (where we map out a training and career plan, often using the Individual Development Plan (IDP) model) or informal (where we have a free-flowing discussion of career and life goals). These sessions occur longitudinally, so a plan can be developed well before completion of PhD studies. This allows for time to identify and enhance each student's repertoire of transferable skills and to create and expand a professional network to leverage during their next career step." (Bill Mahoney)

There have been many positive trends in raising awareness in institutions about the experiences and difficulties faced by today's doctoral students. However, we feel that continued and increased attention should be given to the increasing difficulty of finding employment after completion of doctoral studies and to the creation of institutionalised programmes in career and professional development for graduate students, to the diversity of students from different backgrounds (that is, underrepresented minorities, international and first-generation graduate students and so on) and the diversity within these groups themselves, to power imbalances and potential for harassment in academia, to the mental health and wellness of graduate students and finally, to the need for formal mentor training in universities.

Supervision practices reflected through the four vignettes

Collective supervision

The advantages of collective and collaborative forms of supervision are illustrated by all four vignettes. They show how using multiple supervisors can broaden students' exposure to different perspectives, expertise and experience; how it facilitates the fair treatment of students and makes them less vulnerable when tensions in the supervision relationship or disagreements about the direction of the research project, arise. Collective supervision practices can also be advantageous to the participating supervisors. It stimulates collegiality and may even lead to new research collaborations (Vignette 3, Germany). Vignettes 2 and 4 (South Africa and US) illustrate the importance of co-supervision and supervisor committees for the development of new supervisors.

Furthermore, supervision teams involve people outside of the disciplinary speciality, the institution and even outside of the academic community. The example in Vignette 2 (South Africa) involves collective supervision within a disciplinary community, but across different institutions and countries. It shows how such a collaboration can be instrumental in developing research capacity in resource-poor settings, thereby addressing enduring inequalities across institutions, both nationally and internationally. Vignette 1 (Japan) is a particularly striking example of an alliance that involves role players from multiple disciplines, institutions and countries, as well as from industry. These diverse role players are not just involved in supervision, but also in the evaluation process. This will of course have a profound effect on the outcome of doctoral education, as judgements about the value of the knowledge produced moves beyond disciplinary peer review to multiple stakeholders outside of disciplinary communities. The example on Japan as illustrated in Vignette 1 is also particularly interesting in that it shows quite an advanced form of collaboration between industry and academy in doctoral education. Here the doctorate is not only aimed at serving industry needs, but integral in the renewal of industry itself. Vignette 3 (Germany) reminds us that such changes are not universally welcomed and that there may still be considerable tensions between what German professors regard as their professorial autonomy and external influences and rules.

Structured PhD education and programmes

All the vignettes show how the introduction of programmatic elements can produce positive results. Coursework and other prescribed activities typically precede the independent research phase and serve as an orientation and preparation for it. The use of courses, laboratory rotations, workshops, internships and exchanges allows students to develop an understanding of the scope and limits of their own and others' disciplines or fields of studies and to familiarise themselves with various research methodologies. This helps students to choose a relevant doctoral research project or topic and ensures that they are equipped with the knowledge and skills to carry it out. As illustrated in Vignette 3 (Germany), laboratory rotations also serve as an effective way of matching students to a research group and to a primary supervisor. In systems or projects where coursework is credit bearing (for example, in the US and Japan) and thus makes up an explicit component of the evaluation and the granting of the doctoral degree, the introduction of the above activities is relatively unproblematic. In other contexts, coursework is often felt to compete with the 'real' work of doing research. Vignette 3 (Germany) illustrates how more weight can be given to such 'preparatory' activities by introducing other features of the structured-programme approach, such as having qualifying exams before entering the research and thesis phase. Similarly, Vignette 2 (South Africa) shows an example of a pre-doctoral programme after initial selection, but before final enrolment. The integration of coursework and student support into the doctoral programme itself is a welcome improvement on some types of support that have traditionally been offered by central institutional units or even by private suppliers in these systems. Generic research skills or dissertation writing workshops are often devoid of the actual research context and therefore less valuable. Nevertheless, in the absence of structured cohort-based doctoral programmes, such general offerings are often the only support available to many students.

Cohorts of students and supervisors

The use of cohorts – that is, a group of students all following the same programme at the same time – is shown in all vignettes to have multiple benefits, including peer learning and support and the creation of lifelong relationships and networks. However, our vignettes also show that the creation of cohorts is largely dependent on the ability of doctoral students to study full-time or at least on their having sufficient study-leave opportunities to attend scheduled coursework. In most cases presented in the US example (Vignette 4), faculty's willingness to schedule courses after 4 p.m. or in the evening, can accommodate working students. However, in other cases (Vignette 2, South Africa), graduate students often live too far away from the university campus to attend regular evening classes and short residential courses therefore need to be arranged. Programmes that have funding to pay student stipends or to pay for replacement staff to enable study leave are clearly at an advantage.

Vignette 2 (South Africa) also shares the benefits of a *supervisor* cohort operating in parallel to the student cohort. This enables the deliberate design of collaborative activities among all supervisors attached to the student cohort, beyond the smaller teams supervising an individual student's research project. Co-learning among a group of supervisors is especially useful in a context in which there is a great need for supervisor development.

Standardised experiences and outcomes

The four vignettes all illustrate practices that make the learning outcomes of doctoral education more explicit and transparent and that ensure all students in a programme get the opportunity to achieve these outcomes, through the design of standardised experiences and evaluations. Vignette 1 (Japan) shares an example of a rubric used for self- and peer evaluation and which forms part of the overall evaluation of the candidate. Importantly however, the examples shared here also illustrate that doctoral education needs to be much more than the delivery of a research product and the acquisition of a defined set of skills. The doctoral degree is the highest qualification offered by an academic institution, its key feature being originality and new knowledge. The outcome of doctoral education is thus by definition unpredictable. Rapidly changing environments mean that not just the distant but also the immediate future is uncertain and unknown. The attributes of doctoral graduates cannot be fully predetermined and therefore cannot all be taught. There is also a growing understanding of the diversity of students, their varying needs and the different personal projects that they envisage for themselves, including different career trajectories. The value of mentorship and the creation of more flexible and personal development plans have been stressed (Vignette 4, US).

The environment as education

The practices outlined in the vignettes reflect something more complex and nuanced than just a move towards multiple supervisors, coursework and programme structure. As captured in the Hannover Recommendation 6: 'to advance the institutional environment for doctoral education continuously' – it is the quality and richness of the total environment that offers quality doctoral education and which needs constant and critical review in the light of changing and diverse needs of both students and society. In all of the vignettes, there is an emphasis on the environment, an understanding of the 'eco-social' nature of doctoral education (Green, 2005: 153). For some time now, there have been scholars who have argued that doctoral education is a complex process of socialisation (Chiappa and Nerad, 2020) and that have applied Lave and Wenger's concept of 'communities of practice' (1991) to doctoral education (for example in Golde, 2007; Pearson and Brew, 2002). In this view, learning and identity development occurs through participation in the social practice of the community.

If doctoral education involves learning through participation, then it remains a type of apprenticeship. But as our vignettes illustrate, this apprenticeship now takes place in a community of practice that has broadened beyond the specific discipline and university. The primary supervisor has become one of multiple players involved in helping students navigate their way through complex networks and access resources. In addition, in an increasingly complex multidisciplinary and digitised environment, supervisors and research support staff take part themselves in the learning experience together with the doctoral students. Vignette 4 (US) illustrates the value of a central institutional structure (called a graduate school in that context) to coordinate the doctoral experience by providing support to all these players, supervisors and students and to ensure institutional sensitivity to diversity and potentially harmful behaviours. However, as the reflections of a supervisor in Vignette 4 shows, the role of the primary advisor is by no means diminished by these developments – there remains a lot of opportunity for individual initiative to create and stimulate rich environments for both students and supervisor.

Final reflections on supervision experiences

For all the benefits of adopting certain practices, as illustrated by the vignettes in this chapter, there is one clear area of concern: many of the changes have been made possible through specific grant funding for the creation of specific doctoral programmes. Scholars such as Nerad (2020) have raised concerns that this concentration of research funding in selected institutions or projects within institutions has resulted in the bifurcation of doctoral programmes, leaving the bulk of doctoral education underfunded and unable to benefit from these innovations. Government funding schemes often explicitly state that the funded programme should act as catalyst for the reform of other doctoral programmes in the institution. This has not always been achieved. Even the funded programmes themselves may see a return to old practices once funding has been exhausted, as illustrated in Vignette 3 (Germany). This shows how inert higher education can be but also how financial incentives can be means of speeding up change.

A related concern is the increasing imbalance between funding for the STEM and HSS fields. The vignettes have illustrated the positive effects of broadening doctoral education to include the needs, interests and inputs from the broader social environment. In line with the Hannover Recommendation 4, Vignette 1 (Japan) illustrates a recognition of the contribution of the Social Sciences in a doctoral programme in engineering. However, the risk remains that private industry and economic interests will dominate in the new expanded doctorate described in this chapter. While economic prosperity is of course a central concern for all nations, there is a danger that the inequalities created by global competitiveness will become exacerbated if broader societal interests are not also represented through more public engagement in doctoral education.

Nevertheless there are opportunities for academics who are committed to the academic project, student welfare and social justice to work creatively within the constraints and opportunities of their local contexts. Thus, we see individual supervisors creating and broadening their students' communities of practice beyond that which is offered in the structured programme (Vignette 4, US); we see how a funded programme can share its resources with the broader doctoral student community (Vignette 3, Germany) and we see how universities can collaborate to redress historical inequalities in research and doctoral-education capacity (Vignette 2, South Africa). Given that within any structural constraints there will be openings for individuals to work together to change those structures or to find new opportunities within them, the value of the Hannover process in creating collective action becomes clear.

References

Boud, D. and Lee, A. (2009) 'Introduction'. In D. Boud and A. Lee (eds.), *Changing practices of doctoral education*. Abingdon, Oxon: Routledge, 12–17.

Chiappa, R. and Nerad, M. (2020) 'Doctoral student socialization'. In M.E. David and M.J. Amey (eds), *The SAGE Encyclopedia of Higher Education*. Thousand Oaks: SAGE, 392–5.

Golde, C.M. (2007) 'Signature pedagogies in doctoral education: Are they adaptable for the preparation of education researchers?'. *Educational Researcher*, 36(6), 344–51.

Green, B. (2005) 'Unfinished business: subjectivity and supervision'. *Higher Education Research & Development*, 24(2), 151–63.

Lave, J. and Wenger, E. (1991) *Situated Learning: Legitimate peripheral participation, earning in doing*. Cambridge, UK: Cambridge University Press.

Ministry of Education, Culture, Sports, Science and Technology, Japan. (2021) *WISE Program Doctoral Program for World-leading Innovative and Smart Education*. Accessed 9 June 2022. https://www.jsps.go.jp/j-takuetsu-pro/data/WISEbrochure_en.pdf.

Nerad, M. (2011) 'What we know about the dramatic increase in PhD degrees and the reform of doctoral education worldwide: Implications for South Africa'. *Perspectives in Education*, 29(3), 1–12.

Nerad, M. (2020) 'Governmental innovation policies, globalization, and change in doctoral education worldwide: Are doctoral programs converging? Trends and Tensions'. In S. Cardoso, O. Tavares, C. Sin and T. Carvalho (eds), *Structural and Institutional Transformations in Doctoral Education: Social, Political and Student Expectations*. Cham, Switzerland: Palgrave Macmillan, 43–84.

6
Funding of doctoral education and research

Marc Torka, Ulrike Kohl, William M. Mahoney, Jr, with contributions by members of Working Group 2 at the Hannover Conference[1]

This chapter outlines major dynamics in the global funding landscapes of doctoral education and research, as well as their consequences for doctoral candidates. Funding is a major force in shaping doctoral education and thus a theme that cuts across the recommendations of this book. Funding mechanisms link doctoral education to its wider political, economic and research environments and provide incentives to drive, delay, obstruct or even reverse institutional change. Appropriate funding is therefore essential to realise our sixth recommendation to 'Advance the institutional environment for doctoral education continuously'. Moreover, financial resources determine if students from all disciplines and backgrounds who want to embark on a doctorate can participate in doctoral education, and they shape the scale and composition of the PhD community. Funding also defines what kind of research is deemed as 'doable' (Neumann, 2007) and impacts the knowledge we create. However, this relies on the perspective of the funder and their peer reviewers. Often this can take a very conservative approach and result in funding only where there is a high probability of success. This means that anything considered leading edge or risky may not be funded. Appropriate resources for doctoral students and research environments are crucial to develop promising researchers, research programmes, innovations and careers within and beyond academia. Further, these resources determine whether current political priorities, such as reasonable completion times or increased retention rates, can be achieved. Current developments, such as the global pandemic and a focus on national priorities, demonstrate that the provision of adequate funding for all types of research is uncertain. The chapter argues that stable and enhanced funding is necessary to develop doctoral-education systems and support the next generation of doctoral candidates and, ultimately, their careers and our future workforce.

The chapter aims to stimulate a discussion about suitable funding of doctoral education and is organised in three sections. The first section outlines basic relationships between funding and doctoral education, the second describes major funding trends, and the third addresses five funding-related concerns that shape the future of doctoral education. These concerns emerged from intense discussions with members of the working group, contributors to the chapter and participants in the Hannover 2019 workshop and conference. We have developed general recommendations for each concern which should be reflected upon, refined and adjusted to the various settings in which doctoral education takes place.

In the absence of reliable and detailed international comparative data on PhD funding, this chapter draws on available quantitative information from literature, on the country descriptions that were provided at the Hannover conference (2019) and on data available from the Organisation for Economic Co-operation & Development (OECD) on research and development (R&D) investments, the numbers of researchers and the number of awarded doctorates (OECD, 2021a, 2021b). Although not all doctoral candidates receive funding or complete the PhD, awarded doctorates are considered as a rough proxy for direct PhD funding, which covers the living costs and tuition fees of doctoral candidates.

National research, higher education and doctoral-education funding systems are unique combinations of at least four types of resources: Federal and state funds, private endowments, tuition fees and fixed-term grants from all kinds of funding agencies, charities, government departments and industries. Funding is allocated to institutions, departments and academics through diverse mechanisms, including general block grants often based on student numbers, performance-based formulae such as graduation numbers, research and industry income as well as competitive grants based on funding applications. Depending on the type of system, doctoral candidates work to self-fund their studies, receive support from their families, are provided with internal funding such as teaching and research assistantships and/ or have to apply for external grants and fellowships.

To account for the needs of doctoral candidates and cope with the complexity of diverse funding systems, this chapter primarily focuses on direct PhD funding and briefly addresses general funding of national research, higher education and innovation systems in which doctoral education is ultimately embedded. Specific aspects regarding political considerations of PhD funding for capacity-building strategies are discussed in Chapter 7, with several country-specific examples.

The relation between funding and doctoral education

Doctoral education is located at the intersection between university education and research. It is the last stage of formal higher-education degrees, traditionally the first step into a research career and is increasingly considered as advanced-skill training beyond academia. The intermediate position of the doctorate between education and research, as well as the transitional status of candidates on their passage 'from apprentice to colleague' (Laudel and Gläser, 2008), generates complexity, competing aims and an interplay between multiple funding opportunities. PhD students rely on funding from universities, funding agencies, foundations and industries that are linked to specific purposes, priorities and the timely completion of the degree. Funders, institutions and supervisors must balance competing funding aims to ensure that the basic principles of doctoral education set out in the Hannover Recommendations are not compromised.

As discussed at the Hannover conference, originality of research is at the heart of doctoral education and should remain there. Developing creative critical autonomous and responsible intellectual risk takers is the unique feature of doctoral education and is of great value both to the doctoral graduate and to society at large. This implies that doctoral education must be driven by research challenges as well as societal needs together with the inspiration of the candidates, and not primarily by political considerations.

Previous research has shown the influence of funding on doctoral research. It has been argued that source, type, amount and length of funding affect the selection of research topics (Isaac et al., 1989), research time (Laudel and Gläser, 2008), attrition rates (Lovitts, 2001) and degree completion times (Nerad and Cerny, 1993). The relationship between PhD funding and time to degree is complex. Empirical studies have produced mixed results due to a range of interacting factors (Horta et al., 2019). Whether PhD funding generally reduces (Abedi and Benkin, 1987) or extends (Stock et al., 2011) the time to complete a PhD may depend on the type (de Valero, 2001; Ehrenberg and Mavros, 1995) and length of funding (Skopek et al., 2020; Kim and Otts, 2010), as well as the research productivity and skills accumulated during candidature (Horta et al., 2019) to address labour-market conditions within and beyond academia (Breneman, 1976). The challenge is to find a balance between these factors, because neither generous funding nor time-limited or small grants guarantee reasonable completion times nor quality of the PhD.

Types of funding vary across fields, institutions and doctoral-education systems. A survey from the European University Association (Hasgall et al., 2019) among 311 member institutions revealed that doctoral candidates receive funding from diverse and often combined sources (Figure 6.1). Most European doctoral students are funded through external project-based funding from governments, research councils and foundations, or by internal university scholarships or external stipends. Some candidates are employed in entry-level university positions that are often fixed-term, casual, teaching-based and usually involve work beyond the PhD. This also applies to working PhD students, who are employed in the private, public or non-governmental organisation (NGO) sector, as well as self-funded candidates without any institution-based financial support, usually through loans, savings or part-time work.

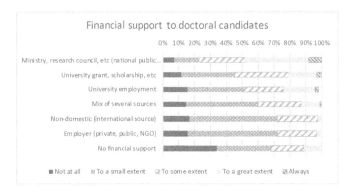

Figure 6.1: EUA 2018 Doctoral Survey: To what extent are doctoral candidates at your institution financially supported by the following sources (stipend, grant, salary, scholarship, fellowship, etc.)? © European University Association. (Hasgall et al., 2019)

In some higher-education institutions, a mix between periods of fixed-term contracts and periods of self-funding is possible; however, depending on the country or institution, self-funding can be limited or even not accepted, for example in disciplines that require high infrastructure or consumable costs. When doctoral candidates are required to support themselves, in addition to their research efforts, they mostly need a longer time to complete their research but gain hands-on experience in other domains.

The type of PhD funding affects the research product. Personal stipends allow greater freedom in the development of research directions. Employed students are likely to combine research activities and work products to allow for more consistency in their efforts. External project or supervisor grants come with a purpose that may predefine PhD themes and outcomes. While funding implications may be similar around the globe, the mix of funding sources varies greatly across countries and disciplines. Funding diversity tends to be greater in large-scale established systems, while PhD funding in small and emerging systems tends to be provided through national programmes. Since doctoral education receives funding from diverse sources, PhD students are subject to high levels of uncertainty due to sometimes uncontrollable changes in the general funding landscape.

To illustrate the diversity of PhD funding situations, here are some examples of funding sources for PhD candidates in different contexts: US graduate students usually receive university internal teaching and research assistantships or apply for external grants to fund their studies. While teaching assistantship is the modal type of support in the arts and humanities, project-funded research assistantships are the major source of support in the 'bench' sciences. In 2019, 21.4 per cent of PhD funding in the US came from teaching assistantships, 33.4 per cent from research assistantships, 24.8 per cent from fellowships, scholarships or grants, 15.2 per cent from own and 5.2 per cent from other resources (National Science Foundation, 2020). In other countries, such as China, Kazakhstan, Bulgaria and Chile, PhD funding is less diversified and covered by government scholarships for most students. Dutch doctoral candidates are usually employed at universities during their doctorate, and in Australia most students receive a personal fellowship provided by either the Australian government (~40 per cent), the University (~40 per cent), supervisors (~10 per cent) or industry (~10 per cent). Only about 10 per cent of PhD students in Japan receive a scholarship that covers their minimum living costs and more than half of doctoral students do not get any financial assistance (Country Descriptions, 2019).

Global trends in PhD funding

Changes in PhD numbers, doctoral-education policies and programmes are tightly linked to a number of long-term global funding trends outlined in this section.

General increase in R&D expenditures, research staff and doctoral degrees

The first trend is an increase in R&D expenditures, research staff and awarded doctoral degrees in many countries. A recent OECD report (OECD, 2021c: 23–5) found that the share of doctorate-level attainment grew on average 25 per cent across OECD countries from 2014 to 2019. Total government budget allocations for R&D have also grown by 44 per cent since 2005 and the number of researchers (FTE) increased by 37 per cent. However, the report also noticed a 'wide variation among countries' and that it is 'not possible to assess how the rate of growth in the number of FTE researchers in the higher education and governmental sectors compares to the rate of growth in doctorates awarded' (OECD, 2021c: 25). Figures 6.2, 6.3 and 6.4 based on OECD data illustrate differences between selected OECD countries (US, China, Russia, Germany, UK, Japan and South Korea) and show that the relationship between R&D expenditure, research staff and conferred PhD degrees is not linear.

While growing R&D investments in the US, China, Germany and Korea correspond with an increase in the number of researchers, the growth of awarded doctoral degrees is not directly linked to these developments. We see a consistent increase of PhD numbers in Korea, a slowdown of growth in the US and China and an actual reduction in awarded doctorates in Germany since 2015. In countries with stagnating R&D investments, such as Japan, Russia and the UK, the development of PhD numbers is also inconsistent. We find a sharp rise in the UK, stagnation in Japan and an obvious reduction in awarded doctoral degrees in Russia. The inconsistent relationship between R&D expenditures in the higher-education sector and researcher and PhD numbers is due to many reasons: not all researchers advise PhD students; R&D investments cover a wide range of costs; the share of international PhD students and related international funding varies between English-speaking and other countries; and doctoral candidates generally receive support from diverse sources, including loans, part-time work and private funds.

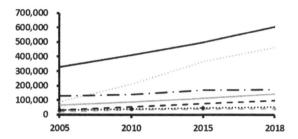

Figure 6.2 R&D Expenditures (in million US Dollars) 2005–2018 in selected countries**

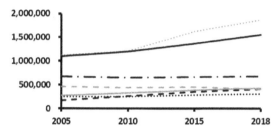

Figure 6.3 Total researchers (FTE) 2005–2018 in selected countries**

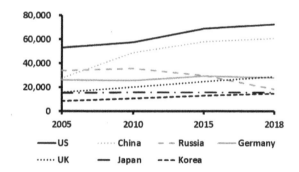

Figure 6.4 Awarded doctoral degrees 2005–2018 in selected countries**
Sources: *OECD (2021), 'Main Science and Technology Indicators'. OECD Science, Technology and R&D Statistics (database). Accessed 21 November 2021. https://doi.org/10.1787/data-00182-en.
**OECD (2021), 'Education Database: Graduates by age'. OECD Education Statistics (database). Accessed 21 November 2021. https://doi.org/10.1787/09b6ea07-en.
Germany: Statistisches Bundesamt, Fachserie 11, Reihe 4.1., 2005–18, China: Ministry of Education, Overview of educational achievements in China, 2005–18, http://www.moe.gov.cn.

As the patterns of growth vary between higher-education systems, it is important to explore country-specific funding dynamics. Rapidly emerging systems, such as China, show a remarkable growth in total R&D funding, researchers and PhD graduates. According to the OECD report, from 1995 through 2018, Chinese R&D investment from public and private sources increased by over 15 per cent a year on average, roughly five times the increases observed in the US and Europe. The number of PhD degrees in China has grown by 119 per cent since 2005, compared to 37 per cent in the US and 15 per cent in Germany. In the same time period, Japan witnessed stagnation with a small increase of 3 per cent more PhD graduates and Russia reduced its PhD pool by nearly 17 per cent, from 34,046 to 28,322 awarded doctorates in 2005 and 2018, respectively. The main sources of R&D funding for higher education differ between these countries, which partly explains national funding dynamics.

Shift from public to private funding

A second trend can be described as a shift from public to private funding in many countries. The private sector makes the largest contribution to national R&D spending in higher education and 'most OECD countries have witnessed a reduction in the rate of growth of public research funding' (Whitley et al., 2018: 110). Although the mix of funding sources varies between countries (UNESCO, 2020), the private sector accounts for around 70 per cent of R&D funding among the 10 largest spending countries. The share of government funding as the second largest source in most countries had been stable in Germany (28 per cent), but slightly declined in Japan and Korea from 17 per cent to 15 per cent and 23 per cent to 21 per cent, respectively. Government funding decreased considerably in China from 26 per cent to 20 per cent, the UK from 33 per cent to 26 per cent and the US from 31 per cent to 22 per cent. In Russia, a reverse trend can be observed as the already high share of government funding increased in the same period, from 62 per cent to 67 per cent (OECD, 2021b).

A high proportion of private funding means that most research takes place outside academia or aligns with industry objectives. In China, only 7 per cent of R&D was carried out in universities in 2018, compared with 13 per cent in the US and 22 per cent in the European Union (Bisson, 2020: 6). Doctoral-education policies moving towards more professional doctorates, transferable skills and intensified university–industry collaborations are directly linked to the increasing importance of private funding and prioritisation of applied research (Jones, 2018).

Shift from block grants to external project funding

A third trend is a shift from block grants towards more external project funding from diverse foundations, government and funding agencies, enforcing the 'projectification of doctoral training' (Torka, 2018). This model implies a project management approach, in which research processes are 'divided into projects that can be articulated in proposals and evaluated' (OECD, 2018: 23). PhD students are expected to take on or develop a PhD project at an early stage and 'carry it out' according to a plan. Within this model, institutions, faculty, supervisors and PhD candidates are expected to ensure that projects are 'doable', stay on track, progress continuously and will be completed on time. While this model may constrain flexibility and is differentially applicable to various research fields (Torka, 2018), it also provides doctoral candidates with structure, opportunities for collaborating and learning in teams, increased interactions with advisors, improved networking opportunities and future job placement because experience in project work is relevant both within and beyond academia (Graddy-Reed et al., 2021). The relevance of project funding varies significantly by discipline and country 'with no observable trend among countries', partly due to data gaps (OECD, 2021c: 25).

Focus on priority research or 'grand challenges'

The fourth trend is a focus on priority research, such as the 'grand challenges' (Kaldewey, 2018) and large grants for research clusters and centres (Bloch and Sørensen, 2015). The concentration of funding reduces the diversity of possible research topics to create a 'critical mass' and enforce collaboration often across disciplines, sectors and stakeholders. Coping with the complexity of interdisciplinary research and collaboration can enrich, but potentially overwhelm, doctoral candidates. External pressures on PhD students may inhibit their development as autonomous 'thinkers', a necessary and required skill for success in their future careers. Finally, the rise in research funding and PhD numbers has not been accompanied by an increase in permanent positions, both inside and beyond the academy.

The share of permanent positions, either conferring civil servant status or tenure, and open-ended positions, is decreasing relative to the number of researchers on fixed-term contracts. In some countries, this is the result of restrictions on public employment. In others, it is the result of institutions not wanting to commit to long-term personnel expenditure in the face of funding uncertainty (OECD, 2021c: 29).

This gap enforces competition among PhD students for casual, fixed-term and project-based employment. In addition, funding gaps may result in elongated and insecure career phases, the delay of tenure, as well as the potential declining capabilities of the academic system to absorb the growing number of PhD holders (Laudel and Bielick, 2018; McAlpine et al., 2018). As a result, transferable skills and career development programmes have been included in many doctoral-education systems.

Taken together, these trends highlight an unmet need for coordination across the education, funding and future employment sectors: funding for training and education should be stably increased, attention to skill development needs to be enhanced and stakeholders should engage in a larger discussion about expanding employment options post PhD.

Five primary concerns in funding of doctoral education worldwide

The aforementioned general funding trends underpin five primary concerns, addressed hereafter by presenting an outline of each concern and developing general recommendations rather than giving detailed country-specific examples. The five concerns are: (a) funding instability during the PhD, in particular in times of crisis; (b) the lack of reasonable funding amounts available to PhD candidates; (c) funding flexibility needed to ensure a certain autonomy for PhD candidates to develop and organise their research; (d) the availability of international funding for mobility and collaboration; and (e) funding beyond the doctorate to address the insecure career prospects of many PhD holders. Interspersed among all of these funding concerns, and highlighted elsewhere in this book, are the impacts on mobility, potential career prospects and the differences in time to degree. Since the funding situation and related concerns vary across doctoral-education systems, the suggestions need to be adjusted to national, regional and institutional conditions.

First concern: funding instability

Doctoral-education funding is subject to unforeseeable social, political and economic dynamics that impact funding (in)stability at country, regional, institutional and individual levels. External shocks, such as the financial crisis or the COVID-19 pandemic, unpredictable shifts in funding policy and the long-term demographic developments and uncertainties inherent to many higher-education funding systems make it difficult for candidates to plan their research, careers and private lives. Doctoral-education institutions around the globe struggle with providing more funding stability in times of dynamic change. The COVID-19 pandemic revealed a lack of long-term funding security and planning in many higher-education systems. In the US, 131 doctoral programmes suspended admission for fall 2021 due to the COVID-19 pandemic, because 'administrators wanted to use the funds they would've awarded to prospective new students in admission packages to ensure current students could stay on track' (Zahneis, 2021). According to a survey at the University of Sydney in Australia, three-quarters of responding PhD candidates anticipate financial hardship and 45 per cent expect to be forced to suspend or withdraw from their studies within six months due to a lack of funds (Johnson et al., 2020). Universities and funders around the globe provided only short (up to six months) scholarship extensions or eased deadlines to mitigate the continuing impacts of the pandemic. In the aftermath of the global financial crisis (2007–8), Malaysia scrapped its ambitious MyBrain15 programme to increase doctoral degree holders to 160,000 by 2020 and ceased funding for stipend, tuition and examination fees. The ageing Japanese population has resulted in the contraction of the entire university sector, a decline of research productivity in the natural sciences and engineering, as well as a shift towards fixed-term employment and a high rate (52 per cent) of self-funded doctoral candidates in 2015. These trends correlate with PhD students feeling unsupported and uncertain about their future.

Many countries also face an imbalance between humanities, arts and social sciences (HSS) and science, technology, engineering and maths (STEM) funding due to a priority for 'relevant' research and 'job-ready graduates'. For example, the Australian Department of Education (2020) has recently doubled tuition fees for arts degrees to 'deliver more job-ready graduates in the disciplines and regions where they are needed most and help drive the nation's economic recovery from the COVID-19 pandemic'. Even prior to the pandemic and the associated financial unrest, inequities between HSS and STEM had impacts across the PhD educational ecosystem, and these inequities have just been accentuated over the past years.

Uncertainties in higher-education funding policy and systems can be observed around the globe. In Germany, for example, specific funding for graduate schools has been discontinued and reallocated to competitive project-based research clusters. The dependency on external grants led to short-term contracts for doctoral candidates. Although doctoral candidates are expected to complete their studies within three years, many PhD students start their doctorates with financial uncertainty. As the median contract length of PhD students is two years (Federal Ministry of Education and Research, 2021: 116), most candidates are supported by a series of contracts, leading to fragmented careers, biographies and publication records (Metz-Göckel et al., 2016). US graduate students often receive funding packages with varied periods of guaranteed funding. While STEM disciplines with large grants may offer funding for the entire candidature time, other packages only cover the initial year(s) and promise further funding through grants or teaching and research assistantships. This uncertain 'economy of promise' (Felt, 2017: 140) makes it difficult for doctoral candidates to plan their long-term research trajectories, career prospects and private life decisions. The 'European Charter for Researchers' (European Commission, 2005) has addressed this issue by defining minimum standards for employers and funders to ensure that all researchers can 'combine family and work, children and career' and 'the performance of researchers is not undermined by instability of employment contracts'.

However, in many countries, funding for doctoral students has not been adjusted to increased PhD production, sometimes transferring the responsibility of obtaining funding to the individual PhD candidate. The sustainability and predictability of funding for doctoral students in all research areas should be ensured to support the creation of new graduates and knowledge within reasonable time frames. This may imply reconsidering reasonable PhD growth rates, the creation of emergency funds in times of increased uncertainty and linking admission to the availability of guaranteed funding. Ultimately, these issues must be linked to ensuring PhD-trained researchers have access to commensurate employment both inside and outside of academia. In addition, PhD candidates have employment and full social security and unemployment benefit rights in some countries, in particular in Europe; however, in the majority of countries worldwide, this is not necessarily the case. The fact that PhD students are entering the labour market with an employment contract relatively late also delays their entitlement to pension rights. This is another indirect effect of funding instability to which most PhD candidates are exposed.

Second concern: reasonable funding

The second concern is that funding amounts need to be reasonable. Available scholarships often do not cover all research, minimum living wages or trainee benefits such as retirement, social security or unemployment insurance. As a result, PhD candidates often pursue part-time work or apply for loans to support their income. However, these actions may lead to rising debts (National Center for Education Statistics, 2018), delays in degree completion and reduction of novel and exploratory research approaches and outcomes. 'Reasonable' funding depends on many factors, such as national and regional living costs, the availability of additional support structures (for example, subsidised housing) and the demographics of the PhD population, as candidates with caring responsibilities have higher living expenses.

Since major universities are often located in expensive cities with premium housing costs, it is unfortunate that, for the most part, scholarship rates have not been adjusted to reflect real cost-of-living expenses in different locations. In Kazakhstan, most students (90 per cent) receive a small monthly stipend (of about US$250) and an additional fixed stipend for mandatory overseas internships, according to the country report. State stipends are too low to cover living costs in most Kazakh cities, and internship funding is not enough to visit high-cost countries for the period of time needed to do research. As a consequence, almost all students work part-time as research assistants, as junior faculty members or in support roles for projects not necessarily related to their research or academic interests. This distracts from the focus of the PhD and negatively affects the time to degree. The Russian government funds doctoral candidates, but stipends are insufficient, amounting to 10–20 per cent of the average salary for Russian citizens, as estimated in the country report. A high percentage of self-funded PhD students (30 per cent) is the observable consequence of insufficient funding at the national level. Funding schemes in South Africa prioritise STEM fields and doctoral students tend to work full time on funded projects in these areas, whereas the majority of PhD students in the HSS are self-funded. The National Research Foundation is South Africa's main provider of postgraduate bursaries and offers a range of scholarships for doctoral candidates (SAURA, 2012), but the annual amounts ($5,000 to $8,750) are inadequate for students to support themselves and their families. As a consequence, a high percentage of doctoral students in South Africa study on a part-time basis (70 per cent) and they are less likely to succeed and complete their PhD, as compared to full-time students (Cloete et al., 2015). In Japan, only about 10 per cent of PhD students receive a scholarship that covers minimum living costs, and more than half of doctoral students do not get any financial assistance. As a result, the number and proportion of working students has increased by almost 25 per cent from 2005 to 2015, according to the country report. Clearly, there are country-to-country variations, but overall, PhD candidates rarely receive sufficient funding to consistently focus on their research and educational pursuits, absent of outside influences.

In many countries with high living costs, PhD students are under financial pressure for an extended period of time. At the same time, a completed PhD provides no more guarantee to obtain appropriate employment in the academic or other job markets (Skakni et al., 2019) which would adequately compensate for the additional invested time and money necessary to pursue a PhD. Although doctorate holders have the highest employment rates (92 per cent) across OECD countries and sometimes enjoy an earnings premium relative to other graduates (OECD, 2021c: 24), the question remains whether a PhD pays off in the long run.

The doctorate is an educational activity, an apprenticeship and an investment to prepare candidates for employment and appropriate remuneration in the future. In theory, this justifies relatively low incomes during the training phase, but inappropriate and inconsistent funding can also compromise the aim of completing a high-quality doctorate in a reasonable amount of time. Ensuring the balance between real living costs and the income of doctoral candidates is necessary to allow graduate students to focus on the PhD experience. Therefore, we recommend universities and research programme leaders review and adjust funding amounts in relation to real local living costs and individual student's needs.

Third concern: funding flexibility

The third concern is the need for funding flexibility to account for personal, field and project-specific needs and to ensure that doctoral candidates have the necessary freedom to develop their research directions. Funding often comes with a purpose and strict timelines, leading to predefined and standardised project cycles enforcing a trend towards the *projectification* of doctoral education and research (Torka, 2018). Projectification describes a model of research in which PhD students are expected to work on predefined projects or develop their own project aims at an early stage before 'carrying it out' in a linear and timely fashion. This model has been adopted by many doctoral-education systems, although it fits to disciplinary research practices and cultures differently. For example, while doctoral candidates in the HSS are indeed expected to develop their PhD projects independently, this is impossible in many STEM disciplines. PhD candidates often mature in the context of research groups because they need to acquire in-depth knowledge of the research field, research methods and the tacit knowledge to run complex experiments. Moreover, the independent development of research directions is limited by costs, access to facilities and other practical issues. The typical PhD project in these disciplines involves a starting problem or project identified by a more experienced scientist, usually the prospective supervisor, which is then gradually taken on by PhD students to develop initial projects further in a flexible manner. In many experimental disciplines, increased research funding has led to a competition of projects for students because students can choose projects that best fit their interest. This means that projectification may actually enhance the range of doctoral-education opportunities.

The projectification trend and model implies a project management approach in which institutions, faculty, supervisors and PhD candidates are expected to ensure that projects are 'doable', stay on track, progress continuously and will be successfully completed in a timely manner. Institutional expectations, external funding and research ethics applications enforce this model that has become predominant in many doctoral-education policies and guidelines across disciplines. Clearly, some research planning is necessary to learn the scientific method, envisage risks, coordinate complex research processes or keep candidates on track, but it is unlikely that planning can eradicate the unpredictabilities inherent in the PhD process that regularly lead to delays.

The time for completing a PhD continues to be longer than desirable in most higher-education systems worldwide. This is a concern for research-funding agencies, universities, academics and doctoral students facing increasingly constrained labour markets, particularly in academia (Horta et al., 2019: 1).

A mismatch between expected and actual completion times can be found around the globe. Expected or normative completion times are linked to funding opportunities and vary according to national doctoral-education systems. Systems that require a master's or honours degree for doctoral programme admission usually expect three to four years to complete the doctorate. Systems in which students can enrol directly in doctoral programmes after obtaining their undergraduate degrees may expect longer completion times. The normative time to degree in the US graduate school system, where many programmes do not award a stand-alone master's degree, is about six years, with many field-specific variations. The first doctoral phase requires coursework and culminates with the qualifying exam, a capstone paper (occasionally), as well as the approval of a prospectus that outlines the PhD project. The second phase, known as 'all but dissertation', is dedicated to individual doctoral research. Although expected completion times are standardised and apply to all kinds of research, the actual time to degree varies along many factors influencing completion, including disciplines, institutions, student characteristics and funding types (Torka, 2020).

Reliable completion time data is not available in all countries, often just estimated or aggregated with expected time to degree, masking a mismatch that exists around the world. For example, in the US, the actual median completion time is eight years since starting graduate school or six years following completion of the qualifying exam (National Science Foundation, 2020). Similarly, in Canada, it takes 5.2 years to complete a PhD, not including the master's degree. Chile's main funding programme (Becas) provides four years of stipend funding, although students complete their PhD after about six years. Australia offers funding for 3.5 years, but the actual median PhD completion time is 4.8 years (Torka, 2020). Universities in South Africa are expected to ensure a three-year completion time for PhDs due to standard funding cycles, although the real average time to degree is close to five years (Cloete et al., 2015). Finally, in the Netherlands, most PhD candidates are employed at universities for four years, while the average completion time is currently above five years, according to the national Association of Universities (VSNU, 2020). Clearly, there is a disconnect between available funding, expected time and actual time to complete PhD training across the globe. Therefore, either increasing the length of funding or realigning educational expectations is necessary to better support PhD candidates.

The mismatch between funded and real completion time is likely to trigger stress and aggravate the already high prevalence of mental health problems among doctoral candidates (Levecque et al., 2017). A realignment of expected and real completion times is necessary to enable students to complete high-quality dissertations in a *reasonable* time. We consider a balanced and more flexible model as one that questions a 12-year-long doctoral study but allows certainly more than three years to complete a doctorate. To identify the best fit between expected and actual completion times, it is necessary to collect and assess reliable completion data that accounts for obvious differences between research fields and student characteristics. Flexible funds can mitigate such differences and support students to focus on the PhD, particularly in the most challenging final stage of writing up and disseminating their research findings.

Fourth concern: availability of funding for international mobility

The fourth concern is the value of and financial support for international exchange. Mobility and collaboration must be ensured and enhanced in times of growing global nationalism and crises. The current pandemic has shown that some national higher and doctoral-education systems depend on international collaboration; these systems are at risk if global mobility ceases. For example, higher education is Australia's third-largest export industry. Due to COVID-19, the sudden 60-per-cent drop in international student fee revenues placed about 17,000 university jobs at risk and diminished PhD student's opportunities to supplement their funding with casual teaching. A recent survey shows that the pandemic led to a decline of international first-time enrolments at US doctoral programmes by 26 per cent (Zhou and Gao, 2021). The loss of international exchange associated with these missing enrolments will be felt for years to come.

National systems and the EU provide most of the funding for international mobility, exchange and collaboration. Funding comes with a purpose and the power to define conditions of access, research priorities and knowledge. The growing number of international students worldwide currently relies on four main types of funding opportunities. Many countries provide special funding schemes to attract international students to pursue a PhD in their national doctoral-education systems. This implies that international students have to match the educational requirements of other systems and they may need to adjust their topics to the priorities of local advisors and national funding opportunities. An example of such a programme is the Australian Research Training Program for overseas students, which has its historical roots in the drive of a remote country to connect with the world (Torka, 2019). Other funding schemes such as the US Fulbright Program, the Chilean Beca Program or the China Scholarship Council support domestic students to study and conduct research abroad. The third type consists of international research collaborations in the context of large research infrastructures (for example, CERN) or projects. PhD students usually pursue the doctorate at a national university while collaborating with other researchers internationally. The fourth type are institutional collaborations between universities in joint PhD programmes. These programmes allow doctoral students to enrol at two universities, where they are jointly supervised by two advisors and achieve a dual degree. Global fellowships for doctoral candidates are still rare. Certain funding schemes such as the European Marie Skłodowska-Curie Actions programme offer interesting opportunities for PhD training without nationality restriction of the candidates, a lot of these being bottom-up and supporting projects across all STEM disciplines, including the humanities and social sciences.

National funding for international mobility, collaboration and exchange is unevenly distributed and leads to two problems. First, emerging doctoral-education systems rely on the collaboration with advanced systems in the Global North to improve the quality of the doctorate, but they can often not afford undertaking research training in these high-cost countries. Kazakhstan, for instance, introduced the PhD degree in 2010 to align its research training to international standards. Doctoral students are required and financially supported to undertake international research internships with a small lump-sum stipend. But the funding is too low to cover high living costs in the most advanced systems to carry out research projects. This results in short visits and attempts to leave the country permanently.

The second problem is that the Global North dominates the global funding landscape and dictates the research agenda of the Global South. This is a hegemonic situation at a global level. Authority may be exercised directly, for instance when Northern funders define the problems for researchers in the South. More generally, it involves indirect control, occurring through such practices as researching within an established methodological framework or forming an intellectual workforce through curricula modelled on those of Northern institutions. It is also realised within the countries of the North, through practices of introversion, where Northern scholars systematically focus only on the knowledge produced by other Northern knowledge workers (Collyer et al., 2019).

International research funding and collaboration in Africa has substantially increased since the turn of the century. This led to an 'over-reliance on foreign funding' (Arvanitis and Mouton, 2019: 12) in many but not in all African countries. The dominance of research funding from foreign countries shapes the form of collaboration. African countries rarely manage these international programmes by themselves and they are more likely to collaborate with international partners than with other African countries. In these Global North/South collaborations, the significance of 'local knowledge' is negotiated.

This knowledge is tied to local needs and local communities, can challenge mainstream knowledge and is subject to coloniality in the form of institutional centrality, control of international agendas through funding and corporate control of publishing, more subtle mechanisms of hegemon, such as belief in the universality of science, and the disciplinary hierarchies created within new domains of knowledge (Collyer et al., 2019: 174).

Taken together, international funding supersedes local knowledge development and removes the autonomy of Global South researchers to fully pursue their own, independent research paths. International funding can enable, but also compromise, the just exchange of ideas. To support international exchange and ensure that PhD projects develop in an appropriate context, international PhD funding should be expanded in all fields. This may include short-term visits and exchanges between doctoral programmes, carrying out entire PhD projects abroad or dual degrees. Importantly, internationally-funded programmes must ensure that collaborations are dictated by the needs of projects and that conflicting national PhD regulations do not infringe on the development of the PhD project. Integrating local researchers and communities in the review of international funding opportunities would support the significance of local knowledge and help to ensure that the research products directly benefit the local community. Chapter 7 more specifically addresses the need of international funding for capacity building during the doctorate by giving a number of specific country and context-specific examples.

Fifth concern: funding beyond the doctorate

The last concern is the fit between doctoral education and its wider environments. The quality of the doctorate depends not only on the value of the research but also on the prospects for the PhD candidate following their training and education, either inside or outside of academia. In recent years, global higher-education policies focused on the growth of PhD numbers and funding. Funding for postdoctoral fellows, permanent academic employment or the transition into other labour markets has not received the same attention. This has led to two distinct trends in emerging and established systems with different funding implications. In established systems, which are likely saturated with trained PhDs, the increased numbers of PhDs result in more competition for scarce academic jobs, more attention to nonacademic careers, a rise of temporary or casual work and increased job insecurity. Many rapidly emerging systems report a mismatch between state-driven increases in PhD numbers and the capacity of the surrounding academic system to supervise doctoral students, leading to quality issues and talent migration.

The very high growth of R&D funding in China (Figure 6.2) goes in hand with a twelvefold increase in doctoral graduates since 1995. As a consequence, China introduced a quality assurance system in 2007 to monitor and address ongoing concerns regarding training and dissertation quality. A shift from increasing the size of programmes to improving the quality of doctoral education has been suggested to remove barriers in the innovative capability of the Chinese doctoral-training system. While the advisor–student ratio in China meets international standards, a lack of qualified supervisors and adequate mentoring remains an issue (Chen et al., 2018). Kazakhstan has increased the doctoral population five-fold since 2007, although 50 per cent of university staff hold Soviet research degrees and less than 2 per cent a PhD. A survey among 7,513 African PhD students revealed a similar picture (Beaudry and Mouton, 2018). A lack of training opportunities and mentoring are the two most important career challenges in Africa, in addition to the general lack of research funding and infrastructures. Even in South Africa, which arguably has the most advanced doctoral-education system on the continent, supervisor capacity is too low to cope with its growing PhD population, since less than 50 per cent of university staff have obtained a PhD degree (Cloete et al., 2015). Therefore, it is not only necessary to address funding inadequacies in these countries, but the capacity to mentor students throughout their training and as they transition to careers must also be considered.

While doctoral students in rapidly expanding systems might find academic employment after completing the PhD, insecure career prospects are one of the most pressing problems in saturated academic systems. As a consequence, highly-contested coping strategies have emerged. Most strategies aim to support the transition of trained PhD students into the wider labour market (see Chapter 7), strengthen university–industry links, develop internship opportunities or provide transferable skill assessment and training. In addition to this 'revamping' of the PhD, Gould (2015) considers the 'splitting' into research and professional doctorates, 'skipping' the PhD in favour of sufficiently qualifying master's degrees or 'cutting' the number of doctoral students as contemporary strategies to better align PhD production and job-market needs. The lack of funding beyond the doctorate further discourages academic career aspirations of doctoral candidates (McAlpine et al., 2018; Metz-Göckel et al., 2016; OECD, 2021c). Early-career researchers often rely on a series of short-term postdoctoral fellowships and highly competitive fixed-term grants (for example, the Marie Skłodowska-Curie fellowships or European Research Council Starting Grants in the EU) to increase the likelihood of securing a small number of tenured academic posts. Jumping from grant to grant implies a change of topics instead of capitalising on primary results to develop PhD projects into more comprehensive research programmes or industry-related innovations after completion (Laudel and Bielick, 2018). While academic careers remain viable for many PhD holders, increased attention to diverse careers both within and beyond academia should be considered during PhD training.

Both dynamics, increased job insecurity in established and quality issues in rapidly-emerging systems, suggest an imbalance between PhD production, available funding and suitable career options. A combination of different, at times opposing, strategies are necessary to ensure this balance. This can imply a reduction or reasonable growth in PhD numbers, incentives and support to embark on careers within and beyond academia, as well as the appropriate funding of research environments to prevent brain drain and to allow for the development of promising candidates, ideas and innovations during candidature and beyond.

Reflecting these concerns in their context

Ensuring stable, reasonable, flexible, international funding and funding beyond the doctorate are core concerns across doctoral-education systems. The core concerns and general recommendations outlined in this chapter are not prescriptive and should be reflected upon, refined and adjusted according to the unique conditions and funding situation within individual national doctoral-education systems and within higher-education institutions. Planning a PhD and its related funding is complex, as individual and institutional or country contexts are difficult to predict over average completion periods of usually more than four years, depending on the environment. This chapter has highlighted some basic PhD funding issues that can be analysed across systems providing the opportunity to compare, learn from each other and start a global discussion about funding mechanisms for doctoral research and beyond. The next chapter will discuss specific considerations regarding capacity building of PhD students in different country contexts highlighting examples of PhD funding to support capacity-building policies.

References

Abedi, J., and Benkin, E. (1987) 'The effects of students' academic, financial, and demographic variables on time to the doctorate'. *Research in Higher Education*, 27 (1), 3.

Arvanitis R. and Mouton J. (2019) 'Observing and Funding African Research'. Ceped Working Paper 43. Accessed 9 June 2022. https://www.ceped.org/IMG/pdf/wp43.pdf.

Australian Department of Education, S. a. E. (2020) 'Job-ready graduates: Higher education reform package 2020'. Accessed 9 June 2022. https://www.dese.gov.au/download/8198/job-ready-graduates-discussion-paper/12326/document/pdf.

Beaudry, C., Mouton, J. and Prozesky, H. (2018) *The Next Generation of Scientists in Africa*. Cape Town: African Minds.
Breneman, D. (1976) 'The Ph.D. production process'. In J. Froomkin, D. Jamison and R. Radner (eds), *Education as an Industry*. Cambridge, MA: Ballinger, 3–52.
Chen, H., Zhao, S., Shen, W. and Cai, L. (2018) 'The quality of Chinese PhDs: Achievements, problems and responses'. *Chinese Education and Society*, 51 (3), 158–68.
Cloete, N., Mouton, J. and Sheppard, C. (2015) *Doctoral Education in South Africa*. Cape Town: African Minds.
Collyer, F., Connell, R., Maia, J. and Morrell, R. (2019) *Knowledge and Global Power: making new sciences in the South*. Clayton, Victoria: Monash University Publishing.
Country Descriptions. (2019) 'Doctoral education in Australia, Bulgaria, Chile, China, Egypt, Italy, Japan, Kazakhstan, Mexico, New Zealand, South Africa, Turkey and the US'. Accessed 9 June 2022. Retrieved from https://www.doctoral-education.info/documents.php.
de Valero, Y. F. (2001) 'Departmental factors affecting time-to-degree and completion rates of doctoral students at one land-grant research institution'. *The Journal of Higher Education*, 72 (3), 341–67.
Ehrenberg, R.G. and Mavros, P.G. (1995) 'Do doctoral students' financial support patterns affect their times-to-degree and completion probabilities?'. *The Journal of Human Resources*, 30 (3), 581–609.
European Commission. (2005) 'The European Charter for Researchers'.
Federal Ministry of Education and Research. (2021) 'Bundesbericht Wissenschaftlicher Nachwuchs 2021 [Federal report on junior scientific staff]'. Accessed 9 June 2022. http://www.buwin.de/dateien/buwin-2021.pdf.
Felt, U. (2017) 'Of timescapes and knowledge scapes: re-timing research and higher education'. In P. Scott, J. Gallacher and G. Parry (eds), *New Languages and Landscapes of Higher Education*. Oxford: Oxford University Press, 129–48.
Gould, J. (2015) 'How to build a better PhD'. *Nature*, 528 (7,580), 22–5.
Graddy-Reed, A., Lanahan, L. and D'Agostino, J. (2021) 'Training across the academy: The impact of R&D funding on graduate students'. *Research Policy*, 50 (5), 104, 224.
Hasgall, A., Saenen, B., Borrell-Damian L. (coauthors Van Deynze, F., Seeber, M. and Huisman, J.). (2019) *Survey: Doctoral Education in Europe Today: Approaches and institutional structures*. Geneva: European University Association.
Horta, H., Cattaneo, M. and Meoli, M. (2019) 'The impact of Ph.D. funding on time to Ph.D. completion'. *Research Evaluation*, 2019.
Isaac, P., Koenigsknecht, R.A., Malaney, G.D. and Karras, J.E. (1989) 'Factors related to doctoral dissertation topic selection'. *Research in Higher Education*, 30 (4), 357–73.
Johnson, R.L., Coleman, R.A., Batten, N.H., Hallsworth, D. and Spencer, E.E. (2020) *The Quiet Crisis of PhDs and COVID-19: Reaching the financial tipping point*. Research Square.
Kim, D. and Otts, C. (2010) 'The effect of loans on time to doctorate degree: Differences by race/ethnicity, field of study and institutional characteristics'. *The Journal of Higher Education*, 81 (1), 1–32.
Laudel, G. and Bielick, J. (2018) 'The emergence of individual research programs in the early career phase of academics'. *Science, Technology, & Human Values*, 43 (6), 972–1,010.
Laudel, G. and Gläser, J. (2008) 'From apprentice to colleague: The metamorphosis of early career researchers'. *Higher Education*, 55 (3), 387–406.
Levecque, K., Anseel, F., De Beuckelaer, A., Van Der Heyden, J. and Gisle, L. (2017) 'Work organization and mental health problems in PhD students'. *Research Policy*, 46 (4), 868–79.
Lovitts, B.E. (2001) *Leaving the Ivory Tower: The causes and consequences of departure from doctoral study*. London: Rowman & Littlefield Publishers.
McAlpine, L. and Amundsen, C. (2018) *Identity-Trajectories of Early Career Researchers: Unpacking the post-PhD experience*. London: Palgrave Macmillan UK.
Metz-Göckel, S., Schürmann, R., Heusgen, K. and Selent, P. (2016) *Faszination Wissenschaft und passagere Beschäftigung: Eine untersuchung zum drop-out aus der universität [Academic Fascination and Temporary Employment: A study of university drop-outs]*. Opladen: Verlag Barbara Budrich.
National Center for Education Statistics. (2018) 'Trends in Student Loan Debt for Graduate School Completers'. Accessed 9 June 2022. https://nces.ed.gov/programs/coe/indicator/tub.
National Science Foundation. (2020) *Doctorate Recipients from U.S. Universities 2019*. Arlington: National Science Foundation.

Nerad, M. and Cerny, J. (1993). 'From facts to action: Expanding the graduate division's educational role'. *New Directions for Institutional Research*, 1993 (80), 27–39.
Neumann, R. (2007) 'Policy and practice in doctoral education'. *Studies in Higher Education*, 32 (4), 459–73.
OECD. (2018) *Effective Operation of Competitive Research Funding Systems*. Paris: OECD Publishing.
OECD. (2021a) *Education at a Glance: Education and social outcomes (Edition 2020)*. Paris: OECD Publishing.
OECD. (2021b) *Main Science and Technology Indicators (Edition 2020/2)*. Paris: OECD Publishing.
OECD. (2021c) *Reducing the Precarity of Academic Research Careers*. Paris: OECD Publishing.
SAURA. (2012) 'Doctoral education: Renewing the academy'. *SARUA Leadership Dialogue Series*, (4) 1.
Skakni, I., Calatrava Moreno, M.d.C., Seuba, M.C. and McAlpine, L. (2019) 'Hanging tough: Post-PhD researchers dealing with career uncertainty'. *Higher Education Research & Development*, 38 (7), 1,489–1,503.
Skopek, J., Triventi, M. and Blossfeld, H.P. (2020) 'How do institutional factors shape PhD completion rates? An analysis of long-term changes in a European doctoral program'. *Studies in Higher Education*, 1–20.
Stock, W.A., Siegfried, J.J. and Finegan, T.A. (2011) 'Completion rates and time-to-degree in economics PhD programs'. *The American Economic Review*, 101 (3), 176–87.
Torka, M. (2018) 'Projectification of doctoral training? How research fields respond to a new funding regime'. *Minerva*, 56 (1), 59–83.
Torka, M. (2019) 'Doctoral education in Australia: Between global trends and national traditions'. *Internationalisation in Higher Education*, 4, 35–54.
Torka, M. (2020) 'Change and continuity in Australian doctoral education: PhD completion rates and times (2005–2018)'. *Australian Universities' Review*, 62 (2), 69–82.
VSNU (2020) 'PhD students'. Accessed 12 September 2021. No longer available. https://www.vsnu.nl/en_GB/f_c_promovendi.html.
Zahneis, M. (2021) 'The shrinking of the scholarly ranks: The pandemic may do lasting damage to the pipeline of academic researchers'. *The Chronicle of Higher Education*, 67 (12).
Zhou, E. and Gao, J. (2021) *International Graduate Applications & Enrollment: Fall 2020*. Washington, DC: Council of Graduate Schools.

Notes

1   Professor Liezel Frick, Stellenbosch University, South Africa; Professor Reinhard Jahn, Max Planck Institute, Germany; Gulfiya Kuchumova, PhD candidate at University of Nazarbayev, Kazakhstan; Professor Susan Porter, University of British Columbia, Canada; Professor Ana Proykova, University of Sofia, Bulgaria: Ronel Steyn, PhD candidate at Rhodes University, South Africa; Professor Aya Yoshida, Waseda University, Japan; Dr Shannon Mason, Nagasaki University, Japan

7
Capacity building through mobility and its challenges [1]

Devasmita Chakraverty, Maude Lévesque, Jing Qi, Charity Meki-Kombe, Conor O'Carroll

This chapter investigates the various dynamics that influence capacity building for doctoral education in the context of mobility and is written from three perspectives. First, a key part of capacity building in many countries is attracting international doctoral candidates. This brings with it new challenges in terms of diversity and cultural sensitivity. Second, funding drives international mobility to migration of talents to regions of existing research excellence and it is hard to bring them home. Virtual mobility has been a necessity during the pandemic but combined with international travel it can be part of bringing greater balance. The concept of mobility itself needs to expand from being purely international to include interdisciplinary and intersectoral movement. These aspects are important in addressing broad societal challenges (for example, climate change) and careers outside academia. Third, there is increasing focus of governments on expanding research activity as part of economic growth. This has led to greater political interference in both the type of research funded and the disciplines supported. Throughout the chapter, examples are given from a wide range of countries and regions to stress the diversity of approaches and underline that there is no one-size-fits-all solution to any of the mobility-related issues. In terms of the Hannover Recommendations, this chapter leads directly to:

3. encourage diverse forms of mobility to develop multiple careers and ensure a more balanced distribution of talent around the globe;
3a. provide international, intersectoral and interdisciplinary as well as virtual mobility opportunities in doctoral education in order to

support exposure to new fields and to empower deep and diverse questioning leading to new ideas, assembling evidence to support these ideas and defending them to peers and to society;

3b. ensure that funding balances existing inequalities between research systems by helping to address unequal flows of talent and by challenging traditional mobility patterns.

This chapter approaches the issue of how to build and maintain capacity for doctoral training contextualised in a global environment where academia has become one of the many career paths for PhD graduates. Here, we consider careers within academia while the following chapter explores in more detail careers beyond academia. Increased investment in research combined with greater participation (due to factors including diversity and underrepresented minorities; see also Chapter 4) has resulted in a high increase in the number of doctoral candidates. National policies have moved from the view of the PhD as a niche academic qualification to a key component of increasing research activity. A negative consequence of these policies can be to treat doctoral candidates as simply research workhorses and with little focus on their career development. This can be resolved through enhanced doctoral education and training that provides opportunities for professional career support to broaden PhD graduates' employment prospects.

There are many factors involved in capacity building, but a major one is the difference in the aims of institutions/regions/countries building doctoral capacity and those of the individual candidate looking for the best opportunity that will further their career. This is where mobility and migration become significant as personal decisions will impact the ability of an institution or organisation to build research capacity.

One can broadly divide the mobility decision-making process into push and pull factors (Bloch, Graversen and Pedersen, 2015). High-quality institutions combined with adequate funding and career opportunities will attract doctoral candidates; an open political environment can also be an attractor. Conversely, a lack of funding, career opportunities or high-quality research in an unstable political environment will push people to consider a PhD in another institution/region/country. The policy discussion often centres on expressions such as brain drain, brain gain or the more recent brain circulation (Vega-Muñoz et al., 2021). All of these miss the point that one is dealing with people who are making life-changing decisions, especially if it is a question of whether to move abroad for their doctorate.

International mobility flows have led to asymmetric patterns that only seem to benefit countries with well-developed research and education systems. Over time, the concept of mobility has been broadened to include interdisciplinary and intersectoral; this is now embedded in many PhD funding programmes (for example, the European Marie Skłodowska-Curie Actions). Returning to transnational mobility, the concept of virtual mobility is introduced and proposed as an effective means to moderate the effects of brain drain. One of the impacts of the COVID-19 pandemic has been to show the value of virtual mobility. Mobility should now be seen not just in terms of *international* but also *interdisciplinary, intersectoral* and *virtual*.

For many years, doctoral education was seen as an elitist training to become an academic. The numbers were small and career prospects in academia were excellent. Governments and national policymakers took little interest, if any, in doctoral education. However, over the past 50 years, this has changed radically because of the increasing national importance of building research capacity, resulting in an increasing number of doctoral candidates that are needed to drive the research effort. Therefore, governments have taken a more proactive role introducing performance indicators and expectations that PhD graduates will have transferable skills to enable them to move to nonacademic employment sectors. As pointed out in Chapter 1, many PhD programmes now offer such skills training and opportunities to engage with a wide range of employers as part of doctoral research or as internships.

In recent years, a new factor, that of explicit political interference in research themes, is having an impact on doctoral education. National policies that limit academic freedom and restrict funding for certain research areas can be a driver for outward migration. The section on the politics governing doctoral education deals with this issue.

Policy and its implementation are driven mainly by data from surveys, national/regional statistics and specific studies. One must be sensitive to the fact that there is a high variation in the quantity and quality of data available from different regions around the world. For regions including the European Union, North America and member countries of the Organisation for Economic Co-operation and Development (OECD), there is a great deal of detailed statistics available. This can mean that any discussion of global policy is strongly influenced by practice in these regions. To add richer and more nuanced insights, this chapter also includes individual examples that show some of the significant differences in other parts of the world. This can reveal very different dynamics that can go against commonly held opinions on doctoral education.

Capacity-building policies

Capacity building in academia is a dynamic process of building, both individually and institutionally, the skills and competencies required to conduct high-impact research (Trostle, 1992; DFHER, 2021). Individually, it can be viewed as a transition process from a doctoral candidate to a scholar with an independent, long-term, sustainable research agenda. Collectively, capacity building can examine several factors, including demographic diversity and discipline-specific trends.

The process of capacity building should be able to provide structured supervision during doctoral training, training in advanced disciplinary and transferable/generic skills, career mentoring within and outside academia and mentoring for mobility across borders, disciplines and sectors. A structured approach to doctoral training leads to benefits in terms of candidate experience and research output. For example, between 2007 and 2010, a three-year longitudinal study of doctoral candidates in Irish universities showed that, in contrast to those with a single supervisor, doctoral candidates in structured programmes were more likely to present at international conferences and publish in internationally peer-reviewed journals (O'Carroll et al., 2012).

A traditional PhD focuses on original research with an average training time globally of anywhere between three and 10 years. However, doctoral training is not monolithic; there are several kinds of doctoral degrees other than a traditional PhD, and each would entail unique training procedures. There is the scholar–practitioner approach (for example, doctorate in public health or DrPH) which emphasises practice. The scientist–practitioner training (for example, MD–PhD dual-degree training) emphasises both research and practice in medicine and biomedical research with an average training time of 8–10 years (Chakraverty, Jeffe and Tai, 2018; Chakraverty, Jeffe, Dabney and Tai, 2020; see also Chapter 1). For a more in-depth discussion on professional and industrial doctorates, see Chapter 8.

Globally, the number of researchers is increasing due to intensifying investment in research and innovation. In the period 2007–15, the global stock of researchers increased by 21 per cent to a total of 7.8 million (UNESCO, 2015). The highest percentage at 22.2 per cent is in the European Union, with 19.1 per cent in China and 16.9 per cent in the US. The latest data show that this further increased between 2015 and 2018 by 13.7 per cent (UNESCO, 2021). With increased investment in research, the main areas of expansion are at the R1 (PhD) and R2 (postdoc) levels, with far smaller increases at R3 and R4, using the classification of the

European Framework for Research Careers (European Commission, 2011a). This means that a bottleneck is created where the demand to progress to R3 and R4 (as a university academic) can only be met for a small number of researchers given the limited number of university academic positions; this trend was emphasised by the UK Royal Society (Royal Society, 2010; European Commission, 2020).

Challenges to PhD capacity building

The challenges of funding, education, training and career support are well known for all doctoral candidates. However, some of the challenges are exacerbated for women, minorities and underrepresented groups. Moreover, there are specific challenges that pertain exclusively to these groups. Even before they begin a PhD, many are discouraged by a highly competitive and unsustainable academic environment with high expectations of acquiring competitive grant funding and publishing research and the uncertainties associated with getting tenure (Golde and Dore, 2001; Fochler et al., 2016; Hansen, 2020). Women and minorities (for example, persons of colour) are more impacted by such decisions and are less likely to aim for or obtain a faculty position compared to their non-minority peers, leading to reduced gender and racial/ethnic diversity. For example, in the United States, women and men from underrepresented minority groups are 54-per-cent and 40-per-cent less likely to report interest in pursuing faculty positions respectively at research-focused universities compared to well-represented men (Gibbs, Jr et al., 2014).

There are other challenges doctoral candidates, and sometimes postdocs and faculty, experience. For example, funding (see also Chapter 6 for further detail on funding) has historically played an important role in doctoral-candidate retention rates, as funded candidates are more likely to be retained and are more likely to graduate through research fellowships (van der Haert et al., 2014), especially in STEM (Ampaw and Jaeger, 2011). Then, there are programmatic challenges including inadequate mentoring, lack of professional development or a dearth of role models (Butts et al., 2012; Piggott and Cariaga-Lo, 2019). Mentoring during doctoral training (Johnson, Rose and Schlosser, 2007; Wadman, 2012; Fisher et al., 2019) should also consider the importance of culturally sensitive faculty–student relationships among underrepresented minorities. Felder and Barker (2013) stated that a candidate's identity (professional, personal and racial) has a bearing on their relationship and interactions with faculty, advisor, department or institution.

Diversity challenges include the challenges faced due to minority status, which could be related to immigration status, gender and race/ethnicity, among others. While immigrant minorities voluntarily move to a country due to better life opportunities compared to their home country, non-immigrant minorities have a history of being forcibly conquered, colonised or enslaved by the society permanently against their will. Capacity building for First Nations, migrant, refugee and culturally diverse doctoral candidates often involves epistemological border-crossing which is deeply embedded in intersected histories (Qi et al., 2021; Qi, 2021). Historically, some of the barriers for women in science and medicine have been attributed to their personal characteristics along with social constructions of gender-role stereotypes (Keller and Dauenheimer, 2003; Chakraverty, 2013). A lack of institutional support makes women unable to balance their family and career, for example inadequate on-site childcare facilities or stringent and inflexible leave policies (McPhillips et al., 2007; Lendák-Kabók, 2020; Montero-Diaz, 2021). Minority students who experience stereotype threats fear being at the risk of conforming to a negative stereotype about their social group (Keller and Dauenheimer, 2003) and being judged by others based on such stereotypes (Shih, Pittinsky and Ambady, 1999; Allen and Webber, 2019). While a strong academic background is fundamental to post-secondary STEM persistence, black people's self-confidence, self-efficacy in their ability to engage in scientific work and identification as a scientist may be even more important to their success in science careers (Funk and Parker, 2018). The following example shows how cultural issues can impact negatively on career development.

In Africa, black people are also hindered from advancing their careers due to 'Black Tax'. Black Tax is a term that is commonly used in some African contexts to refer to the support middle-class professionals (usually first-in-the-family university graduates or 'those who have made it') give to their less privileged or struggling immediate and extended family members (Magubane, 2017). Black Tax is also described as a form of social capital in which the redistribution of wealth is supported by customs and norms such as 'Ubuntu' (Di Falco and Bulte, 2011; Magubane, 2017), an African philosophy of life that embraces human virtues such as compassion, commonality and sharing. This belief pressures many black professionals to share their income with less fortunate family members, which ultimately hinders and discourages many professionals from advancing their higher education. Doctoral studies are the most affected considering that pursuing a PhD is a 'luxury' few people can afford (Bendrups et al., 2020; Burford and Hook, 2019).

Thus, coupled with the Black Tax demands, many black professionals fail to pursue further education, especially doctoral studies.

Academic communication challenges are experienced by many doctoral candidates who are either not fluent English speakers or who have not been exposed to developing skills to communicate with an academic audience (for example, academic writing skills). As a result of the dominance of English in scientific publications, candidates who don't have English at first-language level may struggle with writing, publishing and seeking linguistic support (Cameron, Zhao and McHugh, 2012). The number of publications is widely used as an indicator of individual and institutional productivity and so is imperative for seeking funding for future research and promotion and tenure (McGrail, Rickard and Jones, 2006; O'Carroll et al., 2017).

A new challenge to PhD researchers is the emerging conflict between the traditional means of assessing quality through bibliometrics and the new methodologies of 'open science'. Currently, individual research excellence has been reduced to the one-dimensional metric of the Journal Impact Factor (JIF) (Larivière and Sugimoto, 2018). This takes a very narrow view of research excellence and excludes diverse career pathways.

Open science is being championed by major European research funders including the European Commission under Plan-S (https://www.coalition-s.org). While the focus is now mainly on open access to publications and open data and FAIR data, new methods for assessing excellence are being considered (O'Carroll et al., 2017). This leaves PhD researchers who are trying to establish themselves in the research community in limbo as, while they may desire to fully embrace open science and publish in open-access journals, they are still being assessed in the traditional manner using narrow bibliometrics. A recent survey carried out by the European University Association (EUA) showed that for researcher assessment in over 75 per cent of respondent universities, research publications and securing external research funding were the main criteria (EUA 2019). Metrics measuring research output dominate (82 per cent) followed by qualitative peer reviews (74 per cent). The main metric for publications is the JIF at 75 per cent followed by the h-index at 70 per cent. On a positive note, the Global Research Council (GRC) is moving towards agreement among research funders globally on introducing a far more comprehensive approach to assessment that values an individual's net contribution to research (GRC 2021).

Another challenge to doctoral training includes mentoring those who do not believe in their achievements and feel like intellectual frauds. Also known as impostor syndrome or impostor phenomenon (Clance,

1985), this is a psychological condition experienced by doctoral candidates (Chakraverty, 2020a), postdocs (Chakraverty, 2020b) and faculty (Hutchins and Rainbolt, 2017) who hold self-limiting beliefs about their abilities and potential to become successful in their field (Chakraverty, 2019). Recent research shows that doctoral candidates who feel like impostors tend to struggle with their academic communication, developing collaborative networks and asking for help and judging themselves harshly compared to their peers; the impostor phenomenon tends to amplify with every doctoral milestone crossed or academic recognition received (Chakraverty, 2020a).

Addressing the issues raised above will require country specific and contextual solutions. To address financial challenges such as securing competitive grant funding, institutions can provide support through grant-writing workshops. A study of a diversity-focused, mentored, research-skills training programme showed great success in terms of grant submissions and awards among underrepresented minority participants in cardiovascular research (Fabris et al., 2016). Such mentored-training programmes can be used as a model.

Additionally, Morehouse and Dawkins (2006) have recommended matching mentors with doctoral candidates based on research interests. Doctoral socialisation is a key aspect that shapes doctoral experiences (Kong et al., 2013) and the quality of faculty advising one has access to, emphasising the role of faculty-student mentoring in student success (Felder, 2010). Specifically, same-race connections (as faculty advisors and mentors) are essential for the overall success of underrepresented minority doctoral candidates (Barker, 2011). Campus-wide mentoring can help retain more women, reduce isolation and provide informational and psychosocial support (Chesler et al., 2010).

Finally, departments can better support women's success by identifying peer support groups, mentors and advisors (Dabney et al., 2016). There is an evident need for programmes geared specifically for the underrepresented minorities such as mentor programmes, work-life programmes, family integrated activities and supports and social support groups on campuses (Williams et al., 2018).

Reverse migration post PhD

While countries like the United States are training more PhDs than the labour market can employ, other countries (especially with large economies) have their own challenges. Many doctoral graduates take up jobs they are overqualified for that do not require a PhD at all. Countries like India are not producing enough PhDs in STEM who are skilled, competitive and can serve the needs of a booming economy through research and development. Globally, there is a general lack of quality control, PhD best practices or standards consistency across countries. Some may experience a long and often unstructured training with few financial benefits. Upon completion, few PhD graduates find employment in academia while their hyper-specialised academic focus may not be attractive to other sectors. Formal training varies widely and there is often little focus on teaching skills, networking and academic writing, all of which can help doctoral candidates to be employable in a wide variety of positions and sectors. For example, in Europe, a 2017 survey showed that while 81 per cent of PhD candidates believe skills training is important, only 33 per cent receive such training and this is usually related to communications (European Commission, 2017).

The following example presents how India is looking to bring back PhD graduates who have studied abroad. The Indian higher-education sector is the third largest in the world (in terms of total student enrolment) after the United States and China. Yet, doctoral training is not as consistent or internationally competitive in India, with very few universities and higher-education institutions finding a place among the top 100 in global rankings. Historically, a large proportion of those who obtained PhDs in India did so with the intention to teach at undergraduate and postgraduate colleges. Conducting research was a negotiable requirement even in some of the top institutes. However, with globalisation and the need to be internationally competitive and relevant, such requirements have changed. From 2021, a PhD degree is mandatory for teaching positions in universities. There are new policies in the PhD curriculum, including ethics and misconduct in research and publications.

Capacity building in doctoral education should also closely examine the capacity development of faculty who will be training future doctoral candidates. India experiences significant migration of scholars to other continents such as Europe, North America and Australia, who do not find the option to return sufficiently attractive. The government as well as universities have recently started to look at incentives to attract these scholars, through more and better job openings, competitive salaries, attractive benefits (such as subsidised or free childcare) and greater opportunities for research and professional development. The government has introduced special provisions for recruiting faculty at the assistant professor level who received their PhD from the top 500 universities ranked globally. Incentives include rewarding research productivity (measured through research published in top peer-reviewed journals), additional support to attend and present at international conferences every year and incentivising short-term research visits to other countries to promote collaboration. Additionally, training workshops for new faculty that focus on learning new instructional practices and developing research skills could be beneficial (Stains, Pilarz and Chakraverty, 2015). Other incentives could include better healthcare, longer and more flexible parental leave and better childcare facilities.

While many of the high-ranked institutes and universities in India have now adopted the tripartite areas of research, teaching and service as an evaluation framework to grant tenure to pre-tenured faculty, the requirements for obtaining tenure may vary. For example, some institutions prioritise research output while relaxing teaching and service requirements for pre-tenured faculty substantially. The number of publications required for tenure is lower, and so is the time for obtaining tenure, which is typically between one and three years. However, such policies are not uniform and vary between institutions.

One of the additional initiatives that has opened many lucrative faculty jobs for PhDs in the last decade or so in India is the establishment of many private universities, such as Ashoka University and O.P. Jindal Global University, providing excellent opportunities for teaching and research along with attractive, competitive salaries and benefits. Within Ashoka University, more than 75 per cent of current faculty members have obtained a PhD in the United States, the United Kingdom or another country outside India.

The example for India detailed above shows that there might be value in providing special incentives to early-career researchers living abroad to return to their home country. There is also a negative driver that may induce people to return home or at least leave their current country of residence. This is well exemplified in the stricter immigration policies in the United States that have made obtaining permanent residence and long-term job permits an expensive, time-consuming and harrowing process (including limited opportunities for spouses to find job opportunities due to strict visa rules). This, coupled with cultural alienation, increased xenophobia, hate crimes and discrimination against foreigners, push many to relocate back when competitive opportunities are made available.

The need to embrace all forms of diversity in capacity building

Overall, the main issues in doctoral capacity building include a combination of intrinsic and extrinsic challenges. While intrinsic challenges pertain to skill building, programme challenges and diversity issues, extrinsic challenges include inadequate employment options within and outside academia and not producing globally competitive PhDs. Capacity building is also largely shaped by migration trends for doctoral candidates both to pursue PhDs and to pursue job opportunities post PhD. Overall, it comes down to issues of numbers and quality. After all, doctoral workforce capacity is a function of research outputs and research quality. The challenges around capacity building also relate to the country-specific migratory trends. For example, countries like India experience a phenomenon that is popularly understood as the 'brain drain' where a sizeable proportion of Indians move out to pursue doctoral training and do not return, yet there are fewer PhDs training in India proportional to the population, especially in fields like STEM. In Europe, there is a similar trend where doctoral candidates migrate South-North and East-West.

Also, in the interest of better capacity building, it would be important to acknowledge and welcome diversity – cultural, social, intellectual and in any other forms. Recognising that there is not one single way of knowing things, doctoral education should support cross-cultural ways of learning and cross-talks between institutions, disciplines, education systems and countries. After all, there is not one prescriptive, ideal standard or template of doctoral education, and the different ways in which countries have imagined and reimagined doctoral education mirrors the socio-political contexts relevant to those countries.

International mobility of doctoral candidates

A key part of capacity building is attracting highly talented individuals from abroad to boost the national research effort and increase the quality of research in universities and research performing organisations. In this context of capacity building, one should understand the migratory trends of doctoral candidates at a globalised scale. Policies are indeed influenced by inbound and outbound mobility patterns of a given country's intellectual force as it contributes to national prosperity and growth.

Relations with other nations are additionally key in recognising the value given to different educational structures and the motivational factors at play in doctoral candidates' decisions. Central to this are the push and pull factors that influence the individual's decision to move to another country as part of developing their research career.

Overview of international PhD mobility

Migratory trends in graduate students and fledgling academics are mainly guided by three characteristics bearing influence on the researchers' careers: international networking, career perspectives and high-quality peers (European Union, 2018). The measured trends in mobility for international PhD candidates currently follow the typical patterns observed across educational levels, from South to North and East to West, with the strongest receiver of doctoral candidates being the United States (Bokova, 2015; OECD, 2018). Of all internationalised doctoral candidates, most are enrolled in science and engineering programmes, with a 130-per-cent growth in those enrolments between 2005 and 2012 (Bokova, 2015: 77). This trend can be explained by the active recruitment of STEM graduate students by countries across the world with ageing populations (Nerad and Evans, 2014). While legitimate concerns persist surrounding the potential for 'brain drain', the UNESCO report on the future of graduate education sustains the continuing benefits of brain circulation. It was estimated in 2015 that 2 per cent of all current university students abroad were international students (Bokova, 2015).

In the meantime, the growth of international students has continued. For example, in the United States, the percentage of international students rose from 4.8 per cent to 5.5 per cent between 2014/15 and 2019/20 (Institute of International Education, 2019 and 2020). While this percentage is not enough to pose a threat to the national development of individual countries, it is undeniable that this growing globalisation entangles universities in both highly valuable collaborations and fierce academic competition (Bokova, 2015). Outbound migratory trends of graduate students (brain drain) are of particularly high concern to countries during their economic development. With the advent of the COVID-19 pandemic however, we find promising evidence that virtual mobility could become widespread in doctoral education, thereby anchoring the candidate to their country of origin while establishing a concrete belonging to their institution of choice, irrespective of physical boundaries. Research by Smith McGloin (2021) highlights the strategies adopted by doctoral candidates during quarantine and, so doing, argues for the redefinition of mobility in a fixed setting.

A noteworthy change in mobility pattern is slowly being observed at a global scale, as international enrolments in Asia (for example, in China, Korea, Japan, Singapore, Qatar and the United Arab Emirates) are on the rise. Yet the number of students going to North American, Western European and Australian/New Zealand universities has increased as well, maintaining the general migratory trends of international education from South to North and East to West (Kritz and Gurak, 2018). This evolution can be explained by the fact that tertiary public expenditures and academic supply at home are the greatest determinants of a country's outbound mobility ratio (Kritz and Gurak, 2018). This indicates that given the growing higher-education investments of Asian and Middle Eastern countries, migratory trends for international students may change in the coming decade in favour of these regions.

As student migration ratios rise, so too are expectations in favour of international mobility increasing for doctoral candidates (Bauder, 2015; Bilecen and Van Mol, 2017). While the literature has long favoured the discussions around the benefits of international mobility, there has also been an increasing focus on the civic issues inherent in these expectations (Ackers, 2008; Bauder, 2015; Bilecen and Van Mol, 2017; Gerhards, Hans and Drewski, 2018). As Bilecen and Van Mol (2017) argue, the transnationalisation of education both creates and reproduces social inequalities between student bodies, faculty members and, more largely, their spaces of education. Gerhards, Hans and Drewski (2018) contribute to this discussion by empirically demonstrating how national scientific reputation (a doctoral candidate's country of origin) and symbolic capital (the university's prestige) affect a doctoral candidate's chances of taking advantage of international mobility outside their objective credentials along with their access to quality departments. These discrepancies are now a central focus of the discussion on migration and mobility at all levels of studies in hopes of bettering the future of international academic mobility based on its current shortcomings (Bauder, 2015).

Further, concerns have been raised with regards to international mobility being a prelude to international migration and, ultimately, a non-returning trajectory in doctoral candidates (Reale, Morettini and Zinilli, 2018). Low investments in research and development of the home country paired with the budgetary rollbacks of social sciences and humanities funding are identified as strong determinants of non-returns in researchers (Reale, Morettini and Zinilli, 2018). Overall, age appears to be a strong determinant of international mobility and relocation, as Van Noorden

(2012) found that within new doctoral graduates across regions, only 10 per cent would not consider international relocation in comparison to 40 per cent of those who had completed their PhDs 16 years ago. Finally, matters of forced migration in scholars facing risks in their country of origin ought to be mentioned as not all mobility journeys are undertaken by choice. A few recent significant examples include doctoral candidates in Yemen and Venezuela who have yet to find stability in the context of their country's humanitarian and economic crises (Scholars at Risk, 2020). Turkey and China's political climate, alternatively, pose a great challenge to the pursuit of knowledge and academic freedom as researchers have faced the purging of their institutions, imprisonment and worse (Scholars at Risk, 2020). Additionally, the suspension of campus activities considering the pandemic effectively shut down the research endeavours of communities lacking internet connectivity (Scholars at Risk, 2020.). Each of these matters separately could limit the return options of doctoral candidates while exacerbating the obstacles faced in the pursuit of their degree across the board.

Upon closer inspection of the available literature in distinct regions across the globe, singular trends emerge of the specific challenges, gains and ambitions with regards to the mobility of their doctoral pool. A brief overview of these particularities is essential to provide perspective on the interactions between countries and the effect that policies, economic and academic contexts bear on the development and exchange of knowledge worldwide.

Region-specific migratory patterns of mobile doctoral candidates

In this section, examples of PhD candidates' migratory patterns are presented and the differences between, and indeed within, regions illustrate the different drivers of mobility. Of course, these trends in migration are time sensitive, depending, for example, on changing funding, policy and political considerations. However, the examples presented below illustrate the diversity of factors, both push and pull, that influence the mobility destinations of prospective doctoral candidates.

North America

North America displays a strong inbound mobility ratio, strongly skewed in favour of the United States with Canada competing heavily to attract larger numbers of international researchers (Bokova, 2015). An overview of mobility motivations across nationalities shows that the prestige of a North American education paired with the enticing career opportunities offered within the continent strongly factor into the migration trends from East to West and South to North (Zhou, 2015). Obstacles to a greater outbound mobility include language barriers in Western Europe and the reduced career options in this latter setting (Knight and Madden, 2010). Additionally, a Canadian or American doctoral candidate's financial stability is predicated on a mixture of funding sources held simultaneously (Jones, 2018), thus limiting the emigration of candidates who would have otherwise been reliant on the same sources of income as domestic students.

Latin America

South America is establishing itself as an emerging influence within the international scientific community with some countries rethinking their academic infrastructure to the benefit of their countries' development (Munoz-Garcia and Chiappa, 2017). Much remains to be done for its national academic landscapes to find balance on the matter of student mobility. Fledgling academics rely heavily on international training to complete their education and struggle with steady funding at home (Bokova, 2015). As an example, Chile has incentivised outsourcing doctoral training with limited success in increasing the country's domestic research and development personnel on par with the OECD average (Comisión, 2015). These disappointing results, in turn, have fostered strong debates within the country regarding the efficacy of outsourcing doctoral training and the need for alternative strategies (Pedraja-Rojas et al., 2016). When turning to Mexico, it is found that outside attracting international talent, there is a will to universalise higher education as the current context precludes equal opportunities for citizens to access this training. The pervasive wealth disparities within the population reproduces systems of inequity and sets higher education, even with partial funding, as an impossibility for a vast proportion of individuals, a fact at the forefront of this movement toward greater inclusion (Caregnato et al., 2021). Both Mexico and Brazil, as such, have implemented affirmative action to facilitate their indigenous population's access to higher education, pointing to a positive shift in previously held financial priorities over the diversification of their scholars and the richness of the cultural contribution of indigenous researchers (Oyarzún, Franco and McCowan, 2017). South America thus still faces challenges with regards to 'brain drain' in terms of attracting foreign scholars, bolstering their own citizens into the pursuit of higher education and ensuring the return of their doctoral graduates. However, hopeful trends in doctoral accessibility and management point to the gradual decrease of such difficulties. A persisting obstacle to finding viable solutions to these challenges is the lack of broad and standardised statistics on PhD candidates and international students.

Africa

Doctoral mobility within Africa remains within the African continent (DHET, 2013: from Lee and Sehoole, 2015). Efforts are being made to attract future faculty members to prestigious institutions on the continent, particularly in South Africa. However, inbound mobility ratios from outside the African continent continue to be low at this time, with foreign students being attracted to the continent on vastly different bases than doctoral candidates in the United States or Western Europe (Lee and Sehoole, 2015). The African higher-education system has focused on building international networks by sending their academics abroad to exchange knowledge, good practices and information, building the eventual attractiveness of national institutions in the global market (Woldegiorgis and Doevenspeck, 2015). In South Africa, recruiting international postgraduate students has been declared a national priority under the National Plan for Higher Education and the National Development Plan 2030 (Cloete and Mouton, 2015). This endeavour is mitigated by political uncertainty within the region, which is being counterbalanced by various collaboration initiatives and short-term exchanges to involve researchers across borders in lasting scientific networks (Harle, 2013).

As Zeleza (2017) argues, many universities in Africa are largely not internationally competitive and recognised, considering their low international rankings. In addition, several lack sufficient funding for research. In certain cases, staff in such universities are not aware of how to access research funds due to a lack of information and international collaborations. These deficiencies act as push factors for many African students to study overseas to acquire internationally recognised doctoral degrees as well as to seek prestigious collaborations and engaging research. Their preferred destinations include Western countries such as the United Kingdom, the United States and more recently former Eastern Bloc countries (Woldegiorgis and Doevenspeck, 2015; Jiani, 2017). However, it is important to stress that some African universities offer world-class educational opportunities (Bothwell, 2015). Consequently, universities in countries such as South Africa and Egypt have earned themselves places in the top 1,200 universities in the world (Fomunyam, 2017). Impressively, the Times Higher Education 2016 ranking of BRICS and emerging economies places three South African universities (University of Cape Town 4th, University of the Witwatersrand 6th and Stellenbosch University 11th) in the top 12, while Brazil and Russia have one each and India has none (Fomunyam, 2017: 171).

Europe

With regards to Western Europe, PhD mobility trends are more extensively surveyed in European Union reports and OECD statistics. Globally, Western Europe is, after the United States, the preferred destination for doctoral candidates (Bokova, 2015; Veugelers and Van Bouwel, 2015). As an example, the Netherlands has seen a general increase in PhD graduates, among both domestic and international candidates, with a doctorate conferral rate of more than twice what it was in the year 2000 (VSNU, 2020). Most PhDs are employed by the universities themselves (VSNU, 2020). This trend of increasing international PhD candidates is generalisable to Western Europe as a whole and can be attributed to three broad factors: the English-speaking majority, the prestige of the education and the tertiary academic investments within the European Union (Veugelers and Van Bouwel, 2015). Policies for EU nationals greatly facilitate exchanges between institutions within the Schengen area, establishing a greater balance than anywhere else worldwide in terms of inbound and outbound mobility ratios (European Union, 2018). Scandinavia in general is actively recruiting international candidates to the PhD with an emphasis on research in the STEM fields (Nerad and Evans, 2014).

Eastern Europe has a very different academic context. Findings from two case studies (Bulgaria and Russia) indicate that the 1990s 'brain drain' afflicting Eastern Europe has begun to settle, with the region now regaining its intellectual infrastructure by effectively managing to both maintain and attract doctoral candidates from abroad (Berezina et al., 2018; Bokova, 2015). The creation of international networks from home appears to be a key factor in the current 'brain circulation' that is coming to define Eastern Europe's scientific mobility pattern (Berezina et al., 2018). Bulgaria has become a good example of this trend by encouraging bilateral agreements between countries to tie international institutions in scientific partnerships. These initiatives are however heavily determined by the political climate at hand as, in Russia for instance, collaboration remains mainly within the bounds of the former Soviet Union under the mindset that characterised the last decade of the Soviet regime (Platonova and Semyonov, 2018).

Asia

Further east, there is a steady rise in international enrolments on the Asian continent (for example, in China, Korea, Japan, Singapore, Qatar and the United Arab Emirates) (Kritz and Gurak, 2018). However, with it, the outbound mobility ratios of the United States and other Western countries have also increased, maintaining the continental outbound mobility trends. A prime example of this inclination is India, which is the strongest contributor of foreign scientists abroad but consequently suffers a heavy 'brain drain', with 40 per cent of its home-born researchers working overseas and facing little inbound mobility (Van Noorden, 2012). Chinese nationals are also incentivised to study abroad, however little reciprocal training through joint degrees or collaborating enterprises is observed (Yang, 2020). During the last 10 years, Chinese doctoral students have been encouraged with national or provincial fellowships to study a year aboard, but they are no longer encouraged to complete a doctoral degree outside China. The Chinese doctoral students who study for the entire degree time are funded mostly by the host university. We might conclude from surveying the mobility trends of Asia's PhD holders that, while economic 'push' factors are decreasing as its countries develop and gain prestige within the scientific community, there is yet to be seen a significant reversal of its emigration tendencies within the intellectual elite.

Australasia

Australia and New Zealand have become increasingly attractive destinations for international doctoral candidates, particularly for PhD candidates (Bokova, 2015; Education Counts, 2019). Indeed, they are being actively recruited by governments, either through scholarships, facilitated migration policies or jointly coordinated international programmes. Having previously suffered from brain drain, active efforts are made to reverse the tides and mobilise the intellectual elites to boost the economic development of Australia and New Zealand (Ziguras and Law, 2006). Most recently, the federal government of Australia has devoted extensive resources to facilitating pathways to higher education, namely by addressing educational costs through flexible scholarships, additional funding for industry placements and investments in indigenous candidates to increase doctoral education among its own population (Australian Council of Learned Academies, 2016). New Zealand has followed a similar strategy by allowing international doctoral candidates to pay domestic fees, incentivising professional doctoral degrees across disciplines and introducing creative components to higher-education training (Spronken-Smith, Cameron and Quigg, 2018). Generally, these countries have a definite advantage in attracting international doctoral students and researchers in commerce and natural sciences, since English is the main language spoken. It could be argued that the Oceanian reliance on the inbound mobility of its scholars is precarious and should not be encouraged to the detriment of varied strategies of academic growth. Namely, as has been seen in the COVID-19 pandemic, global disruptions may limit or altogether interrupt the flow of students required for universities to operate. During COVID restrictions, Australia lost most of the income generated by the enrolment of Chinese scholars, leaving its academic institutions critically underfunded (Mercado, 2020).

New Zealand is a small, isolated country in the South Pacific with a population of less than five million. Traditionally, there has been significant outward mobility of high achieving students to undertake their graduate study overseas. Indeed, this was almost seen as a rite of passage to secure an academic position back in New Zealand. However, until the mid-2000s, the inward mobility of international candidates was low. In a move to generate more skilled migrants, in 2006 the New Zealand Government introduced a package of support to attract international PhD students. The package included domestic fees for international PhD students, free education for their children and post-study work rights. Moreover, each university has scholarship support, which is accessible to both international and domestic applicants. Prior to the introduction of this policy, only 14 per cent of doctoral enrolments were international, but over the ensuing years the doctoral programmes experienced significant growth and by 2017, 48 per cent of doctoral students were international (Spronken-Smith, 2019). This government programme has been extremely successful in promoting the mobility of international students into New Zealand.

Mobility beyond borders: i[4] Mobility

The discussion above has focused exclusively on movement across national borders. As was discussed in Chapter 7 (Capacity-building policies) above, doctoral candidates must have the capacity to move across sectoral borders (for example, academia to industry) to further their career development. In order to promote intersectoral mobility, there should be options that, as per the European Commission (2011b: 6), 'include placements during research training; shared funding; involvement of non-academics from relevant industry in informing/ delivering teaching and supervision; promoting financial contribution of the relevant industry to doctoral programmes; fostering alumni networks that can support the candidate (for example mentoring schemes) and the programme, and a wide array of people/technology/knowledge transfer activities'

Doctoral research is often focused on a specific problem within a discipline. However, given the interconnectedness between disciplines and the need to address complex challenges (for example, sustainable development goals), researchers must be able to integrate information, data, techniques, tools, perspectives, concepts and/or theories from two or more disciplines or bodies of specialised knowledge. This highlights the need for doctoral training in an open research environment and culture to ensure that any appropriate opportunities for cross-fertilisation between disciplines, geographic areas and cultures can foster the necessary breadth and interdisciplinary approach.

A major collateral effect of the COVID-19 pandemic has been to bring to the fore the practice of virtual mobility. After an initial disparate approach, universities successfully provided virtual access to courses for students in the academic year 2020–21. This type of virtual mobility could also provide equal access to and for researchers with physical disabilities, while also helping those on parental leave to maintain contact with their national and international networks. Provided high-speed internet is available, it would further enable PhD candidates in the 'brain drain' countries to access well-resourced labs and to collaborate internationally (O'Carroll et al., 2014). Combined with short-term secondments/visits, this form of blended mobility could go some way towards improving the retention of researchers. This would then expand the concept of mobility from the one-dimensional to the four-dimensional: international, virtual, intersectoral and interdisciplinary.

The need for blended mobility

One of the greatest challenges faced when assessing the current mobility trends of doctoral candidates relates to the lack of a standardised measure across regions and the disparity in the available information, also discussed in Chapter 1. Western Europe and the United States, along with a few other OECD countries, provide excellent data on the matter of graduate mobility and the transnational mobility of its intellectual force. When investigating other regions however, the limited data or lack of disaggregation by international or domestic doctoral candidates or by doctoral degree conferred and its limited availability in English compound difficulties in clearly assessing the doctoral context worldwide and drawing representative conclusions.

Outside knowledge-based considerations or improving the surveying of mobility trends, practical concerns should be addressed considering the skewed migration patterns of certain regions and the precariousness that it reproduces worldwide. Indeed, of great concern is the predominantly outbound mobility ratios of developing countries, particularly in the southern hemisphere (for example, Chile, Mexico and South Africa). It has prompted worries surrounding non-return migration trends and debates concerning the policy changes necessary to address them. While it could be tempting to impose an obligation to return, it should be noted that a mandatory return to avoid a definitive divergence (departure) of a nation's doctoral pool is a false imperative: many other policy initiatives can be introduced to encourage the return of new researchers without constraining their freedom of choice and limiting their careers. Reale, Morettini and Zinilli (2018) explore this question in the case of social sciences and humanities scholars and reveal the factors involved in the return of doctoral graduates, namely the research and development funding of the home country, the shrinking job opportunities of their host country or difficulty of obtaining work visas and their family situation. Steps towards improving the academic infrastructure and valuing the doctoral candidates' expertise (through adequate research funding) should be considered ahead of restrictive policies. More specifically, fledgling researchers should be provided with incentives to return home rather than a restriction of their movements. Funding should also not be considered the 'end all' of the problem: there need to be real career opportunities for returning PhD emigrants along with a stable home environment tied to the structural conditions of their native country (Kritz and Gurak, 2018).

It should be stressed that a strong outbound mobility ratio is not exclusively problematic and should be encouraged, even in the case of an 'intellectual exodus'. Indeed, scientific mobility encourages international collaboration (Bokova, 2015: 74) even if doctoral graduates do not return home, as most often, they undertake collaborative research with their home country. While it does not immediately solve the issue of brain drain, expatriated doctoral candidates can be encouraged to work with 'home' universities to raise the quality of the education provided and build national competencies while nurturing academic relations abroad. As an example, Indian expatriates that have gained valuable knowledge overseas have continued to collaborate with their counterparts at home, thus raising the quality of education and technological capacities of universities and enterprises in India (Pande, 2014: from Bokova, 2015). Such global initiatives further persist after graduation as researchers with international experience continue to collaborate globally throughout their careers (Bokova, 2015; Yudkevich et al., 2017).

In the context of capacity building, all four forms of mobility, be it international, virtual, intersectoral or interdisciplinary, and blended mobility should be made available for doctoral candidates. This could further support their career development and build research and innovation capacity both within and outside academia. In the context of transnational migration, virtual mobility can be an effective means to counteract brain drain, particularly considering the new post-pandemic worldwide reality. Similarly, blended mobility could serve to alleviate the demands of migration with a shorter, more achievable mobility while maintaining constant engagement and academic 'mooring' through virtual connectedness and engagement (Smith McGloin, 2021). This section on mobility thus concludes by focusing on the context of today, inciting thoughts on the policies driving doctoral candidates and their implications for capacity building.

Political influence on the PhD

Capacity building for doctoral education is impacted by state political structures and global geopolitical environments. Intensifying global competition and collaboration between nation-states and regions drives the increase in research funding across the world. In the wake of the 2007 global financial crisis, research capacity and innovation are increasingly perceived by nation-states as key investments for economic growth (Hartley, Pearce and Taylor, 2017). Building capacity in research and innovation requires quality doctoral education that provides the human capital for knowledge economy and society. Policy initiatives in many countries have been oriented towards rapidly increasing the number of doctorate holders with a short turnaround time. For example, the Irish 2006 Strategy for Science Technology and Innovation (SSTI) set a target to double the number of PhD graduates by 2013 (Irish Department of

Enterprise, Trade and Employment, 2006). In Chile, graduate programmes form the bulk of human capital for scientific advancement (Besnier, 2012). Australia's most recent review of doctoral education regarded its Higher Degree by Research (HDR) training system as critical to its future economic strength (McGagh et al., 2016).

Many Asian governments consider developing doctoral education as a strategy to enhance national research capabilities and thereby economic competitiveness. Countries including Malaysia, Thailand and China require doctoral candidates to publish before graduation to improve the global rankings of universities (UNESCO-UIS, 2014). By 2013, doctoral training programmes had been implemented in most countries or territories across East and South Asia, except for Bhutan, Laos and the Maldives (UNESCO-UIS, 2013). This points to a growing gap between some countries that independently produce a qualified workforce for its higher education and research systems and others which depend on importing external staff for local capacity building (UNESCO-UIS, 2014).

The increased level of interest in the doctorate has emerged because of the recognition of research and innovation in sustaining economic growth, as well as a global effort towards Agenda 2030 and Sustainable Development Goals (SDGs). In Europe this is manifested in the Green Deal (European Commission, 2019) and through the research and innovation programme, Horizon Europe, that will invest over €95 billion. This shifts the PhD from an individually driven (at least in the STEM disciplines) intellectual pursuit to a societal driven research effort.

Governance, funding and control of doctoral education

The political structures that govern and support doctoral education vary between countries as doctoral education sits at the interface between education and research. Usually, the degree aspect is first the responsibility of the awarding university under regulations from the ministry of education (or devolved higher-education body). However, in general, the bulk of funding for doctoral candidates is provided by funding agencies linked to ministries of research, business and enterprise. In the European Union, policy for doctoral training, for example, is shared between the European Commission's Directorate-General for Education and Culture and Directorate-General for Research and Innovation, including many of the constructs for doctoral education (structured programmes, requirements for thesis supervisory committees and generic/transferable skills training). Higher-education policy for the PhD is through the

Bologna Third Cycle. In the context of European Union research policy, the Innovative Principles for Doctoral Training were developed to provide a framework for best practice in doctoral education and training (European Commission, 2011b).

Public universities are the main drivers in doctoral education in most countries, with a varied level of autonomy. The EUA University Autonomy Tool (https://www.university-autonomy.eu/) analyses 29 higher-education systems in Europe through comparing the four areas of organisational, financial, staffing and academic autonomy. In Mexico, public universities are autonomous from the state and free from religious affiliations. However, the National Council on Science and Technology (CONACyT) has been fundamental in promoting postgraduate training. In mainland China, the policy on doctoral education is mainly formulated by the Ministry of Education. However, colleges and universities have greater autonomy in how to evaluate doctoral candidates' quality (Zheng, Shen and Cai, 2018). In Japan and Malaysia, doctoral-education policies are set and approved by the ministries of education (Arimoto, 2018; Nerad, 2020).

While increased investment in doctoral training is to be welcomed, the view of research and innovation for short-term economic gain is a double-edged sword. With increased funding comes increased control exogenous to academia. Further politicisation of science impacted many countries, where research governance and policy making was relocated to ministries of economy, business or industry. This often reduces the significance of science policy and the relative independence of scientific research (Besnier, 2012). Increasingly, research policies are tied up with government agendas that limit the objectives of and approaches to scientific advancement. This is when research policy making is compromised by 'politics-based evidence' instead of 'evidence-based policy' (Henderson, 2013). This in turn impacts on the disciplinary areas funded and can limit the scope of doctoral research (see also Chapters 1 and 9).

Funding sources for the PhD

An increase in research and development spending and the number of researchers is a key target in the 2030 SDGs. Countries stimulate investment in private and public sectors by setting national R&D spending targets as a percentage of GDP. The UNESCO Institute for Statistics (UIS) has estimated global spending on R&D as almost US$1.7 trillion, and 10 countries account for 80 per cent of spending. North America and Western Europe take the lead with an average R&D spending of 2.5 per cent of GDP. This is followed by East Asia and the Pacific region (2 per cent on average).

Universities in many regions are underfunded, despite increasing enrolments in higher education and HDR programmes. There are exceptions such as Japan, where the number of doctoral candidates has been decreasing since 2008 due to its shrinking young population (Yonezawa, 2020). In Europe since 2000 and the establishment of the European Research Area (ERA), there has been an agreed EU target of 3 per cent of GDP on R&D. While the ERA target has remained at 3 per cent of GDP on R&D since 2000, due to the economic crisis, budgets did not increase in accordance with increasing student numbers. This is linked with scant public budgets and competing demands from other sectors (Dohmen, 2018). Nonetheless in the new ERA policy launched in 2020, the 3 per cent target has been reaffirmed (European Commission, 2020).

In Brazil, Jair Bolsonaro's government froze 42 per cent of the research budget for the country's science and communications ministry in March 2019. Due to this, the country has been losing young researchers who are moving abroad (Angelo, 2019). In Chile, despite the scholarship programmes developed by the government since 2008, the rate of research and development personnel per one thousand people (less than one) remains much lower than the OECD average of 7.6 (Comisión, 2015: 32).

In many countries, international students are not eligible for most national fellowships and so are more likely to be funded through international or personal means. In the US, in the arts and humanities, for example, a teaching assistantship is the modal type of support for the PhD scholar. A clear emphasis on STEM is perceived in many countries as higher levels of funding are available when compared to HSS. Students in the hard sciences have better chances of obtaining graduate teaching assistantships in the US than those in other subjects. Boyce et al. (2016) argue that potential reasons for this include privileging science over other forms of knowledge, including pedagogical knowledge, and, reflecting entrenched mind-body dualism and the privileging of academic subjects. East Asian countries such as China have increased government funding for research in colleges and universities where doctoral candidates are one of the main forces of scientific research. Government scholarships cover the tuition and basic living expenses of students. Malaysia's MyBrain15 programme was introduced in 2007 with the objective of increasing the number of Malaysian doctoral degree holders to 160,000 by 2020. This programme provided funding to cover tuition fees, stipends and examination fees. The programme was subsequently suspended due to an unfavourable economic climate. Consequently, doctoral candidates are mostly self-funded or financed by their employers.

Therefore, increasingly countries are subscribing to a funding framework for doctoral education in which source revenues diversify beyond government fellowships and university project-based funding to include industries and self-funded international students. For example, public investment in the Australian higher-education sector has drastically declined in recent years to the point where it is now 0.7 per cent of GDP, which is 40 per cent below the OECD average of 1.1 per cent (OECD, 2017). The remainder of funding for Australian universities comes from increasingly high student fees, especially for international students and from non-government sources. The COVID-19 pandemic has demonstrated the danger of universities relying heavily on international students for income. Across Europe, one can see the impact of lower government investment in universities with the increase in the number of undergraduate and graduate courses offered in English to attract international students. This is reinforcing the status of English as the global language. Similarly, in South Africa, the government's block grant system is supplemented by fees paid by students. A report by Universities South Africa (USAF, 2016) indicates that government subsidies to universities have declined by over 30 per cent in the last two decades. This decline has put pressure on the other two sources of income available to universities, namely, tuition fee income, which has been contested by the 'fees must fall' movement in South Africa, and third-stream income (typically research grants, contract income, donations and so on).

Geopolitical influence on doctoral education

Over the last few years, the impact of global geopolitical instability on capacity building in doctoral education has become increasingly overt. Global higher education faces a 'wholly different political environment' driven by recent geopolitical events (Van Damme and Van der Wende, 2018: 81) that challenges the principles of capacity building in doctoral education. These include 'the need for a critical mass of research, reciprocity, exposure to other ways of thinking and university autonomy' (Jørgensen, 2012). In the early 2010s, mobility of international doctoral students was shaped by major trends and events such as the slowdown of the Chinese economy, Brexit and the 2016 American presidential election (Choudaha, 2017). In Europe, Brexit, continued terrorist attacks, the refugee crisis and a coup attempt in Turkey seemed to have 'promoted a turn away from internationalism, global collaboration and an open society' (Choudaha, 2017: 91). Meanwhile, China's Belt and Road Initiative facilitated its shift from major importer to rising exporter of international education (Van Damme and Van der Wende, 2018). The Belt and Road Initiative supports research grants and scholarships that enhance the quality of international education and serve the country's international projects in infrastructure building, trade, culture and diplomacy (Qi, 2021).

Since the onset of the COVID-19 pandemic, international student mobilities have been significantly disrupted. Doctoral education has been embroiled in escalating geopolitical tensions that play out as risk assessments and reviews for national security, foreign espionage and intellectual property concerns. The Trump Administration revoked the visas of over 1,000 Chinese students and researchers which it accused of military connections. The crackdown in the US turned international students to other destinations (Leriber, 2019). International student enrolment in the US dropped by 6.6 percent in the 2017–18 academic year, doubling the decline rate of the year before (Institute of International Education, 2018). This made it increasingly difficult for universities to continue to attract talented research candidates from abroad. A study on international doctoral candidates found that the US government's executive orders restricting travel in January 2017 affected not only international doctoral candidates from the six banned countries, Iran, Libya, Somalia, Sudan, Syria and Yemen. Doctoral candidates from other countries also perceived the US political climate as 'stressful, confusing and hostile' (Todoran and Peterson, 2019).

There has also been a push in the West to govern and review international research collaborations. For example, Universities UK has published its guidelines *Managing Risks in Internationalisation: Security related issues* (UUK, 2020). The Swedish Foundation for International Cooperation in Research and Higher Education has released *Responsible Internationalisation: Guidelines for reflection on international academic collaboration* (Shih et al., 2020). The German Rectors Conference (HRK) *Guidelines and standards in international university cooperation* (HRK, 2020) emphasises robust governance and professional management. The implications of these for doctoral education have led to rejections of student visas especially in sensitive fields of research such as emerging technologies.

Figure 7.1 outlines how political instability may have influenced the capacity building of both academics and doctoral candidates. The main

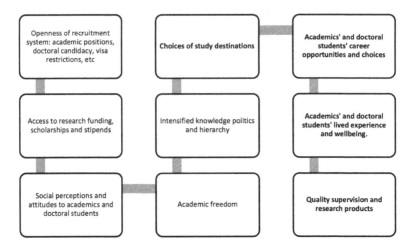

Figure 7.1 Illustration of where the influence of political instability on recruitment, funding and social attitudes impacts on students and academics study and career choices. Jing Qi

issues for any prospective PhD candidate planning to move abroad is the opportunity to access a country/institution with an open recruitment system coupled with good funding opportunities. The choice of study destination is also strongly influenced by the quality of research and supervision coupled with the academic environment and career opportunities. However, now, as illustrated in Figure 7.1, the perception of academia in society, the level of academic freedom and political influence have become all key factors in deciding on a PhD destination.

In Europe, UK universities are experiencing 'consequences of the Brexit vote on international student mobility and in the international collaboration among researchers and at a strategic level' (Van Damme and Van der Wende, 2018: 92). Australia has been ranked as the safest and most welcoming country for international students by the Hobsons International Student Survey (Australian Embassy, 2016). Safety was considered as a key factor by 93 per cent of international students (out of the 65,000 survey participants) for choosing to study in Australia. There was a '14.2 per cent increase in visa applications from Chinese students intending to study in the postgraduate sector for the period 1 July 2017 to 31 January 2018, compared with the same period last year' (Australian Embassy, 2016). However, increasing political tension between China and Australia in early 2016 was perceived to have influenced Australian visa restrictions for some postgraduate research students and research scholars, particularly those on Chinese government scholarships in sensitive science and technology fields (Munro, 2018). Australia's border closure to international students since the outbreak of COVID-19 has also led to a significant drop in international student enrolments.

When governments have significant control over the sources of research funding and universities, areas of research that do not conform with their policies can be negatively impacted. In 2018, the Hungarian government removed gender studies from a list of approved master's programmes (Redden, 2018). This followed a government decree based on the ruling party's ideological opposition to gender studies programmes. In a similar vein, funding for already peer-reviewed and approved grant proposals in the humanities were blocked by a government minister. This was when former Education Minister of Australia Simon Birmingham used his ministerial power in 2017 and 2018 to block 11 Australian Research Council (ARC) grants that were worth a combined total of AUS$4.2 million. All of the grants denied funding were studies in the humanities and selected through rigorous peer review by expert panels. The political interference, in particular its secretive nature, sparked the outrage of Australian universities and researchers and was criticised as undermining the integrity of the peer-review system (Karp, 2018). As Piccini and Moses (2018) said, 'by rejecting only humanities projects, Birmingham has placed this discipline at a decided funding disadvantage'.

In Turkey, current political pressure over universities has an immense impact on existing PhD programmes and candidates. Following a failed coup attempt in July 2016, the government declared a state of emergency and decreed the closure of 15 Turkish universities (among other institutions) and seized their assets. Allegedly these universities supported the Gulen movement which Turkish authorities suggested was behind the attempted coup. 'Authorities have taken a range of actions against the members of the higher-education community – among others – allegedly intended to identify those parties involved with the coup attempt, or to eliminate the Gulen movement's influence within several Turkish institutions. In addition to university closures, these actions reportedly include restrictions on travel, mass suspensions, and arrest and detention of university personnel' (Redden, 2017). A total number of 66,000 students were relocated to continue their education (Turkey Purge, 2017).

Among African countries, South African higher-education institutions and doctoral-education programmes attract many international students across the globe, especially from within the Southern African region. Consequently, the country is growing to be known as a regional higher-education internationalisation hub (Sehoole, 2011; Lee and Sehoole, 2015). While the country continues to put in place measures to attract more international students, recurring xenophobic attacks on foreign nationals stand as a huge obstacle to these efforts. International students and their families back home have expressed frustrations, worries and doubts to study in South Africa arising from the hostile reception due to xenophobic episodes (Zeleza, 2017; Herman and Meki-Kombe, 2019).

Changing mobility policies to remove global inequalities

This chapter investigated the various dynamics that influence capacity building for doctoral education with a focus on mobility and its drivers. It addressed the issue of how to build and maintain capacity for doctoral training in the current global environment where academia has become the alternative career (intersectoral mobility). The particular challenges for women, minorities and underrepresented groups were highlighted.

There are many factors involved in capacity building, but a major one is the difference between the perception of institutions/regions/countries building doctoral capacity and that of the individual candidate looking for the best opportunity that will further their career and fit it with their personal circumstances such as partnership or family concerns. This is where migration (international mobility) becomes significant as the personal decisions of potential PhD candidates will impact on the ability of an institution/region/country to build research capacity.

In the context of the COVID-19 pandemic, online education and collaboration have been widely adopted. Extrapolating to doctoral studies, virtual mobility can offer a new means for capacity building, enabling PhD candidates to access resources abroad and collaborate internationally. Combining short-term transnational and virtual mobility can lead to a blended mobility. This can go some way towards reducing brain drain as it supports PhD candidates remaining in their own university while having the opportunity to access international education/training and research.

Institutions offering an excellent research environment combined with good funding and further career opportunities will attract PhD candidates. In contrast, a lack of funding, career opportunities or high-quality research will push people to consider a PhD in another institution/region/country. In recent years, it has become evident that an open political environment can also be an attractor.

Direct political interference in research themes and the scope of research funding is a new push factor that drives doctoral candidates away from countries and reduces their attractiveness.

The chapter identified a range of good practice examples from around the globe as to how to address capacity building in the context of mobility for a wide range of national and regional structures to improve the global quality of doctoral education.

In terms of the Hannover Recommendations, this chapter leads to Recommendation 3: 'Encourage diverse forms of mobility to develop multiple careers and ensure a more balanced distribution of talent around the globe.'

This chapter has pointed out the challenges in developing PhD capacity and how it can lead to inequality, depletion of talent and increased political interference. However, the underlying assumption is that simply increasing numbers is a good thing as it is a necessary aspect of increasing research activity. It may be argued that the broad global success of increasing PhD numbers has led to new problems as it ignored the lack of academic career prospects for these talented people. The next chapter addresses this issue and considers global labour-market developments and how new employment opportunities for doctoral graduates can be fostered.

References

Ackers, L. (2008). 'Internationalisation, mobility and metrics: A new form of indirect discrimination?'. *Minerva*, 46 (4), 411–35.

Allen, J.M., Webber, M. (2019) 'Stereotypes of minorities and education, stereotypes of minorities and education'. In: Ratuva S. (ed.) *The Palgrave Handbook of Ethnicity*. Singapore: Palgrave Macmillan.

Ampaw, F.D. and Jaeger, A.J. (2011) 'Understanding the factors affecting degree completion of doctoral women in the science and engineering fields'. *New Directions for Institutional Research*, 2011 (152), 59–73.

Angelo, C. (2019) 'Brazil's government freezes nearly half of its science spending'. *Nature*. Accessed 9 June 2022. https://www.nature.com/articles/d41586-019-01079-9.

Arimoto, A. (2018) 'Doctoral education in Japan: Historical development and challenges'. In *Doctoral education for the knowledge society*. Cham: Springer, 167–81.

Australian Council of Learned Academies. (2016) *Review of Australia's research training system*. Accessed 9 June 2022. https://acola.org/wp-content/uploads/2018/08/saf13-review-research-training-system-report.pdf Melbourne: ACOLA.

Australian Embassy. (2016) 'Statement on post graduate research students' and research scholars' visa issue'. Accessed 9 June 2022. https://china.embassy.gov.au/bjng/mr180316.html.

Barker, M.J. (2011) 'Racial context, currency and connections: Black doctoral student and white advisor perspectives on cross-race advising'. *Innovations in Education and Teaching International*, 48 (4), 387–400.

Bauder, H. (2015) 'The international mobility of academics: A labour market perspective'. *International Migration*, 53 (1), 83–96.

Bendrups, D., Diaz-Gasca, S., Ortiz, G.C.M., Sanchez, P.G. and Mena-Maldonado, E. (2020) 'Australia as a destination for Latin American doctoral candidates: Four personal reflections'. *Transitions: Journal of Transient Migration*, 4 (1), 69–85.

Berezina, E.V., Vasil'eva L.V., Lebedev, K.V., Pluzhnova, N.A., Prokhorova, L.V. and Fedin, A.V. (2018) *Highly qualified scientific personnel training in Russia [Podgotovka nauchnikh kadrov vischei kvalifikatsii v Rossii]*. Statistical book, 2013, 2017, 2018.

Besnier, P.A. (2012). 'Politics of science: why governance of research must stay independent'. *The Guardian*. Accessed 9 June 2022. https://www.theguardian.com/higher-education-network/blog/2012/dec/04/politics-science-research-governance-chile.

Bilecen, B. and Van Mol, C. (2017) 'Introduction: international academic mobility and inequalities'. *Journal of Ethnic and Migration Studies*, 43 (8), 1,241–55.

Bokova, I.G. (2015) 'UNESCO Science Report: Towards 2030'. UNESDOC Numeric library. Accessed 9 June 2022. https://unesdoc.unesco.org/ark:/48223/pf0000235406.

Bothwell, E. (2015) 'BRICS & emerging economies university rankings 2016: Results announced'. Times Higher Education World University Rankings. https://www.timeshighereducation.com/news/brics-and-emerging-economies-rankings-2016-results-announced.

Boyce, B.A., Curtner-Smith, M. and Sinelnikov, O. (2016) 'Recruiting, funding and hiring of doctoral students in physical education teacher education'. *Quest*, 68 (4), 394–405.

Burford, J. and Hook, G. (2019) 'Curating care-full spaces: Doctoral students negotiating study from home'. *Higher Education Research & Development*, 38 (7), 1,343–55.

Butts, G.C., Hurd, Y., Palermo, A.G.S., Delbrune, D., Saran, S., Zony, C. and Krulwich, T.A. (2012) 'Role of institutional climate in fostering diversity in biomedical research workforce: A case study'. *Mount Sinai Journal of Medicine: A Journal of Translational and Personalized Medicine*, 79 (4), 498–511.

Cameron, C., Zhao, H. and McHugh, M.K. (2012) 'Publication ethics and the emerging scientific workforce: Understanding 'plagiarism' in a global context'. *Academic medicine: journal of the Association of American Medical Colleges*, 87 (1).

Caregnato, C.E., Santin, D.M., Del Valle, D. and Takayanagui, A.D. (2021) 'Educación superior y universidad en América Latina: Perspectivas temáticas para debates e investigaciones'. *Revista Brasileira de Estudos Pedagógicos*, 101: 670–90.

Chakraverty, D. (2013) 'An examination of how women and underrepresented racial/ethnic minorities experience barriers in biomedical research and medical programs'. DBER Speaker Series. 43. Accessed 9 June 2022 https://digitalcommons.unl.edu/dberspeakers/43.

Chakraverty, D. (2019) 'Impostor phenomenon in STEM: Occurrence, attribution and identity'. *Studies in Graduate and Postdoctoral Education*, 10 (1), 2–20.

Chakraverty, D. (2020a) 'PhD Student Experiences with the Impostor Phenomenon in STEM'. *International Journal of Doctoral Studies*, 15, 159–79.

Chakraverty, D. (2020b) 'The impostor phenomenon among postdoctoral trainees in STEM: A US-based mixed-methods study'. *International Journal of Doctoral Studies*, 15 (329–52).

Chakraverty, D., Jeffe, D.B. and Tai, R.H. (2018) 'Transition experiences in MD–PhD programs'. *CBE – Life Sciences Education*, 17 (3), ar41.

Chakraverty, D., Jeffe, D.B., Dabney, K.P. and Tai, R.H. (2020) 'Exploring reasons that US MD-PhD students enter and leave their dual-degree programs'. *International Journal of Doctoral Studies*, 15, 461–83.

Chesler, N.C., Barabino, G., Bhatia, S.N. and Richards-Kortum, R. (2010) 'The pipeline still leaks and more than you think: A status report on gender diversity in biomedical engineering'. *Annals of biomedical engineering*, 38 (5), 1,928–35.

Choudaha R. (2017) 'Three waves of international student mobility (1999–2020)'. *Studies in Higher Education*, 42:5, 825–32.

Clance, P.R. (1985) *The Impostor Phenomenon: Overcoming the fear that haunts your success*. Atlanta: Peachtree Pub.

Cloete, N., Mouton, J. and Sheppard, C. (2015) *Doctoral Education in South Africa*. Cape Town: African Minds.

Comisión Presidencial Ciencia para el Desarrollo de Chile. (2015) 'Un sueño compartido para el futuro de Chile'. Informe a la Presidenta de la República, Michelle Bachelet. Accessed 10 September 2021. No longer available. http://www.cnid.cl/wp-content/uploads/2015/07/Informe-Ciencia-para-el-Desarrollo.pdf.

Dabney, K.P., Chakraverty, D., Hutton, A.C., Warner, K.A. and Tai, R.H. (2016) 'The bachelor's to PhD transition: Factors influencing PhD completion among women in chemistry and physics'. *Bulletin of Science, Technology & Society*, 36 (4), 203–10.

DFHER (2021) *National Research and Innovation Strategy 2021–27*. Department of Further and Higher Education, Research, Innovation and Science, Government of Ireland.

Di Falco, S. and Bulte, E. (2011) 'A dark side of social capital? Kinship, consumption, and savings'. *Journal of Development Studies*, 47 (8), 1,128–51.

Dohmen, D. (2018) 'Higher education funding in the context of competing demands for government expenditure'. In B. Cantwell, H. Coates and R. King (eds), *Handbook on the Politics of Higher Education*. Cheltenham: Edward Elgar Publishing: 229.

Education Counts. (2019) 'Retention and Achievement'. New Zealand Government, Ministry of Education. Accessed 9 June 2022. https://www.educationcounts.govt.nz/statistics/tertiary-education/retention_and_achievement

European Commission. (2011a) *Towards a European Framework for Research Careers*. Brussels: EC. Accessed 9 June 2022. https://cdn5.euraxess.org/sites/default/files/policy_library/towards_a_european_framework_for_research_careers_final.pdf.

European Commission. (2011b) *Report of Mapping Exercise on Doctoral Training in Europe: Towards a common approach*. Brussels: EC. Accessed 9 June 2022. https://docplayer.net/4078065-European-commission-directorate-general-for-research-innovation-report-of-mapping-exercise-on-doctoral-training-in-europe.html.

European Commission. (2018) *MORE3 Study: Support data collection and analysis concerning mobility patterns and career paths of researchers*. Brussels: European Commission. Accessed 9 June 2022. https://op.europa.eu/en/publication-detail/-/publication/4681ae98-3ba0-11e8-b5fe-01aa75ed71a1.

European Commission. (2019) 'The European Green Deal, COM(2019) 640 final'. Accessed 9 June 2022. https://eur-lex.europa.eu/legal-content/EN/TXT/?qid=1576150542719&uri=COM%3A2019%3A640%3AFIN.

European Commission. (2020) 'A new ERA for Research and Innovation: Communication from the Commission to the European Parliament, the Council, the European Economic and Social Committee and the Committee of the Regions COM/2020/628 final'. Accessed 9 June 2022. https://eur-lex.europa.eu/legal-content/EN/TXT/?uri=COM%3A2020%3A628%3AFIN.

European Union. (2018) 'Education and training monitor 2018: Report from the European Commission'. Accessed 10 September 2021. No longer available. https://ec.europa.eu/education/sites/education/files/document-library-docs/volume-1-2018-education-and-training-monitor-country-analysis.pdf.

European Universities Association. (2019) 'Reflections on University Research Assessment: Key concepts, issues and actors'. Accessed 9 June 2022. https://eua.eu/resources/publications/825:reflections-on-university-research-assessment-key-concepts,-issues-and-actors.html.

Fabris, F., Rice, T.K., Jeffe, D.B., Czajkowski, S.M., Boyington, J. and Boutjdir, M. (2016) 'Junior faculty career development through an NHLBI program to increase diversity in cardiovascular health-related research'. *Journal of the American College of Cardiology*, 67 (19), 2,312–13.

Felder, P. (2010) 'On doctoral student development: Exploring faculty mentoring in the shaping of African American doctoral student success'. *The Qualitative Report*, 15 (3), 455–74.

Felder, P.P. and Barker, M.J. (2013) 'Extending Bell's concept of interest convergence: A framework for understanding the African American doctoral student experience'. *International Journal of Doctoral Studies*, 8 (1).

Fisher, A.J., Mendoza-Denton R., Patt, C., Young, I., Eppig, A., Garrell, R.L., Rees, D.C., Nelson, T.W. and Richards, M.A. (2019) 'Structure and belonging: Pathways to success for underrepresented minority and women PhD students in STEM fields'. *PloS ONE* 14 (1): e0209279.

Fochler, M., Felt, U. and Müller, R. (2016) 'Unsustainable growth, hyper-competition and worth in life science research: Narrowing evaluative repertoires in doctoral and postdoctoral scientists' work and lives'. *Minerva* 54, 175–200.

Fomunyam, K.G. (2017) 'Decolonising the future in the untransformed present in South African higher education'. *Perspectives in Education* 35 (2): 168–180.

Funk, C., Parker, K. (2018) 'Women and Men in STEM often at odds over workplace equity'. Pew Research Centre. Accessed 9 June 2022. https://www.pewresearch.org/social-trends/2018/01/09/women-and-men-in-stem-often-at-odds-over-workplace-equity

Gerhards, J., Hans, S. and Drewski, D. (2018). 'Global inequality in the academic system: effects of national and university symbolic capital on international academic mobility'. *Higher Education*, 1–17.

Gibbs, Jr, K.D., McGready, J., Bennett, J.C. and Griffin, K. (2014) 'Biomedical science Ph. D. career interest patterns by race/ethnicity and gender'. *PloS one*, 9 (12), e114736.

Golde, C.M. and Dore, T.M. (2001) 'At cross purposes: What the experiences of today's doctoral students reveal about doctoral education'. Philadelphia, PA: A report prepared for The Pew Charitable Trusts.

GRC. (2021) 'Responsible research assessment: Global Research Council (GRC) conference report (2021)'. Accessed 9 June 2022. https://www.globalresearchcouncil.org/fileadmin/documents/GRC_Publications/GRC_RRA_Conference_Summary_Report.pdf.

Hansen, D.S. (2020) 'Identifying barriers to career progression for women in science: Is COVID-19 creating new challenges?', *Trends in Parasitology*. 36 (10): 799–802.

Harle, J. (2013) 'Doctoral education in Africa: A review of doctoral student needs and existing initiatives to support doctoral training and research development'. The Association of Commonwealth Universities.

Hartley, S., Pearce, W. and Taylor, A. (2017) 'Against the tide of depoliticization: the politics of research governance'. *Policy & Politics*, 45 (3), 361–77.

Henderson, M. (2013) *The Geek Manifesto: Why science matters*. London: Random House.

Herman, C. and Meki-Kombe, C.L. (2019) 'The role of social networks in the transitional experiences of international African doctoral students at one university in South Africa'. *Higher Education Research & Development*, 38 (3), 508–21.

HRK. (2020) 'Guidelines and Standards in International University Education'. Resolution of the German Rectors Conference (HRK) Board, 6 April 2020. Accessed 9 June 2022. https://www.hrk.de/resolutions-publications/resolutions/beschluss/detail/guidelines-and-standards-in-international-university-cooperation/.

Hutchins, H.M. and Rainbolt, H. (2017) 'What triggers imposter phenomenon among academic faculty? A critical incident study exploring antecedents, coping, and development opportunities'. *Human Resource Development International*, 20 (3), 194–214.

Institute of International Education. (2019) 'Open Doors 2019 fast facts: International students in the US'. Accessed 9 June 2022. https://opendoorsdata.org/wp-content/uploads/2020/05/Fast-Facts-2019.pdf.

Institute of International Education. (2020) 'International Student Enrolment Trends, 1948/49–2019/20'. Open Doors Report of International Educational Exchange. Accessed 9 June 2022. https://opendoorsdata.org/data/international-students/enrollment-trends/.

Irish Department of Enterprise, Trade and Employment. (2006) 'Strategy for Science Technology and Innovation 2006–2013'. Accessed 10 September 2021. No longer available. https://enterprise.gov.ie/en/Publications/Strategy-for-Science-Technology-and-Innovation-2006-20131.html.

Jiani, M.A. (2017) 'Why and how international students choose Mainland China as a higher education study abroad destination'. *Higher Education*, 74 (4), 563–79.

Jørgensen, T.E. (2012) *CODOC, Cooperation on doctoral education between Africa, Asia, Latin America and Europe*. Brussels: European University Association.

Johnson, W.B., Rose, G. and Schlosser, L.Z. (2007) 'Student-faculty mentoring: Theoretical and methodological issues'. In T. Allen and L. Eby (eds), *The Blackwell Handbook of Mentoring: A multiple perspectives approach*. Chichester: Wiley-Blackwell, 49–69.

Jones, G.A. (2018) 'Doctoral education in Canada'. In *Doctoral Education for the Knowledge Society*. Cham: Springer, 147–164.

Karp. P. (2018) '"Disgraceful": university decries "political interference" that blocked $4m in grants'. Accessed 9 June 2022. https://www.theguardian.com/australia-news/2018/oct/30/disgraceful-university-decries-political-interference-that-blocked-4m-in-grants.

Keller, J. and Dauenheimer, D. (2003) 'Stereotype threat in the classroom: Dejection mediates the disrupting threat effect on women's math performance'. *Personality and Social Psychology Bulletin*, 29 (3), 371–81.

Knight, J. and Madden, M. (2010) 'International mobility of Canadian social sciences and humanities doctoral students'. *Canadian Journal of Higher Education*, 40 (2), 18–34.

Kong, X., Chakraverty, D., Jeffe, D.B., Andriole, D.A., Wathington, H.D. and Tai, R.H. (2013) 'How do interaction experiences influence doctoral students' academic pursuits in biomedical research?'. *Bulletin of science, technology & society*, 33 (3–4), 76–84.

Kritz, M.M. and Gurak, D.T. (2018) 'International student mobility: sending country determinants and policies'. In M. Czaika (2018), *High-Skilled Migration: Drivers and policies (First ed.)*. Oxford: Oxford University Press.

Larivière, V. and Sugimoto, C.R. (2018) 'The Journal Impact Factor: A brief history, critique and discussion of adverse effects'. Accessed 9 June 2022. https://arxiv.org/ftp/arxiv/papers/1801/1801.08992.pdf.

Lee, J.J. and Sehoole, C. (2015) 'Regional, continental and global mobility to an emerging economy: the case of South Africa'. *Higher Education*, 70 (5), 827–43.

Lendák-Kabók, K. (2020) 'Women's work–life balance strategies in academia'. *Journal of Family Studies*.

Leriber, N. (2019) 'Foreign students sour on America, jeopardizing a $39 billion industry'. Bloomberg. Accessed 10 September 2021. No longer available. https://www.bloomberg.com/news/articles/2019-01-17/foreign-students-are-a-39-billion-industry-trump-is-scaring-them-off

Magubane, N.N. (2017) 'Black tax: the emerging middle-class reality'. Doctoral dissertation, University of Pretoria.

McGagh, J., Marsh, H., Western, M., Thomas, P., Hastings, A., Mihailova, M. and Wenham, M. (2016) *Review of Australia's Research Training System*. Melbourne: Australian Council of Learned Academies.

McGrail, M.R., Rickard, C.M. and Jones, R. (2006) 'Publish or perish: A systematic review of interventions to increase academic publication rates'. *Higher Education Research & Development*, 25 (1), 19–35.

McPhillips, H.A., Burke, A.E., Sheppard, K., Pallant, A., Stapleton, F.B. and Stanton, B. (2007) 'Toward creating family-friendly work environments in pediatrics: Baseline data from pediatric department chairs and pediatric program directors'. *Pediatrics*, 119 (3), e596-e602.

Mercado, S. (2020) 'Coronavirus coverage: International student mobility and the impact of the pandemic'. BizEd – AACSB international. Accessed 10 September 2021. No longer available. https://bized.aacsb.edu/articles/2020/june/covid-19-and-the-future-of-international-student-mobility.

Montero-Diaz, F. (2020) 'Swimming upstream: Balancing motherhood, academia and well-intentioned policies'. *Ethnomusicology Forum*, 29:3, 292–95.

Morehouse, L. and Dawkins, M.P. (2006) 'The McKnight doctoral fellowship program: Toward a seamless approach to the production of African American doctorates'. *The Journal of Negro Education*, 563–71.

Munoz-Garcia, A.L. and Chiappa, R. (2017) 'Stretching the academic harness: Knowledge construction in the process of academic mobility in Chile'. *Globalisation, Societies and Education*, 15 (5), 635–47.

Munro, K. (2018) 'Dutton's department denies delaying Chinese student visas for political reasons'. *The Guardian*. Accessed 10 September 2021. No longer available. https://www.theguardian.com/australia-news/2018/mar/23/duttons-department-denies-delaying-chinese-student-visas-for-political-reasons.

Nerad, M. and Evans B. (eds). (2014) *Globalizing Forces and the Evolving PhD: Forces and forms of doctoral education worldwide*. With introduction and conclusion and a separate chapter, 'Fit to be Used' by M. Nerad. Rotterdam: Sense Publishers.

Nerad, M. (2020) 'Governmental innovation policies, globalisation, and change in doctoral education worldwide: Are doctoral programmes converging? Trends and tensions'. In *Structural and Institutional Transformations in Doctoral Education*. Cham: Palgrave Macmillan, 43–84.

O'Carroll, C., Scholz, B., Nogueira, M.M., Avellis, G., Marin, L., Dan, M.B. and Theodoridou, M. (2014) 'Careers: Virtual mobility can drive equality'. *Nature*, 511 (292), 292.

O'Carroll, C., Purser, L., Wislocka, M., Lucey, S. and McGuinness, N. (2012) 'The PhD in Europe: Developing a system of doctoral training that will increase the internationalisation of universities'. In *European Higher Education at the Crossroads*. Dordrecht: Springer, 461–84.

O'Carroll C., Rentier B., Cabello Valdez C., Esposito F., Kaunismaa E., Metcalfe J., McAllister D., Vandevelde K. (2017) 'Evaluation of Research Careers fully acknowledging open science practices'. European Commission.

OECD. (2017) *Education at a Glance 2017: OECD Indicators*. Paris: OECD Publishing.

OECD. (2018). 'International migration outlook 2018'. Accessed 9 June 2022. https://www.oecd.org/migration/international-migration-outlook-1999124x.htm.

Oyarzún, J.D.D., Perales Franco, C. and McCowan, T. (2017) 'Indigenous higher education in Mexico and Brazil: Between redistribution and recognition'. *Compare: A journal of comparative and international education*, 47 (6): 852–71.

Pedraja-Rojas, L., Rodriguez-Ponce, E. and Araneda-Guirriman, C. (2016) 'Doctoral education and government funding in higher education institutions: An approach from Chile'. *Contemporary Issues in Education Research*, 9 (2): 67–75.

Piccini, J., Moses, D., (2018) 'Simon Birmingham's intervention in research funding is not unprecedented, but dangerous'. Accessed 10 September 2021. https://theconversation.com/simon-birminghams-intervention-in-research-funding-is-not-unprecedented-butdangerous-105737.

Piccini, J., Moses, D. (2018) 'Simon Birmingham's intervention in research funding is not unprecedented, but dangerous'. Accessed 10 September 2021. https://theconversation.com/simon-birminghams-intervention-in-research-funding-is-not-unprecedented-but-dangerous-105737.

Piggott, D.A. and Cariaga-Lo, L. (2019) 'Promoting inclusion, diversity, access and equity through enhanced institutional culture and climate'. *The Journal of Infectious Diseases*, 220 (Suppl 2), S74–81.

Platonova, D. and Semyonov, D. (2018) 'Russia: The institutional landscape of Russian higher education'. In *25 Years of Transformations of Higher Education Systems in Post-Soviet Countries*. Cham: Palgrave Macmillan, 337–62.

Qi, J. (2021) 'China's international higher education policies 2010–2019: Multiple logics and HEI responses'. *Higher Education*. Accessed 10 September 2021. https://doi.org/10.1007/s10734-021-00695-7.

Qi, J., Manathunga, C., Singh, M. and Bunda, T. (2021) 'Transcultural and First Nations doctoral education and epistemological border-crossing: Histories and epistemic justice'. *Teaching in Higher Education*, 26 (3), 340–53.

Reale, E., Morettini, L. and Zinilli, A. (2018) 'Moving, remaining, and returning: International mobility of doctorate holders in the social sciences and humanities'. *Higher Education*, 1–16.

Redden, E. (2017) 'Threats to universities worldwide'. *Inside Higher Ed*, 26 September 2017. Accessed 10 September 2021.https://www.insidehighered.com/news/2017/09/26/annual-report-scholars-risk-analyzes-attacksstudents-academics-and-universities.

Redden, E. (2018) 'Hungary officially ends gender studies programs'. *Inside Higher Ed*, 18 October 2018. Accessed 9 June 2022. https://www.insidehighered.com/quicktakes/2018/10/17/hungary-officially-ends-gender-studies-programs.

Royal Society (2010) *The Scientific Century: Securing our future prosperity*. Accessed 9 June 2022. https://royalsociety.org/topics-policy/publications/2010/scientific-century/.

Scholars at Risk. (2020) 'Free to think: Report of the Scholars at Risk Academic Freedom Monitoring Project'. Accessed 9 June 2022. https://www.scholarsatrisk.org/wp-content/uploads/2020/11/Scholars-at-Risk-Free-to-Think-2020.pdf.

Sehoole, C.T. (2011) 'Student mobility and doctoral education in South Africa'. *Perspectives in Education*, 29 (1), 53–63.

Shih, M., Pittinsky, T.L. and Ambady, N. (1999) 'Stereotype susceptibility: Identity salience and shifts in quantitative performance'. *Psychological science*, 10 (1), 80–3.

Shih, T., Gaunt, A. and Östlund, S. (2020) *Responsible internationalisation: Guidelines for reflection on international academic collaboration*. Stockholm: STINT, 2020. Accessed 9 June 2022. https://www.stint.se/wp-content/uploads/2020/02/STINT__Responsible_Internationalisation.pdf.

Smith McGloin, R. (2021) 'A new mobilities approach to re-examining the doctoral journey: Mobility and fixity in the borderlands space'. *Teaching in Higher Education*, 26 (3), 370–86.

Spronken-Smith, R.A., Cameron, C. and Quigg, R. (2018) 'Factors contributing to high PhD completion rates: A case study in a research-intensive university in New Zealand'. *Assessment & Evaluation in Higher Education*, 43 (1), 94–109.

Spronken-Smith, R.A. (2019) 'New Zealand's doctoral education system'. Paper for Revisiting Forces and Forms of Doctoral Education Worldwide 2019 Conference, Hanover, Germany 5–6 September 2019. Accessed 9 June 2022. https://www.doctoral-education.info/dl/Country-description-New-Zealand.pdf.

Stains, M., Pilarz, M. and Chakraverty, D. (2015) 'Short and long-term impacts of the Cottrell scholars collaborative new faculty workshop'. *Journal of Chemical Education*, 92 (9), 1,466–76.

Todoran, C. and Peterson, C. (2019) 'Should they stay or should they go? How the 2017 US travel ban affects international doctoral students'. *Journal of Studies in International Education*, 24 (4), 440–55.

Trostle, J. (1992) 'Research capacity building in international health: definitions evaluations and strategies for success'. *Social Science and Medicine*, 35 (11), 1,321–4.

Turkey Purge. (2017). '66,000 students relocated after Turkish government shut down 15 universities over coup charges'. Accessed 10 September 2021. No longer available. https://turkeypurge.com/66000-students-relocated-as-turkish-government-shut-down-15-universities-over-coup-charges.

UIS. (UNESCO Institute of Statistics) (n.d.) 'How much does your country invest in R&D?' Accessed 10 September 2021. No longer available. http://uis.unesco.org/apps/visualisations/research-and-development-spending/.

UNESCO-UIS. (2014) *Higher Education in Asia: Expanding out, expanding up: The rise of graduate education and university research*. Quebec: UNESCO-UIS.
UNESCO. (2015) 'UNESCO science report towards 2030'. Accessed 9 June 2022. https://unesdoc.unesco.org/ark:/48223/pf0000235406_eng.
UNESCO. (2021) 'UNESCO science Report: The race against time for smarter development'. Accessed 9 June 2022. https://unesdoc.unesco.org/ark:/48223/pf0000377433.
UUK. (2020) 'Managing risks in internationalisation: Security related issues'. Universities UK. Accessed 9 June 2022. https://www.universitiesuk.ac.uk/policy-and-analysis/reports/Pages/managing-risks-in-internationalisation.aspx.
Van Damme, D. and Van der Wende, M. (2018) 'Global higher education governance'. In B. Cantwell, H. Coates and R. King (eds) *Handbook on the Politics of Higher Education*. Cheltenham: Edward Elgar Publishing, 91.
Van Der Haert, M., Arias Ortiz, E., Emplit, P., Halloin, V. and Dehon, C. (2014) 'Are dropout and degree completion in doctoral study significantly dependent on type of financial support and field of research?' *Studies in Higher Education*, 39 (10), 1,885–1,909.
Van Noorden, R. (2012) 'Global mobility: Science on the move'. *Nature News*, 490 (7,420), 326.
Vega-Muñoz, A., Gónzalez-Gómez-del-Miño, P., Espinosa-Cristia, J.F. (2021) 'Recognizing new trends in brain drain studies in the framework of global sustainability'. *Sustainability 2021*, 13, 3195.
Veugelers, R. and Van Bouwel, L. (2015) 'Destinations of mobile European researchers: Europe versus the United States'. In *Global Mobility of Research Scientists*. London: Academic Press, 215–37.
VSNU. (2020) 'PhD students'. University Association of the Netherlands. Accessed 10 September 2021. vsnu.nl/en_GB/f_c_promovendi.html.
Wadman, M. (2012) 'NIH tackles major workforce issues'. *Nature News*, 492 (7,428), 167.
Williams, S., Thakore, B.K. and McGee, R. (2018). 'Providing social support for underrepresented racial and ethnic minority PhD students in the biomedical sciences: A career coaching model'. *CBE – Life Sciences Education*, Vol. 16, No. 4.
Woldegiorgis, E.T. and Doevenspeck, M. (2015) 'Current trends, challenges and prospects of student mobility in the African higher education landscape'. *International Journal of Higher Education*, 4 (2), 105–15.
Yang, P. (2020) 'China in the global field of international student mobility: An analysis of economic, human and symbolic capitals'. *Compare: A Journal of Comparative and International Education*, 1–19.
Yonezawa A. (2020) 'Challenges of the Japanese higher education amidst population decline and globalization'. *Globalization, Societies and Education*, 20, 1.
Yudkevich, M., Altbach, P.G. and Rumbley, L.E. (2017) *International Faculty in Higher Education: Comparative perspectives on recruitment, integration and impact*. New York: Routledge
Zeleza, P.T. (2017) 'Internationalization of higher education in the era of xenophobic nationalisms'. From NAFSA 2017 Annual Conference and Expo. Los Angeles: NAFSA, 1–10.
Zheng, G., Shen, W. and Cai, Y. (2018) 'Institutional logics of Chinese doctoral education system'. *Higher Education*, 76 (5), 753–70.
Zhou, J. (2015) 'International students' motivation to pursue and complete a PhD. in the US'. *Higher Education*, 69 (5), 719–33.
Ziguras, C. and Law, S.F. (2006) 'Recruiting international students as skilled migrants: the global "skills race" as viewed from Australia and Malaysia'. *Globalisation, Societies and Education*, 4 (1), 59–76.

Notes

1 The authors would like to acknowledge the contributions of the Hannover Conference Policy Dimension Working Group members, Rachel Spronken-Smith, Roshada Hashim, Akiyoshi Yonezawa and Wenqin Shen.

8
Global labour market developments

David Bogle, Igor Chirikov, Miguel S. Gonzales-Canche, Annamaria Silvana de Rosa, Nancy L. Garcia, Stefaan Hermans, Joyce Main, Suzanne Ortega

Increasing numbers of doctoral candidates, particularly in the biomedical sciences and engineering, have produced a number of tensions in the expectations of doctoral candidates given the wide range of roles they proceed to within and beyond the academy. It has produced challenges for the way that they are educated and in some cases the ability to maintain a vigorous training environment. This chapter presents recent trends and data on the initial career destinations of doctoral graduates to seed the discussion of the nature of doctoral training. We consider the changes made over the last decade and whether doctoral education as currently practised is meeting the needs of the doctoral graduates and those who employ them. We reflect on the effectiveness and how to improve. With research and the recruitment of doctoral candidates now so international, some degree of consistency in doctoral training processes and outcomes between countries and between disciplines would be beneficial for aspiring researchers, while respecting and gaining value from differing academic and cultural traditions.

The chapter leads particularly to the third of the Hannover Recommendations:
3. 'Encourage diverse forms of mobility to develop multiple careers and ensure a more balanced distribution of talent around the globe.'

It also supports the following recommendations:
6a. 'Continually review and enhance the way doctoral candidates are educated to ensure that they meet the needs of our times, especially

in view of the increasingly complex and urgent problems, the rapidly changing digital environment, and the need for understanding and interaction across cultures and disciplines.'

6g. 'Raise the awareness of employers around the world of the changes in doctoral education in recent decades and the value of doctoral graduates in the workforce.'

The rationale for increasing investment resulting in significant growth in many regions is to help drive innovation. As has been explored in Chapter 5, there have been significant changes in doctoral education in preparing candidates for a wider range of careers. But are these the right changes and are they sufficient? What should the distinctive skillset be for doctoral graduates so that they may fulfil these roles? Is the skillset the same across the developed and developing world? Are there new forms of doctoral education that might supplement and enhance graduates in this role? Should this be distinct from the historic PhD leading to an academic career? How can we better persuade society and employers, especially small employers, of the value of doctoral graduates? From the context of the developments in the labour market and its implications, including the precarity of academic careers and the absorption of the wider economy in different countries, in this chapter we consider the skillsets that should be developed, including those arising from recent technological innovations. We also discuss the potential role of professional doctorates and set out features of the environment that are conducive to high-quality doctoral education as an experience leading to a wide range of potential roles. Much of the data available is for Europe and the US, which influences the discussion, but where we can we have drawn also from information from the Global South.

The changing context of careers in research

Numbers of doctoral graduates have swelled in recent years, particularly in the developed world. The countries graduating the largest numbers in 2016 were the US, where from 1998 to 2016 the numbers swelled from around 45,000 to nearly 70,000; Germany where the numbers rose only slightly from 25,000 to 29,000; the UK from 10,000 to 27,400; and India, where they rose from almost zero to around 25,000 (OECD, 2016). In China, PhD graduations have also grown significantly to 44,000 in 2008, with a period of rapid growth from 1999 to 2004, but still remain lower than the United States (Chen et al., 2018). The growth has been the result of a considerable increase in funds for doctoral study in the developed world, particularly in science, technology, engineering and medicine (STEM) subjects. Many governments aim to increase the numbers of researchers as a means of driving innovation leading to greater social and economic development and greater prosperity. There seems to be no shortage of talented candidates keen to undertake a doctorate. The academic world is tackling the need to train researchers more broadly and to reach out to society to involve others from society in cocreating their research questions and projects. Undoubtedly, this wider role of doctoral education has led to some challenges.

Research budgets, including for doctoral education, have increased in many countries, and with this come higher expectations and a greater scrutiny from the funders and from society more generally. With this can also come greater volatility of funding, as money is more closely tied to specific outcomes rather than given for flexible open-ended use and guaranteed as core funding. Funding can also be directed to achieve more explicitly political agendas which may not align with the primary purpose of doctoral education. The more the value of doctoral education can be explicitly highlighted and demonstrated and the role that doctoral graduates play in the labour market and society generally, the more likely there will be secure and stable funding. It will also open career paths into industry, business, government and charities.

Hence an important change needed is to clarify the mindset of candidates and employers to see doctoral graduates as competent professionals and drivers of innovation, in addition to their traditional role as replenishing the academic pipeline (European Commission, 2017b, p34): 'One of the elements that directly channels into economic growth is the skills development by training researchers. It is a crucial mechanism for the transfer of knowledge from public research to companies, especially when this knowledge is embodied in the researcher that carries out the specific research. More precisely, one of the wider economic benefits from publicly-funded basic research is associated with scientists' migration into the commercial sector of the innovation system. The benefits are notably associated, not only with applying the latest theoretical knowledge accruing from scientific research, but rather, scientists [transferring] elements of problem-solving strategies that are fundamental in basic research'.

This has been happening in some countries for many years (in Western Europe and the US for example) but not in others, and, even where it has been, the perception of some employers has not necessarily changed.

Political developments around the world are resulting in rejection of evidence-based policy, which seems to indicate a need for more and better trained researchers to assemble and critique the evidence. The reputation of doctoral study has been tarnished in some countries where there is evidence that doctoral degrees can be bought. In Russia, for example, there is evidence of plagiarism but without resulting in any action (Rostovtsev, 2017). It is unclear how widespread this is around the globe, with some notable cases of German politicians, but clearly it has the potential to damage the reputation of all doctorates.

Labour market trends

The doctorate is a crucial stepping stone towards a research career, both within and beyond academia. Doctoral graduates are trained to be original and creative, both of which are needed to find ways forward to confront the key questions facing our planet, particularly on climate change and sustainability, and to tackle increasing inequality as well as other grand challenges. The global scenario affected by the COVID-19 pandemic – which has caused discontinuity in lifestyles and in the world economy – has also highlighted the differences that potentially disadvantage the career trajectories of some academic researchers and has exacerbated inequalities (Euroscientist, 2021). Here, we look first at trends in academic careers and then at wider roles for doctoral graduates, highlighting various data sources.

The short-term nature of many roles within academia led the OECD recently to propose measures for 'reducing the precarity of research careers' (OECD, 2021). It identified requirements to better equip governments with the instruments and capabilities to direct innovation efforts towards the goals of sustainability, inclusivity and resilience. Responses to the *OECD Science Flash Survey 2020* suggested that the pandemic is having a detrimental effect on academic job security and career opportunities in the physical and social sciences, humanities and arts, as well as affecting research funding and the time available for doing research. Younger researchers and women have been more vulnerable to these effects. Addressing the problem of precarity will help improve the resilience of science systems and better prepare them to address future shocks. The OECD report notes that:

1. researchers (including doctoral candidates) are the most important resource of the research system;
2. many OECD countries are preoccupied with the future of research careers;
3. the move away from core basic funding to project-based funding is

making research systems increasingly dependent on a cohort of junior staff employed on casual contracts;
4. the traditional academic career path can no longer absorb the increasing number of doctorate holders in many systems.

The OECD 2020 Report relates the precarity of the research careers to various drivers of change affecting the contemporary research world, including:
a. a stagnation in public funding in many countries;
b. the increasing number of doctorates awarded;
c. the emergence of a dual labour market with the coexistence of a shrinking protected research elite and a large precarious academic cohort;
d. and the rapid worsening of working conditions of postdoctoral researchers.

The report lists a series of initiatives taken to address the precarity of academic research careers, including the European Charter and Code for Researchers, the German tenure-track programme, the Chinese guidelines to address the 'publish or perish' mentality encouraging their researchers to publish in 'leading' journals (specified as those with high-impact factors) or research with particular benefit to Chinese society, Japan's LEADER scheme funding 'Leading Innovative Excellent Young Researchers' and *Nature*'s survey of postdoctoral researchers around the world. The OECD report concludes with an important open question emerging from the COVID-19 crisis: 'how to protect academic researchers on fixed-term employment that are at risk of losing their jobs'. Current European Union policy focuses on the renewal of the European Research Area and stresses the key role of researchers: 'to develop attractive career frameworks for researchers, equip them with the skills they need in a fast changing global world' (European Commission, 2020). The US has recently announced a major increase in research funding through government sources. But will these be enough to secure a confident future for early-career researchers?

Prior to the COVID-19 era, the career outcomes of PhDs across multiple countries were documented through a joint data collection initiative in 2010 by the OECD, Eurostat and the UNESCO Institute for Statistics. The data from 'Careers of doctorate holders' (Auriol, Misu and Freeman, 2013) spans 25 countries from around the world and uses 2008/9 survey data to analyse the labour market outcomes of doctorate holders. They found that employment rates continue to be high among doctorates and that PhD holders experience a labour market premium compared to others with higher-level qualifications. Consistent with previous trends, the most likely first destination for PhDs is the academic/education sector, although there is ample evidence of employment in other sectors. Following higher education, the second most prevalent employment sector is in business or government.

Temporary postdoctoral positions at academic institutions are becoming more prevalent worldwide, particularly in Portugal, Germany and the Netherlands. PhDs who graduated within five years of the survey were more likely to hold temporary contracts compared to those who graduated more than five years after the survey. Across many countries in the survey, over 50 per cent of PhDs continue in academic research-related positions (Auriol, Misu and Freeman, 2013). Portugal (85 per cent) and Poland (over 90 per cent), in particular, have higher proportions of their PhDs working in research in higher education. As expected, the job market outcomes vary by PhD discipline. PhDs in the sciences and engineering are more likely to hold research-related occupations, while PhDs in the social sciences are less likely to do so. However, the work of those holding non-research occupations is still generally related to their doctoral education.

The United States has information on the long-term career trajectories and outcomes of PhD holders collected in the biannual NSF *Survey of Doctorate Recipients*, but it is limited. This survey tracks only 10 per cent of awarded PhDs holders of the particular years until age 76. Due to funding cuts of the US National Endowment of the Humanities, this tracking covers now mainly natural sciences and engineering and a few social-science fields, but no arts and humanities PhDs. The biggest drawback of this survey is that the selection criteria are based solely on demographics and not on institutions, departments or programmes. No analyses at the doctoral programme or institutional level can be made, and 90 per cent of the career information is missing.

In general, limited knowledge in the longitudinal career trajectories of PhDs stems from challenges associated with uniform and longitudinal data collection (that is, difficulty and costs of tracking individuals over time). Changes in workforce norms, where careers are now less likely to progress linearly and where employment in foreign countries is becoming more common, also make data collection challenging. However, there are several ongoing efforts to collect longitudinal data in the United States – the Council of Graduate Schools is administering surveys across institutions, the American Association of Universities Data Exchange encourages the use of a common set of questions, and the National

Science Foundation has revised the Survey of Earned Doctorates to collect longitudinal data from PhD holders. While many of these efforts are still in progress, several longitudinal studies (over five years out) have been completed by the Centre for Research and Innovation in Graduate Education (CIRGE) (for example, Nerad and Cerny, 1999; Nerad et al., 2008; Nerad, 2009), the Andrew W. Mellon Foundation (Ehrenberg, et al., 2010; Main, Prenovitz and Ehrenberg, 2019) and the Wisconsin Centre for Education Research (for example, Connolly, 2016).

Several reports on the development of doctoral education in Europe have been published by the European University Association Council for Doctoral Education (EUA-CDE). Their reports have focused on particular issues, including the link between doctoral education, research and innovation and its impact on Europe's economic, scientific, technological and social development. The EUA-CDE's recently published report 'Career development and tracking in doctoral education' (EUA-CDE, 2020) gathered findings from 14 institutions across several countries in Europe (Austria, Belgium, France, Germany, Ireland, Italy, Latvia, Poland, Spain, Switzerland). It highlights both national and institutional methods and their limitations regarding both the success rate in data collection and their comparability, as well as some examples of good practice. The project aimed to investigate the career outcomes of its doctorate holders up to 10 years after the doctoral degree. The most substantial insights have come from talking to PhD alumni with high-level positions in international research organisations or innovative companies, presented as testimonials showing a broad range of career paths beyond academia for PhD graduates.

The European Science Foundation undertook a pilot career-tracking project in 2015 which has produced some interesting findings. Postdocs who remained at the R2 level (posts entered immediately post PhD) for four or more years were more likely to end up in very precarious working conditions than others that had been promoted beyond R2 or had moved out of their postdoctoral position. Also, postdocs in Europe were facing greater job instability until they were in their forties when compared to postdocs in the Global South (European Science Foundation, 2015).

The doctorate for labour markets within and beyond academia

In the previous section, we outlined some of the literature and data sources that have been published about global labour-market trends for doctoral graduates. In this section we will delve more closely into the data.

In the US, the NSF reports that around 50 per cent of their scholars stayed in academia on graduation from 1996–2011, while in 2019 this had dropped to 41 per cent. In the UK around 50 per cent of doctoral graduates take up jobs beyond academia immediately after their doctorate (Vitae, 2013); in Germany the figure is 65 per cent (Bundesbericht Wissenschaftlicher Nachwuchs); in Austria 80 per cent (Auriol et al., 2013); and in France 37 per cent, but after five years only 53 per cent of those remain in French academic research (ADOC). The Royal Society reported in 2010 that in the UK, only 3.5 per cent of science PhD graduates end up in permanent academic positions (Royal Society, 2010). Even from the prestigious Marie Skłodowska-Curie scheme, only around 30 per cent end up in permanent academic employment. However, comprehensive data collection is not performed in most countries – or if it is, it often only covers a few months after graduation, which is not representative. The range of roles beyond academia that graduates enter is very diverse and of course discipline dependent: industrial research, healthcare, policy, consultancy and university administration are all significant. Collecting such data across geographies, disciplines and employment sectors is very difficult with many inconsistencies. The data itself is rather sparse.

As mentioned above, the NSF undertakes regular surveys of graduate destinations of doctoral recipients in the US (NSF, 2019), and around 70 US universities track career pathways of most of their doctoral alumni. The Council for Graduate Schools is encouraging more programmes to increase awareness and exposure to career paths beyond academia. The Council is considering the effects of partnering with industry and particularly exploring early-career industry experiences in engineering. In contrast to other programmes, engineering doctoral graduates do mostly go to industry. There are significant differences in outcomes across different institutions, varying particularly with the research ranking of the university.

In Europe, universities are less well developed in their doctoral alumni tracking. The MORE3 and MORE4 studies on researchers' mobility and careers provide some data, with continuing follow-up studies planned (MORE4). The European Commission has collected data for its Marie Skłodowska-Curie Alumni Association MCAA Fellows (Souto-Otero et al., 2019). The drive in the EU has also been to encourage careers beyond academia in order to help drive innovation in the economy.

Vitae has produced a number of reports in a series 'What do PhDs do' in the UK (Vitae, 2013). They show that three-and-a-half years after obtaining their doctorate, around 17 per cent are in research roles and 21 per cent teaching in higher education. All the rest were working in roles beyond academia, with 12 per cent in research roles and 23 per cent in 'other doctoral occupations'. In Italy, for the AlmaLaurea V Investigation (AlmaLaurea, 2020), a survey of the profile of 3,938 PhDs was undertaken involving 24 Italian universities. The results show that 73 per cent believe that there are more job opportunities abroad for their disciplinary sector. Only 7 per cent believe they have more opportunities to establish themselves in Italy. This focus on the relation between perception of the career opportunities and the country where the doctoral training has been pursued is also linked to the fact that the networked doctoral training structures – based on the international, interdisciplinary and intersectoral mobility (the so-called triple 'I' model) as promoted by the European Commission's Principles for Innovative Doctoral Programs (EU-DGR&I, 2011) – are still quite rare in doctoral programmes across the EU (de Rosa, 2016).

There is less information about doctoral destinations in the developing world, where such tracking is even less well developed. In developing countries, most institutions are preparing their doctoral graduates for academic teaching careers because of a shortage of research skills in universities. In Brazil, the evaluation of doctoral programmes by funding agencies tracks outcomes of the programmes they fund. CAPES, the official Brazilian governmental agency for Co-ordination for the Improvement of Higher Education Personnel, has destination information which confirms that very few go to the private sector. Mexico currently directs its system to develop candidates for faculty careers (either to continue as professors or to become new professors) and less well for careers beyond academia. Many developing countries are growing and strengthening their higher-education provision and so are in need of more recruits with research training for academic positions. This is very much in contrast to the developed world where academic recruitment is static and, in some cases, decreasing due to shrinking undergraduate cohorts, the removal of the compulsory retirement age and an increase in the use of adjuncts and temporary academic contracts. This was discussed in Chapter 7.

The decline in the number of permanent academic positions per researcher at universities and increasing dependency of researchers on temporary and short-term third-party funding is well documented (Nature, 2019). There is also evidence of the effects of job insecurity (Vogiatzis, 2017), concern about a 'lost generation' of postdocs (Nature, 2018) and of a growing number of postdocs and few places in academia

(Powell, 2015). The Graduate Student Experience in the Research University (gradSERU) survey, which analyses current doctoral students in the US and Europe, tells us that doctoral students generally rank the quality and quantity of information about career opportunities outside universities as poor (Douglass and Chirikov, 2021).

Career tracks inside academia and beyond are quite varied across disciplines and across the world. Almost everywhere in the natural and life sciences, it is common for researchers to undertake several postdoctoral posts before they obtain a permanent or tenured academic position (and increasingly even for temporary positions). There is a trend in the US to encourage industry professionals to come back to academia. This requires education of search committees about the very different nature of publication records. In many European countries (notably Germany), recruitment from industry to academic engineering positions is common. However, increasing emphasis on research performance is reducing this trend, most notably in the UK where research evaluation (the Research Excellence Framework) has the effect of discouraging recruitment of practitioners to permanent academic posts.

The recent EURODOC-MCAA declaration on sustainable careers strongly recommends more systematic career tracking (Kismihók et al., 2019). The Next Generation Life Sciences Coalition (NGLS) commits its members to tracking career destinations of both PhD graduates and postdocs. The problems of career tracking of researchers are well documented by Blanck et al. (2017). There were 1.88 million researchers employed in the EU28 in higher education, business and government (Eurostat, 2016) demonstrating that many opportunities beyond academia are indeed available.

In order to persuade governments to collect the data, the higher-education sector needs a more compelling case for the need. Why should governments collect the data? Given the increasing emphasis on innovation and the role that doctoral graduates should have, the data is needed in order to guide investment in developing researchers for enhancing their contribution to innovation. The Hannover Recommendation 5 stresses the importance of more research on doctoral education and its effects. An important reason for universities to collect such data is to provide current doctoral candidates information to make informed career decisions and to help their planning processes. It also enables close contact with alumni for fundraising and in seeking their support for career education of researchers. It is often thought that doctoral alumni are typically not so generous, so they are less of a focus for alumni offices, but recent evidence in the US shows that this is not the case and they are just as generous. The need for longer-term longitudinal surveys is also important in order to really track the longer-term experience of doctoral graduates.

So far, the complex data collection exercises have not proven to be sustainable in the long term, and yet such data is needed to make strategic decisions about doctoral education. A stronger case needs to be made to ensure resources are available for this. Who might do this? Universities must have a stake, but is it adequate for each country to rely just on universities with the inevitable heterogeneity in coverage, quality and detail that this would bring? The EUA-CDE 2020 report proposes a web-based application created in-house by universities or based on a commercial career network such as LinkedIn. It provides suggestions as to how to develop career-tracking practices and strategies. The key points concern the need to clarify the specific information sought and its purpose, to plan the process and include all necessary stakeholders, to understand the limitations of the data received and to contextualise and communicate the results. This continues to be a significant challenge for the sector that needs to be addressed collectively.

Finally, our current understanding of careers is based on the current economic system, but this too is changing. Long-term stable career trajectories are probably not the future. What is the future of work within and beyond academia? Will instability be the norm? Many doctoral graduates in fact value flexibility. Some are looking for stability and clarity about where the future is leading them. Graduate aspirations are mixed. The next section considers the skills that they may need in this broad context.

Skills development for the doctoral labour market across the world

A doctoral programme's unique point is to develop 'creative critical autonomous intellectual risk takers' (Bogle et al., 2010). The unique element of a doctorate is to develop original independent thinking in the candidate, and this is the main criterion by which most thesis defences are judged – on the basis of the candidate and their ideas as evidenced by the defence, the thesis and in some cases publications.

It is important to encourage PhD candidates to take intellectual risks as part of their journey. Risk taking as such is a vital element of training the thinkers and researchers for future unknown significant challenges facing the world. It seems that in the current context of intense competition for funds, a tightening of peer review and expectations of guaranteed outcomes, projects without intellectual risks are often given priority. It is vital, however, that the PhD retains a significant element of intellectual risk-taking and passion, without being entirely speculative, and that candidates learn to manage the uncertainty inherent in research. According to the European Research Council (ERC) Qualitative Evaluation (ERC, 2019), 'A strong positive correlation was found between the high-risk/high-gain feature and the overall grade of projects.' Finding a balance to manage risk allowing sufficient creativity is the challenge.

As part of the doctorate comes a set of skills that are of value in academic research jobs, in research jobs beyond academia, but also in all jobs which require creative thought based on careful and rigorous analysis of conflicting evidence. A list of skills developed during a doctorate is given in Table 8.1 (Bogle et al., 2010). These skills are developed largely through undertaking supervised research while being supported and supplemented by formal training. A key skill for researchers in particular is embracing uncertainty (Novotny, 2016).

For any future role, it is important to help graduates articulate this unique skill set to potential employers. Doctoral graduates must take responsibility for choosing and developing their skills, with support from their advisors, and be able to articulate their particular strengths and experience. Universities too need to articulate more strongly and widely the skills that researchers can offer employers. Some employers are reluctant to hire researchers due to a lack of experience or even as a result of prejudice, but possibly also due to a lack of preparation of doctoral candidates to operate in ways needed by employers beyond academia.

Table 8.1: Skills developed by doctoral candidates
(Bogle et al., 2010)

- intellectual skills, which comprise the ability to:
  - think analytically and synthetically;
  - be creative, inquisitive and original;
  - take intellectual risks;
  - deploy specific technical, research-related tools and techniques.
- academic and technical skills, which comprise the ability to:
  - understand, test and advance complex theories or hypotheses and to deploy sophisticated concepts, methodologies and tools in the chosen subject to a very high level;
  - identify issues and translate them into questions amenable to scholarly enquiry;

- successfully pursue original research in the chosen field;
- use critical judgment in an objective manner based on verifiable evidence;
- apply highest standards of rigour in the proof of ideas;
- manage a high degree of uncertainty both in method and in outcomes;
- develop and demonstrate academic credibility and become recognised as a member of an international scholarly community;
- understand the workings of a specific high-level research-intensive environment;
- transfer new knowledge to scholarly communities and communicate it to society;
- work according to ethical principles;
- work in an interdisciplinary setting or on an interdisciplinary topic.
• personal and professional management skills, which comprise the ability to:
- persist in achieving long-term goals;
- manage projects with uncertain outcomes in diverse settings and organisations;
- take a project through all its stages: from developing the original idea, to developing a plan, gathering the evidence, and communicating the results and their significance;
- be self-motivated and autonomous;
- work to achieve results with minimum supervision;
- be flexible and adaptable in approaching complex and uncertain problems;
- communicate very complex concepts;
- network internationally;
- work in a team;
- speak and present effectively in public.
• The following skills are sometimes also developed:
- the ability to lead other researchers;
- the ability to teach and train others;
- the ability to organise conferences and workshops.

While once a candidate would rely on their supervisor/advisor for all their training, this greater focus on the skills, which they develop both for the undertaking of their project but also for future careers, has led to the development of frameworks and to training programmes provided by universities and collaborating institutions and companies. Researcher career-development teams need to tackle many aspects: identifying researchers' and employers' needs in order to train researchers accordingly, encouraging lifelong learning as employers' needs invariably will change, raising awareness of skills development among the different stakeholders, providing the necessary frameworks to facilitate joint efforts towards better trained researchers and agreeing on who takes on which of the responsibilities.

The EC's research portal EURAXESS provides a career development and career orientation tool to help guide skills development and competence profiles for PhDs. The EURAXESS initiative is currently exploring how the network can support career development at different levels through different EURAXESS projects. The first results include a set of recommendations for different stakeholders on how to foster researcher career development, case studies where different European institutions share their approaches, and a few tips on how to measure the impact of the strategies. For example, the UK community, coordinated by VITAE, developed a researcher skills taxonomy called the Researcher Development Framework (Vitae, 2011) which forms the basis of researcher development also in some countries beyond the UK. The new European Research Area (ERA) policy intends to transform and broaden the EURAXESS services to an ERA Talent Platform. This will be an online one-stop shop with links to EURES (the network of European public employment services) for researchers to manage their skills acquisition and careers.

These generic skills are needed by researchers everywhere, although each individual may seek to develop particular strengths according to their needs and aspirations. There is now a greater emphasis on providing this broader set of skills required for the doctorate and those required by potential employers beyond academia for driving innovation in the economy while still allowing complete freedom with regards to the PhD topic. Modern societies are seeking intellectual leadership and risk taking together with people who can drive topics and agendas towards desired outcomes. The precise need for such skills will of course be context dependent, depending on discipline and country needs. It is recognised that R&D spending drives innovation, but labour markets are not static, and it is important to create dynamism in the economy and society rather than just more research jobs.

There are some new skills currently less well covered that are vital for doctoral graduates to take their place in the workforce within or beyond academia (Nerad, 2015). These are set out in the rest of this section.

While once the doctorate was very much an isolated experience, it is important for researchers to know how to collaborate. It is widely recognised that in future, discoveries are unlikely to come in isolation. This applies just as much within academia as beyond – in making progress on society's grand challenges, in working together in collegiate multidisciplinary environments mixing physically and virtually, and in developing and delivering new curricula and new teaching methods which rely increasingly on problem-solving approaches and 'flipped' classrooms as well as peer learning.

Communication to the wider world has become more important for academic researchers as they fight for profile and impact, especially internationally. Since talent is now so mobile, it is important to allow for and understand different cultures and ways of working. The researchers need to be able to translate research ideas and outcomes into a broader context and to explain this context. Also important is social media as a platform, particularly given the high levels of misinformation bred by its immediacy. Many doctoral candidates are more skilled in social media than their advisors.

A new set of skills that is becoming prominent is in the use and manipulation of large datasets and in understanding the complexities and weaknesses of sophisticated algorithms, particularly those involving artificial intelligence (AI). Once the preserve of science and engineering, it is becoming clear that all researchers, and indeed all professionals whatever their disciplinary background, will require these skills. Recent research indicates that the digital revolution has contributed significantly to job creation: four out of 10 jobs were created in digitally-intensive industries over the past decade (OECD, 2019). At the same time, the demand for AI talent nearly doubled between 2016 and 2018 with two roles open for every AI expert available (MMC Ventures, 2019). Technological progress has occurred in parallel with an increase in overall employment, albeit being directly responsible for substantial job destruction in certain sectors. The troubling prediction that radiologists will disappear (Hinton, 2016) was not confirmed, and in July 2020 no radiologist had been replaced by AI (OECD, 2021). The recent US National Academies report (National Academies, 2018) lays out some of the additional data skills doctoral students will need. This is now being explored at undergraduate level and will result in major changes to education. New PhD programmes and their formal training will need to place much more emphasis on data and programming skills, regardless of discipline. PhD candidates in all disciplines will increasingly need the capacity to work with big datasets. 'Systems thinking' – the ability to understand and analyse whole systems and the way they interact – is also an important element.

The past two years have seen a clear acceleration in the adoption of new technologies by companies across the world (WEF, 2020). AI-related jobs continue to proliferate across nearly every industry, while robotics is a growing sector of the $1.2 trillion artificial intelligence industry (LinkedIn, 2020). Businesses seem to support the view that decisions to adopt AI are motivated more by the aim of complementing human capabilities than by the aim of substituting workers (business surveys by Bessen et al., 2018; McKinsey, 2019; Accenture, 2018; reviewed in OECD 2021 Report).

Highly-skilled jobs are deemed to be among the most exposed to AI (OECD, 2021; Grubanov-Boskovic et al., 2021). Targeted research on the health and long-term care workforce (Grubanov-Boskovic et al., 2021) suggests that most AI exposure is driven by its impact on tasks that require abilities dealing with ideas, such as comprehension, attention and conceptualisation, supporting the assumption that highly-skilled medical doctors will probably be more exposed to AI than workers in medium-skilled occupations such as nursing and paramedics. There is evidence also that highly-skilled research occupations which require either reasoning about novel situations (Webb, 2020) or some manual activities (for example, animal scientists and archaeologists) are only lightly exposed to AI (Brynjolfsson, Mitchell and Rock, 2018). On the other hand, social interaction skills seem to future-proof exposure to AI in any job, independent of qualification level. Doctoral training should help early-career researchers in leveraging a set of generic multidisciplinary competencies, including self-management skills such as active learning, resilience, stress tolerance and flexibility, along with social interaction skills to help them take their place and make a contribution in the workplace within and beyond academia.

A worker's skill set will be an important variable in the disruptive impact of technological progress on their job. AI is deemed lacking most of the metacognitive capabilities that are intrinsically human: what counts as knowledge; how to acquire and create it; how to regulate cognition, attention and emotion in learning processes; and what the social and practical motivation for learning is (Tuomi, 2018). Research seems to concur on the tasks which cannot easily be automated: perception and manipulation, especially when performed in unstructured situations; creative intelligence and social intelligence; understanding others and caring for others (OECD, 2019; Servoz, 2019).

Today's public policy focus will also need to address the question of how to turn technological progress to our advantage, with the understanding that policies will determine the impact of AI and not the other way around. This topic currently is generating a lot of interest, with UNESCO hosting the recently created International Research Center on AI (IRCAI) launched in 2020, the European Parliament running the STOA Observatory exploring AI in education and Eurofound publishing a report in December 2021 on 'Work organisation and job quality in the digital age'. Also, the OECD is preparing a call for project proposals with the aim to explore how universities use AI to better match research strands with the labour market (Labour Market Relevance and Outcomes of HE initiative). EU-level initiatives point to the need for doctoral education to increase the focus on skills from data management, to training in ethical and human aspects of AI and to entrepreneurial and self-management competences.

To make the most of their skills and to demonstrate their unique skillset, doctoral candidates will need to work in an environment where there is less distinction between 'inside' and 'outside' universities. In Europe, outreach by doctoral candidates is considered to be a 'horizontal duty' of all as part of responsible research and innovation, although not all doctoral candidates should necessarily be expected to reach out to all three of industry, schools and the wider public. Increasingly, there are links with schools, but most institutions lack sufficient time and resources to reach out very far, geographically or in terms of numbers. Bringing the excitement of new discoveries to schoolchildren and teachers, for example via appropriate 'low budget publications' as well as through direct contact, helps raise the credibility and recognition of research and researchers. But what skills are needed for this and are they being developed routinely? For this, doctoral candidates need to be able to translate concepts and practices into language that very young people can understand. Related to this is citizen science, where the public participates and collaborates in scientific research, which will also require a new set of skills. In the public humanities movement in the US for doctorates in the humanities and arts (https://en.wikipedia.org/wiki/Public_humanities), researchers engage with society in the cocreation of research and its execution, for example. Should public service be part of the doctoral degree requirements?

Open science (sometimes known as open scholarship and which includes responsible research and innovation), where scientific research is made freely available to all, is changing the landscape through supporting open access and open data for greater openness and transparency of published results. The recommendation on access to and preservation of scientific information (European Commission, 2018) reflects developments in areas such as research data management (FAIR data), text and data mining (TDM) and technical standards that enable reuse incentive schemes. It reflects ongoing developments at the EU level of the European Open Science Cloud and the increased capacity of data analytics of today and its role in research. The University of California at Berkeley Reproducibility and Open Science Working Group is leading change in the US. The European Commission recommendation also clearly identifies as two separate points the issue of reward systems for researchers to share data and commit to other open-science practices on the one hand, and skills and competences of researchers and staff from research institutions on the other. The development of open scholarship, necessary to demonstrate transparency in research and to help enhance trust in the research world, will require training a new range of programming, data-archiving and data-management skills. The role of institutional support for open scholarship is being debated around the world (for example, Ayris et al., 2018).

Universities aim to train researchers to be original, to be able to support and defend their original ideas and also to use these ideas to drive innovation. Innovation is a key part of enhancing prosperity in modern developed societies. Extremely rapid development of automation will see changes made that result in much quicker innovation cycles. So, what is the difference between research and innovation? Innovation ('the application of better solutions that meet new requirements, unarticulated needs or existing market or social needs') requires taking ideas into practice for the benefit of society. Sometimes it is easier, with more rapid impact, to advance someone else's research question as opposed to come up with a research question that has not been addressed before. What are the skills required to take one's ideas forward as opposed to ideas of others and are they different? We need to try to instil all these in our 'researchers as innovators'. Not all will succeed. On top of this there is an increasing need to develop entrepreneurial and business skills that support innovation. Programmes funded through the European Institute of Technology (EIT) for example particularly emphasise entrepreneurship and innovation skills.

Many of these ideas are being adopted in the developing world. However, it is an open question as to whether the skill sets are the same in different stages of a country's development. Currently, countries do not measure the extent to which specific skills are developed and do not have the instruments to measure and benchmark skills development. Interdisciplinarity is also a major challenge for many developing countries, especially when disciplines are not themselves strong within a university. It is also true that there are skills from the Global South that might help change societies in the Global North for the better, for example moving economies more in a way to serve the common good rather than maximising profit (Duflo and Banerjee, 2011). This speaks to the first of the Hannover Recommendations to 'establish a global joint value system for doctoral education based on an ecology of knowledges which recognises and seeks to overcome existing inequalities in the access to doctoral education and the provision of knowledge'.

There is a recognition of the key role of public funding in driving innovative practices in academia which is mostly rather conservative. Innovation within academia is largely driven by major funding schemes, for example, NSF, the Marie Skłodowska-Curie Actions (MCSA) programme, German Excellence Initiative, the Japanese Global Centres of Excellence Programme and other national programmes. A feature that differentiates specific universities as being more successful in their social mission is the existence of offices which encourage outreach, knowledge transfer and innovation. Among US research universities, there is a movement supported by the Carnegie Foundation to engage more closely with their local environment in all fields. (Annually participating universities receive an award for their local research engagements.) This should also include arts and humanities and social science research and innovative ideas, although this is rarer (as encouraged by Hannover Recommendation 4). MSCA, through its bottom-up approach, contributes towards tackling societal challenges: 63 per cent of the budget was awarded to sustainable development, 23 per cent to climate change and 6 per cent to biodiversity (Souto-Otero et al.). In general, we are seeing a mixed situation – pressure for change is in some cases coming from within universities, often from young researchers. Since they embody the future and have so much at stake how best should we empower ECRs?

Given these changes to the system and the extra requirements of doctoral candidates, are we now expecting too much? Given the pressure to deliver a successful doctoral project outcome and the uncertainty that underpins this, we can only expect introductions to some of these skills while a few are taken to a more sophisticated level. Given that many postdoctoral researchers also will not pursue academic careers, it is important that this stage clearly builds on the doctorate and adds new skills that will be useful in the workplace, in academia and beyond (Bogle, 2018). The recent Eurodoc-MCAA Declaration on Sustainable Research Careers (Kismihók et al., 2019) shows that researchers are increasingly vocal on the need for change. A postdoctoral stage that only gives narrow technical skills and some publications will increasingly be seen as pointless for those not seeking an academic career. If candidates were put off research positions, this would be damaging to a research system that relies on postdoctoral researchers for delivery of research projects. Research 'talent' mostly wishes to be allowed to work independently and with international mobility.

Communicating about the competencies and transferable skills of the researchers to future employers is crucial. It is important to do this in the language and terminology of current and future employers. Several universities are collaborating with HR staff from companies and other nonacademic sector entities to develop skills profiles for their young researchers as part of their career guidance.

Seeking change in political systems which are regulated more centrally is difficult, particularly in order to obtain meaningful and flexible skills development together with disciplinary development and cross-disciplinary work. Where regulation is light and institutional autonomy strong, some confident institutions can lead.

Skills development is now firmly embedded in many universities of the Global North, helping to prepare PhD candidates for the wider roles in society expected of them. However, there are other research doctorates, professional doctorates, which can train researchers for specific research-based careers in some professions. They also develop generic skills but also some specific research skills for their profession. These are discussed in the next section together with 'industrial doctorates'.

The potential of professional and industrial doctorates

Professional doctorates are typically three-year (full-time or equivalent duration part-time) doctorates with some advanced courses, a portfolio on introducing new practices in a professional environment and a research project (much shorter than the PhD) anchored in professional practice (see also Chapter 1). They are growing in certain areas where the doctorate can be done while in professional practice. They still follow doctoral principles of originality and rigour but are clearly linked to professional practice. In the US, they are mostly in health-related disciplines which can lead to a professional licence. In Europe, the most common are education, clinical psychology and other health-related disciplines, with growing interest in the doctor of business administration. Professional doctorates are very new in Brazil, with certification through CAPES only becoming allowed in 2018.

There are a number of benefits with professional doctorates: candidates can do them more easily alongside an active job; the research is more directly driven by societal needs and typically they are shorter with a more defined timescale. There is a risk of expectation management – that employers expect the same as a PhD, which it is not – and a need to prevent inflation of titles. Universities are the custodians of quality of all degrees and need to be clear about the expected outcomes to potential and current employers. There is a desire in the professional world for real relevance in research degrees but with high standards. They can also be seen as a way of extending links with society.

Professional doctorate candidates are often practitioners with significant administrative workloads. The aim of these awards is not necessarily for the pursuit of knowledge but rather for advancement in professional and in some cases managerial roles. In the US, they are expensive for students as often there is no institutional or federal financial aid and students invest in these costs almost always directly out of pocket. In the UK, some clinical doctorates are funded by the National Health Service as part of professional development, for example in clinical psychology. Mostly, professional doctorate candidates come with more professional experience than those directly from master's and PhD programmes. They tend to be older and come with years of work experience and a greater level of skills development, although not necessarily of research skills, so the programmes are inevitably of a different nature to the PhD.

There has long been a tradition of 'industrial' doctorates. These are typically a PhD but undertaken within an industrial context and judged in the same way as a traditional PhD. They are done in Denmark, the UK, France, Japan and Germany. Sixty-two per cent of MSCA fellows benefit from some form of cross-sectoral mobility or exposure of benefit to their research or their career development largely through secondments and research staff exchanges outside academia. Industry is increasingly interested because of a desire to increase research and links with universities to help keep ahead of competitors. The objective of the MSCA European Industrial Doctorates (EIDs) and the MSCA Initial Training Networks is to involve the nonacademic sector in doctoral training, especially enterprises. EIDs help PhD candidates step outside academia and develop skills in industry and business. This type of network is provided by at least one academic partner together with partners from the business world. Individuals are enrolled on a doctoral programme at the academic partner and are jointly supervised by staff of the academic and nonacademic partners. Similar schemes occur in Europe in France (CIFRE), the UK (CASE and EngD) and other countries. The EC reviewed its EID scheme (European Commission, 2017) finding that:

1. the scheme helps develop new and strengthen existing intersectoral collaborations;
2. the quality of applications was commended resulting in a larger talent pool; and
3. those interested in industrial careers from the start reported that the EID fellowship helped strengthen their career prospects.

In industrial doctorates, it is recognised that there can be a danger of too much direction by a company. Where this is the case, this is inimical to the PhD, which must allow the candidate to drive the research and to develop and prove their own ideas. Universities as custodians of the standards of their doctoral degrees are conscious of this tension. Regulators license universities to award degrees and they cannot be awarded by industry or by research organisations (such as the Max Planck Society or CNRS). In Brazil, the Institute for Pure and Applied Maths can grant doctoral titles, but this is a rare exception.

The differences between PhDs, industrial doctorates and professional doctorates need to be articulated more clearly and with clear statements about expectations of output standards. Possibly, professional doctorate programmes with their shorter research period could provide a more cost-effective – in both financial terms and in time spent by candidates – way of encouraging research-informed practice and innovation. We must ensure that the standards are still at doctoral level, which some do question.

In the following section, we consider the features that are necessary for a rich experience for all these different types of doctorates.

Features of research environments to enhance the employability of doctoral graduates

The insertion into a strong environment is recognised as the most important factor in ensuring high-quality doctoral education (European Commission, 2005; Bogle et al., 2010; Byrne et al., 2013). The Principles of Innovative Doctoral Training of the European Commission highlight the importance of interdisciplinary, international and intersectoral opportunities to develop researchers, and this chapter particularly considers intersectoral experience. The mechanisms for ensuring strong research environments vary greatly across the world with funding, assessment, regulation and quality-assurance regimes all playing a part. Some aspects have been considered in Chapters 4 (Quality Assurance) and

5 (Supervision), but here we look more broadly at the environment and particularly the way it supports preparation for a wide range of careers.

Awareness of the wide range of careers and a reasonable understanding of the opportunities is important for the candidates to be able to make informed choices. Intersectoral mobility (to employment sectors beyond higher education) during the doctorate where possible very much assists this. In Europe, the majority of EU Member States do not have a dedicated national funding system to support this, although a number do have national public or private funding sources to support intersectoral mobility within the country (European Commission, 2018b). The EC review of the 9th Framework Programme (2018c) found a strong demand for PhD and postdoctoral researchers from industry, especially in STEM subjects, and a stronger demand for researchers in non-STEM subjects (social sciences, arts and humanities) in the public and third sectors. However, there are proportionately more schemes targeted at industry than at the public and charitable sectors. There is also a higher level of awareness among larger firms than within SMEs about the benefits of engaging with PhD and postdoctoral researchers. The study also found a lack of interest among researchers in developing a career outside of the academic setting. This increases the need to raise awareness amongst researchers in academia to open doctoral candidates' horizons to careers beyond academia. This is done in some universities by connecting with alumni and with employers interested in hiring doctoral graduates which inevitably focuses on existing relationships and mostly with large companies. However, employment growth is concentrated in smaller companies. Enterprise units also give information and support for startups, but launching companies arising from research ideas can be daunting for those starting out.

Since research is international, mobility is also important to train researchers to be comfortable to move beyond national borders. European-level funding is the only financing source for schemes which combine intersectoral and international mobility. The Marie Skłodowska-Curie Award programme has been particularly successful in this regard. It is also seen as a vehicle for breaking down cultural barriers in Europe and beyond and enhancing European integration.

Structured programmes, long the norm in US doctoral education, have developed over recent years in Europe. While there are many models of such programmes, they all aim to embed doctoral training into a cohort experience, with some element of formal training programme, while retaining the primacy of the individual original research project. The benefits of structured PhD programmes have been highlighted by many (Eurodoc, 2019), resulting in changes in funding schemes such as the

Centres for Doctoral Training in the UK, the École Universitaire de Recherche doctoral programmes in France and the National Science Foundation Research Traineeship (NRT) Program in the US, which encourages collaboration with the private sector. As well as aiding orientation and induction and alleviating the well-known dangers of isolation, a structured programme allows for a more targeted way of bringing in employers who seek specialist skills in specific areas.

Quality assurance is covered in depth in Chapter 4, but here we consider how it can enhance employability. The effectiveness with which doctoral programmes prepare their candidates for a broad range of careers should be considered as part of the quality assurance process. LERU's report on 'Maintaining a quality culture of doctoral education' (Bogle et al., 2016) gives four necessary components: clearly stated expectations, scrutiny processes involving independent experts, measurements to inform the scrutiny, and feedback and enhancement to improve the culture. Preparation for a wide range of careers should be one of the expectations. Data on the career destinations of doctoral graduates should be part of the assessment of research organisations. This data should not be just first destinations but also longitudinal data tracking careers. Having narratives about the impact that doctoral graduates make on society is important for universities to demonstrate that their role is valued. This helps to ensure that sufficient finance is available to ensure a high-quality research training system.

Are there specific needs associated with particular levels of a country's development and its trajectory and aspirations? There was a strong view at the Herrenhausen Conference that doctoral programmes for the developing world should be at the same level and include the same generic skills as in the developed world – currently developing countries gain a lot from researchers who return from undertaking research training in the developed world. The developed world also needs to accept the particular knowledge and viewpoint that doctoral students from the Global South bring with them. It is crucial that they are all trained to be creative in research – but also creative as to how to develop relationships with colleagues and collaborators in other universities and in companies. It is also true in the developing world that doctoral candidates should be prepared to work in companies and other organisations beyond academia. The need to initiate innovative companies is vital for prosperity for these countries. The practical ways to do this may be different, but the need is the same across the world.

If research and research training aim to help society tackle its grand challenges, training and activities should be based on collaboration rather than competition. We have been arguing that collaboration with companies, government and charities enriches the doctoral candidates' training experience. Also, collaboration within and between universities, locally, nationally and globally, enriches candidates' experience and strengthens efforts to tackle grand research challenges. There will inevitably be an element of competition in the research world, but this should not hinder appropriate collaboration. It is normal for the private sector to work in collaboration in some aspect while competing in others. The research system has become more competitive in recent decades, which has decreased some willingness to cooperate. Research training environments should be promoting collaborating mindsets and highlighting mechanisms that help to alleviate the damaging effects of competition. The Russian system, for example, lacks competition and yet does not enhance collaboration either. The grant system and peer review are not well developed in Russia, so there is no opportunity to compete and learn from success, failure and feedback. Collaboration is needed as it strengthens quality, yet human nature can be both collaborative and competitive. The research system needs to encourage collaborative working while managing a certain degree of competition where it is constructive. Immersing doctoral candidates in such an environment will help prepare them for the reality of the wide range of roles they will pursue.

Getting greater value from doctorate education

We have presented data on global labour-market trends for doctoral graduates along with some recent thinking that highlights some of the challenges that face universities and research systems in countries at all stages of economic development. There has been considerable reorientation towards producing doctoral graduates to help drive innovation in all sectors of society. The training, while still primarily focused on producing and defending a piece of substantive original research, has seen a significant growth in skills training both for better execution of research but also for future career needs and prospects. These opportunities are quite variable between countries. There is certainly a need to celebrate the very wide range of potential careers open to doctoral graduates.

These changes are widely recognised within the university sector but less so by potential employers. A key challenge for the community is how can we better persuade society and employers, especially small employers, of the value of the new doctoral graduates (Recommendation 6b). They are still sometimes seen as 'overqualified'.

The new emphasis on skills has been highlighted. But are we developing all the right skills? The need for research and trained researchers is widely recognised as an engine for prosperity but the skills needed are inevitably changing and we have highlighted some of the changes that are needed (Recommendation 6a), in particular around data-management skills, artificial intelligence, systems thinking and innovation in policy and practice. Doctoral candidates everywhere need to be helped to develop career agency skills while reviewing the opportunities in their local context. All the skills are needed by doctoral graduates for their careers both within academic research and for roles beyond academia. It is important for universities and their staff to communicate more widely the changes that have occurred, as outlined in the last three chapters, to explain to employers the broad skill set that is developed in the doctorate to produce 'creative, critical, autonomous responsible intellectual risk takers'. Universities also need to support doctoral graduates to recognise these skills in themselves. This will help them convey to their potential employers the evidence that they have developed these skills and how they will be valuable in the workplace.

With research and recruitment now so international, some degree of consistency would be beneficial for aspiring researchers, between countries and between disciplines, while respecting and taking value from differing academic traditions (Recommendation 3).

This chapter has aimed to consider how best to think about the doctorate on a global scale for the wider role expected of doctoral graduates. The situation is variable across countries, hence there is a need for universities and their funding systems to have flexibility while recognising the potential for international mobility that doctoral graduates have. We do need more evidence to give more confidence on which to base our decisions (Recommendation 5), particularly on short- and long-term career destinations and pathways. Are we preparing global PhD citizens who are also able to address local needs? Are we preparing them to be innovators as well as researchers? Are they prepared for smaller companies which have little tradition of research and innovation? While some large companies have many PhDs employed, some have very few. Are there ways to improve awareness of doctorate-level skills and even perhaps the status of doctoral education? Are we doing this effectively and optimally? There is much progress but still work to do in reforming doctoral education and in raising candidates' and employers' awareness of the distinctive skill set of doctoral graduates.

The next chapter considers the doctorate in a wider social and political context. We are preparing doctoral graduates for a wide range of often influential leadership roles in society, so their ethical framework can have a significant impact on those around them. The chapter considers the context, particularly given the significant crises that affect us all today, and the way that doctoral education gives an ethical framework and transcultural perspectives for the future roles expected for these intellectual leaders.

References

ADOC. (2017) 'Emploi 2017'. Talent Management. Accessed 9 June 2022. https://www.adoc-tm.com/emploi-2017?lang=en.
AlmaLaurea. (2020) Indagine V 'Profilo dei dottori di ricerca 2019'. Accessed 9 June 2022. https://www.almalaurea.it/universita/indagini/dottori/profilo/profilo_dottori2019.
AlmaLaurea. (2019) Accessed 9 June 2022. https://www.almalaurea.it/universita/occupazione/occupazione17/volume 26/3/2022
APAC. (n.d.) 'Academic pathways across Europe'. Accessed 9 June 2022. https://www.academiccareermaps.org/.
Auriol, L., Misu M. and Freeman R. (2013) 'Careers of Doctorate Holders: Analysis of Labour Market and Mobility Indicators'. OECD Science, Technology and Industry Working Papers, No. 2013/04. Paris: OECD Publishing. Accessed 9 June 2022. https://doi.org/10.1787/5k43nxgs289w-en.
Ayris P, San Roman A.L., Maes K., Labastida I. (2018) 'Open science and its role in universities: A roadmap for cultural change'. https://www.leru.org/publicat ions/open-science-and-its-role-in-universities-a-roadmap-for-cultural-change.
Banerjee, A.V. and Duflo, E. (2011) *Poor Economics: A radical rethinking of the way to fight global poverty*. New York: Public Affairs.
Blank, R., Daniels, R.J., Gilliland, G., Gutmann, A., Hawgood, S., Hrabowski, F.A., Pollack, M.E., Price, V., Reif, L.R. and Schlissel, M.S. (2017) 'A new data effort to inform career choices in biomedicine'. *SCIENCE* 358 (6,369), 1,388–89. Accessed 9 June 2022. https://science.sciencemag.org/content/358/6369/1388.full?ijkey=PT03zTJ1cla7U&keytype=ref&siteid=sci.
Bogle I.D.L., Eggermont J., Dron M., and van Henten J-W. (2010) `Doctoral degrees beyond 2010: Training talented researchers for society'. https://www.leru.org/publications/doctoral-degrees-beyond-2010-training-talented-researchers-for-society#
Bogle I.D.L., Shykoff J., von Bulow I., Maes K. (2016) `Maintaining a quality culture in doctoral education'. https://www.leru.org/publications/maintaining-a-quality-culture-in-doctoral-education-at-research-intensive-universities.
Bogle, I.D.L. (2018) 'How could universities and funders improve the situation for postdoctoral scientists'. Accessed 9 June 2022. http://blogs.nature.com/naturejobs/2018/06/27/how-could-universities-and-funders-improve-the-situation-for-postdoctoral-scientists/#/.
Brynjolfsson, E., Mitchell, T. and Rock, D. (2018) 'What can machines learn and what does it mean for occupations and the economy?'. *AEA Papers and Proceedings*, Vol. 108, 43–7. Accessed 9 June 2022. http://dx.doi.org/10.1257/pandp.20181019.
Bundesbericht Wissenschaftlicher Nachwuchs. (2021) Accessed 9 June 2022. https://www.buwin.de/ 26/3/2022
Byrne, J., Jørgensen, T.E. and Loukkola, T. (2013) *Quality Assurance in Doctoral Education: Results of the ARDE project*. Brussels: European University Association.
Chen H., Zhao, S., Shen, W. and Cai L. (2018) 'The quality of Chinese PhDs: Achievements, problems and responses'. *Chinese Education & Society*, 51, 158–68.
CIRGE (n.d.) 'PhD career path tracking'. Accessed 9 June 2022. https://www.education.uw.edu/cirge/phd-career-path-tracking/.

Connolly, M.R., Savoy, J.N., Hill, L., Lee, Y.G. and Associates. (2016) *Building a better future STEM faculty: How doctoral teaching development programs can improve undergraduate education*. Executive summary. Madison, WI: Wisconsin Center for Education Research, University of Wisconsin–Madison.

de Rosa, A.S. (2016) 'The European/international joint PhD in social representations and communication: A triple "I" networked joint doctorate'. In D. Halliday and G. Clarke (eds), *Proceedings of the 2nd International Conference on Development in Doctoral Education and Training*, London: Epigeum, 47–60.

Douglass, J. and Chirikov, I. (2021) 'Pathways for improving doctoral education--Using data in the pre- and post-COVID era'. In S. Schwaag, A. Malmberg and M. Benner (eds.), *Renewal of Higher Education: Academic leadership in times of transformation*. CALIE Project.Lund: Lund University. Accessed 9 June 2022. https://calieproject.files.wordpress.com/2021/05/renewal-of-higher-education_final210505.pdf

Ehrenberg, R., Zuckerman, H., Groen, J. and Brucker, S. (2010) *Educating scholars*. Princeton, NJ: Princeton University Press.

ERC. (2019) 'Qualitative evaluation of completed projects funded by the European Research Council 2019'. Accessed 9 June 2022. https://erc.europa.eu/sites/default/files/document/file/2020-qualitative-evaluation-projects.pdf.

EUA-CDE. (2020) 'Tracking the careers of doctorate holders: EUA-CDE Thematic Peer Group Report'. Accessed 9 June 2022. https://eua-cde.org/reports-publications/945:tracking-the-careers-of-doctorate-holders-eua-cde-thematic-peer-group-report.html.

EU-DGR&I. (2011) 'Principles for innovative doctoral training'. European Commission Directorate-General Research and Innovation. Accessed 9 June 2022. https://euraxess.ec.europa.eu/sites/default/files/policy_library/principles_for_innovative_doctoral_training.pdf.

Eurodoc. (2019) 'Declaration on sustainable researcher careers'. Accessed 9 June 2022. https://zenodo.org/record/3082245#.XRzDe0xuKUm.

Eurodoc. (2019) 'Eurodoc survey on the structure of doctorates across Europe'. Accessed 9 June 2022. http://www.eurodoc.net/news/2019/eurodoc-survey-on-the-structure-of-doctorates-across-europe.

European Commission. (2005) 'Charter and Code for researchers'. Accessed 9 June 2022. No longer available. https://euraxess.ec.europa.eu/jobs/charter.

European Commission. (2017a) *European Industrial Doctorates – Towards Increased Employability and Innovation: Final report*. Luxembourg: Publications Office of the European Union.

European Commission. (2017b) *The Economic Rationale for Public R&I Funding and Its Impact: Policy brief series*. Luxembourg: Publications Office of the European Union.

European Commission. (2018) 'Commission Recommendation (EU) 2018/790 of 25 April 2018 on access to and preservation of scientific information'. Accessed 9 June 2022. https://eur-lex.europa.eu/legal-content/EN/TXT/?uri=CELEX:32018H0790.

European Commission. (2018b) 'Study on fostering industrial talents in research at European Level'. Accessed 9 June 2022. https://cdn5.euraxess.org/sites/default/files/policy_library/final_report_intersectoral_mobility.pdf.

European Commission. (2018c) *A New Horizon for Europe: Impact assessment of the 9th EU Framework Programme for Research and Innovation*. Brussels: European Commission, 70.

European Commission. (2019) 'The EU's open science policy'. Accessed 9 June 2022. No longer available. https://ec.europa.eu/info/research-and-innovation/strategy/goals-research-and-innovation-policy/open-science_en.

European Commission. (2020) 'A new ERA for research and innovation: COM(2020) 628 final'. Accessed 9 June 2022 https://eur-lex.europa.eu/legal-content/EN/TXT/PDF/?uri=CELEX:52020SC0214.

European Science Foundation. (2015) *Career Tracking of Doctorate Holders*. Strasbourg: European Science Foundation.

Euroscientist. (2021) 'Exploring inequities that affect academic output and career trajectories in the aftermath of COVID-19'. Accessed 9 June 2022. https://www.euroscientist.com/inequities-academic-output-career-trajectories/.

Eurostat. (2016) Eurostat statistics explained. Research and Development: R&D Personnel. Accessed 9 June 2022. No longer available. https://ec.europa.eu/eurostat/statistics-explained/index.php?title=Category:Research_and_development 26/3/2022.

FAIR4S capability and skills framework - https://eosc-fair4s.github.io/#. Accessed 9 June 2022.

Grubanov Boskovic S., Ghio D., Goujon A., Kalantaryan S., Belmonte M., Scipioni M., Conte A., Gómez-González E., Gómez E., Tolan S., Martínez-Plumed F., Pesole A., Fernández-Macías E., Hernández-Orallo J., Health and long-term care workforce: demographic challenges and the potential contribution of migration and digital technology, EUR 30593 EN, Publications Office of the European Union, Luxembourg, 2021, ISBN 978-92-76-30233-9, doi:10.2760/33427, JRC121698.

Hinton G. (2016) 'Geoff Hinton: On radiology'. Accessed 9 June 2022. https://www.youtube.com/watch?v=2HMPRXstSvQ.

Kismihók, G., Cardells, F., Güner, P.B., Kersten, F., Harrison, S., Shawrav, M.M., Huber, F., Trusilewicz, L.N., Mol, S.T., Bajanca, F., Dahle, S., Keszler, Á., Carbajal, G.V., Kretzschmar, W.W., Björnmalm, M., Stroobants, K., Hnatkova, E., Cophignon, A., Degtyarova, I., Zwierzyńska, B. and Parada, F. (2019) *Declaration on Sustainable Researcher Careers*. Brussels: Marie Curie Alumni Association and European Council of Doctoral Candidates and Junior Researchers. Accessed 9 June 2022. https://zenodo.org/record/3194228#.YkAhdnrMKUk

LinkedIn. (2020) 'Emerging jobs report'. Accessed 9 June 2022. https://business.linkedin.com/content/dam/me/business/en-us/talent-solutions/emerging-jobs-report/Emerging_Jobs_Report_U.S._FINAL.pdf.

Main, J.B., Prenovitz, S. and Ehrenberg, R. (2019). 'In pursuit of a tenure-track faculty position: Career progression and satisfaction of humanities and social sciences doctorates (CHERI Working Paper 180)'. *The Review of Higher Education*, 42 (4): 1,309–36.

MMC Ventures. (2019) 'The State of AI 2019: Divergence'. Accessed 9 June 2022. https://medium.com/mmc-writes/introducingthe-state-of-ai-2019-divergence-14d69cb3b16c.

MORE4. (2020) *MORE4 study: Support data collection and analysis concerning mobility patterns and career paths of researchers*. Luxembourg: Publications Office of the European Union. Accessed 26 March 2022 https://cdn4.euraxess.org/sites/default/files/policy_library/more4_indicators_report.pdf

National Academies. (2018) 'Graduate STEM education for the 21st Century'. National Academies of Science, Engineering and Medicine. Accessed 9 June 2022. https://www.nsf.gov/attachments/245525/public/Graduate_STEM_Education_21st_Century_Rudin.pdf.

Nature. (2018) 'Track the fate of postdocs to help the next generation of scientists'. 18 July. Accessed 9 June 2022. https://www.nature.com/articles/d41586-018-05745-2.

Nature. (2019) 'Tenure denial, and how early-career researchers can survive it'. 22 January. Accessed 9 June 2022. https://www.nature.com/articles/d41586-019-00219-5.

Nerad, M. (2015) 'Professional development for doctoral students: What is it? Why now? Who does it?'. *Nagoya Journal of Higher Education*, 15, 285–318.

Nerad, M. and Cerny, J. (1999). 'From rumors to facts: Career outcomes of English PhDs: Results from the PhD's ten years later study'. *CGS Communicator*. Accessed 9 June 2022. Retrieved from https://depts.washington.edu/envision/resources/TenYearsLater.pdf.

Nerad, M., Rudd, E., Morrison, E. and Picciano, J. (2007–9) *Social Science PhDs – Five years out*. Seattle, WA: Center for Innovation in Research in Graduate Education.

Nerad, M. (2009) 'Confronting common assumptions'. In R. Ehrenberg, and C. Kuh (eds) *Doctoral Education and the Faculty of the Future*. Ithaca, NY: Cornell University Press, 83.

Nowotny, H. (2016) *The Cunning of Uncertainty*. Cambridge: Polity Press.

NGLS. (n.d.) 'Next Generation Life Sciences Coalition'. Accessed 9 June 2022. https://nglscoalition.org/

NSF. (2019) Science and Engineering Doctorates 2016 Doctorate Recipients from U.S. Universities | US National Science Foundation – nsf.gov. Accessed 9 June 2022. [online] Available at: https://www.nsf.gov/statistics/2018/nsf18304/.

OECD. (2016) *Education at a glance 2016: OECD Indicators*. Paris: OECD Publishing

OECD. Employment Outlook. (2019) 'OECD employment outlook 2019L The future of work'. Accessed 9 June 2022. https://www.oecd-ilibrary.org/sites/9ee00155-en/index.html?itemId=/content/publication/9ee00155-en.

OECD. (2020) 'The precarity of research careers'. Accessed 9 June 2022. http://www.oecd.org/sti/science-technology-innovation-outlook/research-precariat/.

OECD. (2021) 'The impact of AI on the labour market: Is this time different?' Accessed 9 June 2022. https://www.oecd.ai/wonk/impact-ai-on-the-labour-market-is-this-time-different.

OECD. (2021) 'Reducing the precarity of academic research careers'. *OECD Science, Technology and Industry Policy Papers*, 113.

Powell, K. (2015) 'The future of the postdoc'. *Nature*. 520, 144–7.

PWC. (n.d.) 'Do you want to help making education fit for today's and tomorrow's job market? Unleashing the power of educational data'. Accessed 9 June 2022. https://www.pwc.be/en/making-education-fit.html.

Rostovtsev, A. (2017) 'Plagiarism in the dissertations and scientific publications in Russia'. In *Plagiarism across Europe and beyond 2017: Conference proceedings*. Brno: Mendel University in Brno, 107–12. Accessed 9 June 2022. https://academicintegrity.eu/conference/conferenceproceedings/#year2017

Royal Society. (2010) *The Scientific Century: Securing our prosperity*. London: The Royal Society.

Rudd, E., Morison, E., Nerad, M., Sadrozinski, R. and Cerny, J. (2008). 'Equality and illusion: Gender and tenure in art history careers.' *Journal of Marriage and the Family*, 70 (1), 228–38.

SERU (Student Experience in the Research University). https://cshe.berkeley.edu/seru/seru-mission 26/3/2022

Servoz M. (2019) 'AI, the future of work? Work of the future!'. Accessed 9 June 2022. https://op.europa.eu/en/publication-detail/-/publication/096526d7-17d8-11ea-8c1f-01aa75ed71a1.

Souto-Otero, M., Humburg, M. and Francke, J. (2017) *FP7 ex post and H2020 interim evaluation of Marie Skłodowska-Curie actions (MSCA): Final report*. Luxembourg: Publications Office of the European Union.

Tuomi I., (2018) *Impact of Artificial Intelligence on Learning, Teaching and Education. JRC Science for Policy Report*. Luxembourg: Publications Office of the European Union. Accessed 26 March 2022. https://publications.jrc.ec.europa.eu/repository/handle/JRC113226

Vitae. (2011) 'About the Researcher Development Framework'. https://www.vitae.ac.uk/researchers-professional-development/about-the-vitae-researcher-development-framework.

Vitae. (2013) 'What do researchers do? Early-career progression of doctoral graduates 2013'. Accessed 9 June 2022. https://www.vitae.ac.uk/vitae-publications/reports/what-do-researchers-do-early-career-progression-2013.pdf/view.

Vogiatzis A. (2017) 'Permadocs: an illusion of eternity'. https://artemiosv.info/permadocs-illusion-eternity/ 26/3/2022.

Webb, M. (2020) 'The impact of artificial intelligence on the labor market'. Accessed 9 June 2022. https://papers.ssrn.com/sol3/papers.cfm?abstract_id=3482150.

World Economic Forum. (2020) 'Future of Jobs Report 2020'. Accessed 9 June 2022. http://www3.weforum.org/docs/WEF_Future_of_Jobs_2020.pdf.

9
Social, ethical and cultural responsibility as core values for doctoral researchers in the twenty-first century

*Roxana Chiappa, Daniele Cantini,
Yasemin Karakaşoğlu, Catherine Manathunga,
Christian Peters, Beate Scholz, Betül Yarar*[1]

With the dramatic events of a global pandemic, the beginning of the twenty-first century's third decade has underlined that the world is facing universal challenges. The worldwide crisis scenario that COVID-19 has produced makes us realise that science and research do not function and operate in an independent sphere hidden within the proverbial ivory tower, but, on the contrary, are closely linked to the social, cultural and political systems they reside in. This creates opportunities and great tensions and, while exploring those, Chapter 9 connects to and builds on most of the dimensions described in the previous sections of the book. We refer primarily to Hannover Recommendations 1 and 7:

1. Establish a global joint value system for doctoral education based on an ecology of knowledges which recognises and seeks to overcome existing inequalities in the access to doctoral education and the provision of knowledge.

7. The pivotal goal of doctoral education must be and remain the development of original, responsible, and ethical thinkers, and the generation of new and original ideas and knowledge.

Research and doctoral education in the 'age of perpetual crises'
Christian Peters and Beate Scholz

The age of perpetual crises...

In his essay 'The age of perpetual crisis: How the 2010s disrupted everything but resolved nothing' published in December 2019 in the British newspaper *The Guardian*, journalist Andy Beckett describes a rather frightening review of the second decade of the twenty-first century:

> How will we remember the last 10 years? Above all, as a time of crises. During the 2010s, there have been crises of democracy and the economy; of the climate and poverty; of international relations and national identity; of privacy and technology. …All these crises, so close together, have made the 2010s seem much longer than the two previous decades. Sometimes, a single day's events – a Brexit showdown, a Donald Trump meltdown – have felt more dramatic and more exhausting to follow than entire years did during the 1990s and 2000s. (Beckett, 2019)

Indeed, the early twenty-first century is characterised by a rising awareness of and the simultaneous aversion to global ecological, economic and political complexity. Coupled with fears of loss/change of status and identity (Bauer, 2018), this uncertainty coincides with the rise of authoritarianism, antielitism and nationalism and provokes unprecedented threats to both universal and academic freedom. Increasingly, in liberal democracies like the US, France, the UK, Italy and Germany, we observe profound social and cultural polarisations accompanied by distrust of the neutrality of political, scientific and economic elites (Manow, 2019; Rudolph, 2019; Müller, 2016; Levitsky and Zieblatt, 2019). In other countries like Hungary, Brazil, Russia, China and Turkey (Dultra and Rangel, 2019; Devi, 2019; Karakaşoğlu and Tonbul, 2015), universities and scientists are under overt pressure, with authoritarian governments having direct influence on research agendas, academics and higher-education policies and institutions.[2]

Yet, in a dramatic manner, the beginning of our current decade has underlined that the world is one, at least in facing global challenges. It seems as if the COVID-19 pandemic has evidenced that neither nation-states as focus points of particular interests nor individual egotism are appropriate to cope with challenges of that order. As under a magnifying glass, the pandemic can be seen as a tracer of grand challenges: an increasing social divide resulting from imbalanced access to resources such as the COVID-vaccine, hitting the Global South more severely than the Global North; the deterioration of formerly stable democracies; and institutionalised racism accompanied by physical and symbolic violence against black, minority, indigenous peoples and other people of colour.

Equally dramatic is the intensifying impact of climate change, whose worldwide consequences and causations were – again – revealed in the summer months of 2021: despite a renewed increase in the global COVID risk due to highly infectious mutations, it was the heat wave in North America, news of the melting of the Greenland ice shield, the thawing of the Siberian permafrost, catastrophic forest fires in the Mediterranean region and massive floods in China and central Germany that kept media, politics and science in suspense for weeks. 'Human-induced climate change is already affecting many weather and climate extremes in every region across the globe.' (IPCC 2021, 10). The warning from the Sixth Report of the Intergovernmental Panel on Climate Change (IPCC) could not be clearer: either the world reacts as a whole and quickly or the harmful consequences will reach civilisational dimensions in only a short period of time. The report, a collaboration of more than 100 renowned scholars in the field of climate research, underlines that there is no alternative to a swift and globally concerted reaction to the anthropogenic climate crisis.

Both the global pandemic and the climate crisis have shifted public attention towards research and education in a polarised manner. On the one hand, we observe a broad and global loss of trust in the institutions of knowledge production and distribution; on the other hand, we also witness an amazing acknowledging of the crucial role of researchers and their abilities for cross-disciplinary and cross-border interaction, communication and policy advice. For instance, cutting-edge research has paved the way for developing vaccines and treatments, while research results have impacted on legislation, social-security systems, schooling and art, to name just a few.

But not just in coping with the worldwide pandemic or the climate catastrophes, we see societal resilience as well as organised resistance, on all sides of the political spectrum. Thousands around the globe stand up against institutionalised racism as highlighted by the Black Lives Matter movement. People of all age groups protest against autocratic regimes in Russia, Belarus and Myanmar. Often enough, researchers, artists and writers have become role models or guiding spirits of such movements, and in Hong Kong, it is students who play a key role in the protests against the Chinese government's suppression of free elections.

All this has effects on doctoral education. Under illiberal regimes as well as in the polarised sociocultural strata of Western democracies, wherever anti-intellectual dynamics prevail, science seems to have lost its objectiveness and gets overly politicised. The freedom of research and its safeguarding institutions are becoming fragile, and fundamentalist policies may have long-lasting impacts on local academic cultures and the attractiveness of the job profile *researcher*. An atmosphere of suspicion may, in turn, influence early-career researchers, limiting their striving for independence of thought and creativity.

On the other hand, anti-intellectualism and the pressure of authoritarian regimes on scientific systems generate an unprecedented wave of (inter)national solidarity and raise the consciousness of researchers to fight for their own cause and to involve the public in this struggle. In an interview on the Central European University's losing battle against the Orban government, the university's rector Michael Ignatieff describes this vividly:

> Without a doubt, the struggle to stay in Budapest gave our organisation energy and brought us closer together. It was a great battle, because it reminded us why universities are important to a society, why academic freedom is important, and why our university is especially important – we became a symbol. You can't have 80,000 people on your doorstep shouting 'free universities in a free society' in chants without tears in your eyes. (Loudun, 2021)

In addition, our times will in the future be known as the *era of digitalisation*. And no sooner has the world recognised the challenges of Web 2.0, such as market monopolisation in the platform sector or the dangers of political polarisation of large population groups through cognitive self-isolation and disinformation, than the next revolution is just around the corner: the augurs of technological change expect an even more significant transformation of human perception and information processing with the growing role of a completely virtual interaction space for internet users in the so-called metaverse. This Web 3.0 is essentially based on three layers of innovation: edge computing, decentralised data networks and artificial intelligence (AI). The political and epistemological consequences can only be guessed at – or feared.

As the amount and the complexity of information available increases constantly, so does the educational profile of societies where this happens.

The above-mentioned research breakthroughs in AI and robotics as well as the omnipresence of social media are changing the practices of knowledge generation and diffusion and *open science* (European Commission, 2016) has become a leading paradigm of the research and knowledge-transfer processes.

We are convinced that these perpetual crises and technological advancements will have deep and lasting effects on educational structures, with strong implications for teaching and, not to forget, supervision. Such impacts must be considered because they determine not only what society wants to understand and consequently authorises and funds – but also because times of crisis manifest themselves deeply in the worldviews of younger researchers and thus shape the science agenda of futures that are not yet foreseeable.

. . .and how we deal with it

Against the backdrop of massive global calamities, our chapter discusses new frames for doctoral education, its research environment and particularly the public and personal role of the doctoral graduate. Our focus lies primarily on the intended outcomes and impacts of doctoral research, namely research results and highly-qualified persons. In a pars-pro-toto relation to the whole book, this chapter addresses both determinants and the freedom of science based on a multi-perspective approach through complementing essays.

The dependence of research on its environment – or its susceptibility to inappropriate influences – becomes obvious whenever political systems instrumentalise, inhibit or ideologically shape science on a massive scale (see the essay 'On hegemony and global doctoral education' in this chapter). In democracies, external influence is present because politically 'hot topics' such as digitalisation tend to set research agendas for the long term.

We also observe that the moulding of scientific innovation into economically exploitable technology is a default setting of our globalised knowledge-production systems. For many good and just reasons, one may deplore certain effects of this economisation of knowledge. At the same time, we have to acknowledge that the market is a highly-efficient distribution system and that in the foreseeable future, solutions to problems of a global nature will have few chances without our economies' role in mediating innovation. In other words, progress in the twenty-first century is perhaps more than ever understood both as an economic and technological process, and even basic research will sooner or later have to prove its legitimacy against the background of societal relevance. Is this an inevitable development? And what does that mean for the intrinsic motivation of young researchers?

The relationship to the political and cultural context can also be considered in terms of the motivation of the scientist who, in order to contribute to solving problems, wants to engage in a crisis-ridden and unjust world, ideally without losing sight of the evidence orientation and neutrality of the researching mind. That is not an easy thing to do. Certain types of crises, as the pandemic shows, require reliable, fast and robust knowledge. Since any such situation fundamentally is defined by a lack of orientation on what to do (and why), crises also have the potential to strongly politicise science and scientists alike.

This can be detrimental to politics, which risks losing its normative role under the pressure of the lack of alternatives to scientific facts. The caveat here is that 'facts' in the scientific sense are not per se political. They prove their value in an ongoing process of verification and falsification, and what may be consistent and *right* in a paradigmatic sense may prove inhumane when applied unfiltered to questions of the common good. Science and politics require translation and moderation in their mutual relationship. At the same time, politicisation burdens science, which, under the pressure of the dramatic consequences of its insights, could be tempted to adapt findings, to select them or, even worse, to manipulate the investigation process altogether to receive supposedly intended results.

To doctoral students, the power to intervene in the political process may appear as a career opportunity, for example in playing an advisory role in civil societies, in the corporate world, in politics or in the consulting business. The political system *imports* expertise via members of their scientific advisory boards and by using written reports and assessments from scholars and bases executive decisions on them. Therefore, in the process of defining their own social role, early-career researchers must be always aware of this challenge (or temptation). It requires inner strength, self-confidence and having had or having good role models.

Knowledge is a valuable resource, but unlike many other commodities in the political barter system, it needs to be interpreted and protected. Scientists must be sensitive to identifying potential misuse, perceiving consequences and communicating this in an understandable way. 'With great power comes great responsibility' – this piece of pop cultural wisdom also describes the reality of aspiring scientists who want to meet the challenges of our complex present.

The Austrian sociologist Alexander Bogner has published an essay underlining the ambivalent and seductive interplay between knowledge production and political systems. By renewing the concept of *epistemocracy* to analyse some of the pitfalls of the information age, he starts with the observation that democracies in crisis situations are in the danger of relying too much on the power of knowledge. Thus, political crises and conflicts are primarily understood as epistemic problems, that is, as a question of knowledge, expertise and competence. The idea of epistemocracy is underpinned by the belief that political problems can only be properly formulated and convincingly solved if we understand them as problems of knowledge. This is a dangerous tendency, because the focus on knowledge may lose sight of what actually constitutes political problems and what fuels social conflicts – namely divergent values, interests and world views (Bogner 2021, 15ff.).

Bogner's reflections also reveal a dilemma that has continuously accompanied the collaboration at the Hannover conference: the framework for scientific knowledge production as we know it is deeply rooted in rationalist, Western traditions of thought. Scientific objectivity and neutral value judgement go hand in hand. Normative orientation and an open knowledge process seem to stand in each other's way, and the history of the twentieth century shows many examples of how the intervention of one side into the domain of the other has restricted free thought. And yet, we finish this chapter – and started this book – with an attempt at value-guided recommendations. It is important that we do not want these recommendations to be understood as binding rules, in the sense of a fixed and concrete law of good scientific education, but as an invitation to reflect on the framing and conditionality of doctoral education. In this sense, our recommendations may be exploited for creating a catalogue of concrete measures. They should be considered in the same way as research ethics, that is, as an intellectual tool and a necessary form of introspection and, possibly, also as a map marking potential limitations of the researcher in the quest for knowledge (see the section on research ethics in this chapter by Roxanna Chiappa and Daniele Cantini). We hope they may provide orientation to individual researchers and larger institutions when navigating in the contested (politicised) areas outside the academic *safe zones*.

In one way or another, the sections that follow address the extent to which, and the measures by which, researchers and research institutions may monitor and regulate themselves in a contested social, political and cultural environment. However, we have to ask ourselves: how just and open are these institutions we are working in? How valuable can our recommendations be when the system is not fully aware of its own historical, cultural and socioeconomic *conditions of production*? Although many universities in the Western hemisphere have recognised the importance of diversity policy, not only in staffing but also in terms of concrete jurisprudence, some academic subcultures and gatekeeping individuals still apply strong hierarchical structures that go far beyond professional competencies. Gender, sexuality, worldview and ethnic background possess the power to predetermine professional success, and the high-end global knowledge market clearly prefers Western rituals, benchmarks and qualification signals over others. The dominance of certain scientific media outlets and the accumulation of knowledge capital (financially and in terms of the academics attracted) by the world's leading universities can certainly be understood as a hegemonic structure from which an egalitarian global knowledge system will find it difficult to free itself. There still is a lot to do.

In the previously described ambivalent situation of permanent, even accelerating crises on the one hand and sheer unlimited modes of generating new knowledge on the other, research leaders and managers together with policymakers have a special role in ensuring equality, justice and fairness in the access to and the provision of knowledge (resources). At systemic and institutional levels, this brings about a comprehensive responsibility, for example, for modifying institutional cultures in research and higher education, reaching agreement on what may count as knowledge, enabling the use of infrastructure and resources or regulating ownership of results. Hence, the question is how a more just research system could be created. This will be the focus of the next section.

Creating a more just research system
Catherine Manathunga

Doctoral education is the educational site where new researchers learn to engage in the research practices, discourses and debates of their (inter) disciplines. As a result, it is a crucial point of entry into knowledge production and the world of research. However, doctoral-education and the research system remains a space of global inequality and injustice. The first step towards ensuring that all doctoral-education stakeholders contribute towards creating a more just research system involves acknowledging the historical and contemporary dimensions of the global inequities that continue to be perpetuated within the current research system.

Doctoral education, like most forms of higher education globally, remains dominated by Eurocentric, Northern or Western knowledge systems (Connell, 2019; Santos, 2014 and 2018). These international trends began with the European Enlightenment and the concurrent colonisation of much of Africa, the Middle East, Asia, the Americas and Australasia. As Said (1994) convincingly argued, while encounters with difference have always occurred in human history, what was new about Orientalism or Enlightenment knowledge about 'the other' was that it was a systematised, formal and institutionalised method for interpreting difference in order to achieve ideological and cultural domination and control. This period of colonisation wiped out or diminished the significance of ancient systems of higher learning evident in most of the world's civilisations including, among others, Confucian, Hindu, Buddhist, Islamic, Ethiopian, Aztec, Incan and Japanese institutions of higher learning. This also includes indigenous institutions of higher learning around the globe such as the whare-wānanga of the Māori people in Aotearoa New Zealand (Whatahoro, 2011). While these ancient systems of higher learning do not completely replicate modern universities, they were certainly designed to fulfil some of the functions of higher education. The Al-Azhar University in Cairo (Egypt), which was established in 970 CE and continues into the present, is regarded as the oldest continually operating university in the world (Lulat, 2005). Doctoral education is an ancient practice as evidenced by the awarding of doctoral degrees in Confucian-heritage countries such as China and Vietnam as a result of the highest level of palace examinations (*tien-shih*) which were presided over by the emperor (Reagan, 2000).

In contemporary times, the forces of globalisation, neoliberalism and managerialism have only served to reinscribe Northern or Eurocentric knowledge hierarchies. The competition for global rankings, the dominance of the English language in global academic publishing, the unequal distribution of research funding, resources and personnel (Connell, 2019) have the effect of further entrenching global inequities in the research system.

The reinvigorated Black Lives Matter (BLM) movement has also provided renewed global impetus to end institutionalised racism and physical and symbolic violence against black, minority, First Nations peoples and other people of colour in public organisations including universities. The death of George Floyd in the US was a recent catalyst that brought instances of gross injustice against peoples of colour around the globe to the forefront of public attention. In June 2020, there were mass protests supporting the BLM movement on every continent (except Antarctica) and at a time during the COVID pandemic when people were strongly discouraged from attending mass gatherings because of the risk of infection, especially amongst First Nations, minority and black populations. People felt the immediate need to demonstrate solidarity despite the risk of infection (Isaacs et al., 2020). The George Floyd incident has enabled local activists to draw mass public attention to ongoing Aboriginal deaths in custody in Australia and other instances of gross injustice around the globe. In Australia, there have been at least 439 Aboriginal and Torres Strait Islander deaths in custody between 1991 (the year of a Royal Commission report into this issue) and 19 March 2021. No Australian police personnel have ever been convicted for any of these deaths.

Globally, we are at a critical turning point in the fight against institutional and all other forms of racism and unconscious bias (Isaacs et al., 2020). As Isaacs and colleagues (2020: 1, 327) argued, 'the time for nice words and good intentions is over'. A number of scholars have sought to address 'anti-blackness and liberal white supremacy' in universities (for example, Bell et al., 2020). Their arguments build upon kihana ross's (2020) definition of anti-blackness as 'a theoretical framework that illuminates society's inability to recognise our humanity – the disdain, disregard and disgust for our existence'. Bell and colleagues (2020: 4) define white supremacy as 'an institutional system of power that normalises, privileges and maintains whiteness and white advantages in all spheres of life, including higher education'. The BLM movement, then, provides renewed urgency to the need to create a more just research and doctoral-education system around the world.

The second step towards creating a more just research system involves drawing upon the significant theoretical resources developed in the Global South to propose philosophical and practical change. The work of Boaventura de Sousa Santos (2014, 2018) on the need for epistemic or cognitive justice is particularly useful in generating practical strategies to strive towards a more just global research system. Epistemic or cognitive justice involves the need to recognise the inherent equality of all the world's diverse knowledge systems. Santos (2014, 206) argues that there can be 'no global social justice without global cognitive justice'.

Active application of the equality of different knowledge systems

These 'epistemologies of the South' (Santos, 2014) make a compelling case for the active recognition and application of the principle of equality for *all* knowledge systems from Southern, Northern, Eastern and Western sources, including indigenous knowledge systems. Santos calls this an 'ecology of knowledges' approach, which challenges the current monocultural focus on (Northern) scientific knowledge (Harding, 2011) by instead locating scientific knowledge within a broader ecology of knowledge systems (Santos, 2014). In such an ecology, *all* knowledge systems are accorded 'equality of opportunity' to 'maximise their respective contributions towards building... a more just and democratic society as well as one more balanced in its relations with nature' (Santos, 2014: 190). Such knowledge systems would be used in dialogue with each other. This approach to knowledge also accepts the partiality and incompleteness of each knowledge system and the ways in which the complexity of the world's environmental and social problems requires interaction between all knowledge systems to create innovative new research strategies.

The concept of ecologies of knowledge has informed the first Hannover Recommendation (2019), which states that the experts attending the Hannover Conference on doctoral education recommended that 'we establish a global joint value system for doctoral education based on an ecology of knowledges which recognises and seeks to overcome existing inequalities in the access to doctoral education and the provision of knowledge'. More specifically, this recommendation included an argument to 'establish a joint value system rooted in the universal principles of the United Nations Human Rights Charter. It should be based on respect for the individual and aim for an equilibrium of knowledges from South, North, East and West including indigenous knowledge systems in an 'ecology of knowledges" (Hannover Recommendation 1a, 2019). These recommendations also specify that knowledge includes 'that which is defined and assessed by international and intercultural peer communities' (Hannover Recommendation 1c, 2019). The recognition of the significant role of intercultural peer communities is a crucial addition to routine understandings of the role of international peer review in the research system. By intercultural, we are referring to the need for peoples who may have access to diverse Southern, Eastern and indigenous knowledge systems to engage in peer review as well as those from the Global North/West (Manathunga, 2014). In more recent times, the term transcultural has also been used to foreground the hybridity and cultural interfaces (Nakata, 2007) that many people experience in their own bodies and in the postcolonial complexities of transcultural communities. The prefix *trans* (meaning across, beyond or through) is an attempt to foreground the liminal, in-between, hybrid spaces where cultures, histories, geographies and languages *meet* in a contact zone of possibilities.

The third step towards creating a more just research system is to broaden current understandings of who counts as stakeholders of doctoral education. Typically, the key stakeholders of doctoral education are regarded as including doctoral candidates and supervisors, universities, governments, public sector organisations, business and industry. Occasionally, there are references to academic disciplines more generally as a stakeholder of doctoral education. However, if we are to bring about the genuine democratisation of research, then we would need to think of First Nations, migrant, refugee, culturally diverse and all other *communities* as significant doctoral-education stakeholders (Smith, 2012). We would need to think critically and creatively about how non-governmental organisations, not-for-profit groups, protest and social justice movements, lobby groups and other organisations might also be recognised as important stakeholders of doctoral education. These arguments are premised on a broad and inclusive definition of citizenship that is reflected in Hannover Recommendation 1b (2019) that 'realise a broader concept of education in the sense of *Bildung* by including political, social and ethical dimensions to prepare engaged and wise global citizens working to extend and translate knowledge for the public good'.

Fair and just access to research data, resources and intellectual property

Creating a more just research system also involves working towards ensuring fair and just access to research data and resources and ownership of intellectual property (IP). This is reflected in Hannover Recommendation 1d (2019) to 'promote open science where research data and other research results are freely available in such a way that others can collaborate and contribute, with just access to data, research resources and ownership of intellectual property'. This will be particularly challenging to actualise because of the powerful vested financial interests, mostly located in the Global North, controlling academic publishing, university rankings and the unequal distribution of research funding, resources and personnel (Connell, 2019).

There continue to be a number of initiatives designed to support open access, open source and open science (Willinsky, 2005). These approaches are dedicated to the open exchange of knowledge and economic beliefs supporting 'the efficacy of free software and research; … the reputation-building afforded by public access and patronage; and … the emergence of a free-or-subscribe access model'. They 'represent a common commitment to a larger public sphere' and 'foster a global exchange of public goods' (Willinsky, 2005). Linked with this is the notion of a global research commons or 'global research assets governed by a group of information producers and/or users under non-exclusive use conditions' (Dedeurwaerdere et al., 2016: 3). Research commons are based upon ideas of social production and collaborative economic approaches that need to be supported by 'soft law arrangements like codes of conduct and community norms that build consensus on the core values of the system' (Dedeurwaerdere et al., 2016: 9).

The need to go beyond Northern/Western notions of intellectual property to support indigenous and local community resource rights and defensive and positive protection approaches to traditional knowledge are also essential to fair and just access to research data and resources (Dutfield, 2004). As Dutfield (2004) clarifies, traditional knowledge refers not only to ancient sources of wisdom but also to new developments and refinements of this material. Many First Nations groups have traditional proprietary systems of intellectual property ownership and these are often very diverse between groups and complex (Dutfield, 2004). There may be some knowledge that is secret, known to only a few people or known to many, and the responsibilities of elders to use this knowledge appropriately are often permanent after initiation regardless of whether the knowledge is public or not (Dutfield, 2004). This is where defensive and positive protection approaches become vital to protect indigenous and local community resource rights and knowledges (Dutfield, 2004).

While all of these initiatives might be steps in the right direction, great ethical care needs to be exercised in the provision of global access to research data, particularly biogenetic and biocultural data and traditional knowledge, to prevent issues like biopiracy, racial profiling and the inappropriate use of secret or protected indigenous knowledges (Dutfield, 2004). Increasingly, there are requirements that more research should be conducted by indigenous, black, minority and other people of colour and that any nonindigenous and/or white researchers conduct collaborative coresearch with and for First Nations peoples and people of colour so that respectful and culturally safe research processes can be undertaken and that fair and just access to research data, resources and intellectual property and resource rights can be ensured.

Working towards a joint value system in research and education and specifically doctoral education needs to happen at the systemic (macro) as well as the institutional (meso) levels. Yet, paradigmatic changes in the direction of an ecology of knowledges necessitate that at the micro level they are carried forward by the individual researcher. This implies questioning and putting into perspective current predominant research paradigms considering the historical, cultural and disciplinary contexts and circumstances in which they have developed, as the subsequent expert interview elucidates.

On hegemony and global doctoral education
Mark Juergensmeyer and Christian Peters

There are two ways of looking at the global reach of higher education.[3] One is to say that the last vestige of colonialism is in academia, where – particularly in the social sciences and humanities – Western paradigms of analysis are implanted in the rest of the world. Everybody is supposed to adopt certain Western-based research models in the way we analyse social data and relationships.

On the other hand, one can argue that there is nothing more global than the production of knowledge. It is fluid, always changing, it never stays the same. For instance, the way of looking at political science in the late 1960s and 1970s is vastly different from today. Fifty years ago, we thought of the world system exclusively in terms of the nation-state. After World War II and the creation of the United Nations, there was a sense of exhilaration over the fact that the world no longer consisted largely of empires. It was the high point of twentieth-century nationalism. Now, scarcely 50 years later, this enthusiasm seems both naive and untrue. Today, the nation-state of the Bretton Woods era is under siege: we are experiencing new forms of imperial ambitions, and our precious secular democracies threaten to collapse into all sorts of populist, religious and ethnic reconfigurations of xenophobic nationhood and transnationality.

We need to analyse the world differently now. One of the reasons for the rise of Global Studies as a field is this demand and desire to understand and develop new ways of looking at the world and to learn from other people in other parts of the planet who see the world differently. So, which of these two ways of looking at the global reach of higher education is correct? Is it the last vestige of colonialism or is it the best example of globalisation in terms of a real shared participation? Probably both are true, and they are dynamically connected.

To take an example from the field of social theory, it was in the middle of the twentieth century when people like Mao Tse-Tung in China and Jayaprakash Narayan in India picked up Marxism and reshaped the notion of socialism in non-Western contexts. It is fair to say that this represents an alternative theorisation carried out by non-Western thinkers who produced an enormously rich intellectual conversation that has made an impact throughout the academic world. Again, this can be seen in two ways: one is that, yes, they were Chinese and Indian, but they were theorising on a Western Marxist model. On the other hand, they were theorising against the background of living in very old class and caste systems with their religious and ethnic diversities, and they needed to reconceive this theory for non-Western contexts. These scholars were looking for a way to understand social theory in the Chinese and Indian settings, and it produced kinds of scholarship that may not have been possible in different parts of the world.

While it is no doubt good that Chinese Marxism is taught in China and that Indian political thought is being taught in India, what about a reciprocal recognition: should not Indian and Chinese political theory be taught at Harvard and other Western universities, too? And if so, how can we approach and integrate this knowledge into our own systems, how should we translate an observation of the unfamiliar into a language that targets our wider public? Is not the very idea of conversion already a colonial gesture, making a specific regional knowledge adapt to a world system of converging concepts?

Political theory or political thought or ideas about politics are contextual. They are culturally delivered, culturally shaped and are related to both the social and philosophic trends and flows within the milieus from which they arise. On the other hand, there is a drive towards a scientific analysis of politics based on survey research and quantitative data. We would argue that one should be cautious about the idea that you can have a universal methodology that is culture-free. The very creation of mathematical modelling of social phenomena assumes a certain understanding of the nature of society and the limited range of questions that make sense within that context. In the worst-case scenario, such models define what to ask before you would ask questions that help you to know what are the right questions to ask, thereby limiting what you are going to know or how you are going to understand a particular phenomenon. The problem is not with statistical surveys or with mathematics in general. It is the assumption that by using these tools you have a more scientific and closer understanding of a universal truth than without it. For both cases, however, what you structure with those tools determines what you will find.

So, returning to the central theme of this essay, there is a need to decolonise doctoral education worldwide. Considering that academia falls somewhere between true globalisation and Western intellectual hegemony, diversification is a good idea. But how is this to be realised? One approach is the pragmatic option: to diversify the people working in the field. Yet we must acknowledge the investment that migrating scholars have to make upon entering other academic systems, adjusting to the other's rules and cultures. In addition, many studies show that in the majority of countries, internationalisation of faculty is far from perfect.

While there are cosmopolitan hot spots all over the world, few local academic systems demonstrate deep and wide internationalisation.

But there is a more insidious problem. If a scholar is caught in the situation where to make their field respectable is to follow an American-European way of doing things, one may not easily be able to escape, as the dominant paradigm is the only resource known to you that confers respectability. This is a Gramscian reality.[4] This is how hegemony works. Indian professors learned this in their own graduate schools, and they are determined not to succumb to a native idea that might be considered unprofessional. They learn the professional rubric, they observe the attitude, the habitus. And then there are scholars in fields like Global Studies who are trying to escape the Western paradigm, who are convinced that we are limited by our own background and that we should be more malleable. What happens when both groups meet? Sometimes it is frustrating to encounter scholars in other countries who should have a local paradigm but who do not because they are trying so hard to be like us. This is a serious problem.

Therefore, beyond respecting the variety of perspectives, the dehegemonisation of scholarship has to begin with problematising the dominant paradigm. Simply bringing in people – not least junior scholars – who are ethnically diverse or who carry a different passport will not create truly diverse intellectual environments. It is about increasing the ability to articulate a perspective that is different from the dominant one. Unfortunately, in many developing countries education is about memorising the teachings of the old masters, and they are probably the least capable to actually bring about change. So, the transformation has to come from within the dominant paradigm. The question is, how do we get it to be more open? The emergence of Global Studies as a research field suggests that there are many of us who value seeing the world from diverse perspectives. Hopefully this will encourage scholars working outside the dominant paradigm to gain more self-confidence to cherish and develop modes of analysis from within their cultural heritage. Bringing in some of this background can not only challenge but improve dominant paradigms, making them more flexible. Thus, overcoming hegemony in higher education is a shared responsibility.

Overcoming global inequalities in research and higher-education systems seems to be ever more urgent in times of a pandemic threatening humankind in the same way, but with uneven consequences. The emphasis on and the need for research to find solutions and remedies involving all fields and disciplines calls for reassessing and, where appropriate, redefining the (ethical) standards and modes of self-observation (and, potentially, self-limitation) governing the development of new knowledge. Given the likelihood of further crises and pandemics to occur at least in the same if not at higher levels of magnitude, finding suitable answers will be the task of the next generation(s) of researchers whom we are qualifying from now on.

Fostering a culture of ethical and responsive doctoral researchers in a context of crises
Roxana Chiappa and Daniele Cantini

At the time of writing, the world faces one of the worst economic recessions and sanitary crises of the last century due to the global COVID-19 pandemic. The virus has exacerbated old and more systemic crises of social and economic inequalities across societal groups in many industrialised and emerging countries (Rose-Redwood et al., 2020). Across world regions, COVID-19 has unveiled the power asymmetries existing among countries to cope with the consequences of the virus, whereas at the same time this health crisis has shown the uneven research and technological capacities to participate in the competition to generate a vaccine against COVID-19. Before COVID-19 spread out across the globe, uprising nationalist governments, migratory displacements in the Middle East and Central and South America and a major environmental crisis, among other major societal pressures, had already called into question the role of research and technology to respond to such societal issues.

With this background, we ask what is the role of doctoral education in an increasingly complex, interconnected and still very uneven global society? Doctoral education is the most advanced level of education that individuals can achieve and one of the formal academic spaces where different types of knowledge are discovered, passed on from one generation of scholars to the next and reinterpreted in the process. These functions give doctoral education an extra responsibility in two regards: (a) the formation of the new generation of scholars who will likely exert some authority in different societal endeavours; (b) being a catalyst for a research agenda that might proactively respond to major societal problems. Without an attempt to reduce complexity nor simplify the heterogeneity and diversity of doctoral programmes existing in different world regions and disciplinary fields, we believe that doctoral education should promote a culture of responsible ethical researchers in which the meaning of *research ethics* is recognised in its contested and contextual nature.

Our argument here draws from two strands. First, as we have indicated earlier, scientific and technological research is never carried out for the sake of knowledge alone. Issues of funding, patronage, academic productivity pressures and government/political agendas, among others, directly or indirectly shape scientific and technological agendas and research practices of individual researchers (Cantini et al., 2019). These forces inevitably influence the meaning of what constitutes ethical research in an increasingly complex social reality frequently affected by major societal crises (Nowotny, 2016). Second, some empirical studies show that the discussion about ethical research in doctoral education is mainly guided by an increasing number of regulatory frameworks and ethical codes, dictated by national scientific agencies and professional disciplinary fields (Pennock and Rourke, 2017). While ethical research codes and regulatory frameworks are needed to guarantee basic ethical principles (for example no harm, respect for human dignity and integrity of research processes); we argue that the meaning of research ethics should not be reduced to a compliance activity of the research process, but it should be understood as one of the cornerstone attributes of doctoral graduates.

The scholarship around research ethics differentiates research ethics from research integrity (Shaw, 2019). Research ethics typically includes aspects associated with the research design, the respect of research participants and the implications of research for wider society; research integrity alludes to the honesty and verifiable methods used during research (fabrication, falsification, plagiarism). Other authors (Löfström and Pyhältö, 2020) have argued the importance of adopting an ethical lens in doctoral supervision, referring specifically to the pedagogical and relational aspects of the relationship between PhD advisor and advisee. Here, we refer to research ethics as the overall set of principles and values that inform the multiple roles of the researchers.

To support our argument, we divided our section in four parts. The first part includes a brief overview of the history of research ethics and an increasing number of regulatory frameworks emerging in different industrialised and emerging economies. The second part briefly discusses the multifaceted role of doctoral researchers and highlights the importance of conceptualising research ethics by its contextual and contested nature. The third part describes the case of Middle East countries, where the current political crises have restricted possibilities for conducting research. Finally, we offer some final reflections about the role of doctorate education in a context of crises.

Increasing regulatory frameworks of research ethics

The history of science abounds with examples of scientists' unsuccessful attempts at convincing the general public of the ethical soundness of some of their studies, as well as of examples in which subjects have been mistreated under the approval of government authorities, at times criminally (for instance, the Nazi and Japanese military experiments on prisoners during World War II, the Tuskegee syphilis study funded and conducted by the US Public Health Service). In the aftermath of World War II, a powerful social movement emerged which emphasised the notion of the individual moral responsibility of researchers, regardless of the dictates of state officials or other organised bodies. There emerged the notion of monitoring the conduct of physicians and biomedical researchers through universal *mandates* and *codes* of research ethics, so that researchers did not abuse or exploit their patients in the name of science or any other ideological principles (see Belmont Report, 1979; Nuremberg Code, 1947; UNESCO's Universal Declaration on Bioethics and Human Rights, 2005; World Medical Association Declaration, 1964).

Since the 1980s, this view of research ethics in the biomedical field has spread to other scientific disciplines and has been adhered to by an increasing number of national scientific agencies in industrialised countries; more recently, emerging economies have also developed their own regulations. For instance, a review of regulatory ethics research frameworks developed by scientific agencies in the European Union, in China, in the US and in India shows that there is a predominant view of research ethics that entails three pillars: the individual responsibility of researchers; minimising risks; and the protection of human subjects, with special emphasis on human subjects who are in vulnerable situations (Cantini et al., 2019a).

We selected these countries because of the leadership position they have in scientific knowledge production in their respective world regions. With different nuances and institutional capacity to guarantee research ethics, the regulatory frameworks on research ethics in the mentioned countries highlight the individual responsibility of researchers to guarantee the integrity of the entire research process and avoid any misconduct (fabrication, falsification and plagiarism) across all research stages. The notion of minimising risk is primarily discussed when research projects involve humans, animals, plants, toxic chemicals, radioactive materials and technological developments that can represent a future danger for the societies. Finally, these documents discuss the conditions of consent and confidentiality when research includes direct and/or indirect relationships with human subjects, paying particular attention to when the research involves infants, people in conditions of imprisonment and indigenous peoples.

Toward a culture of responsible ethical researchers: the contextual and contested meaning of research ethics

Along with the increasing number of regulatory frameworks dealing with research ethics, a number of courses about research ethics also emerged. Empirical studies in some countries about the effects research ethical training has on the prevalence of research misconduct or unethical behaviours show contradictory results (see Anderson et al., 2007; Hoffman et al., 2015). On the one hand, some research shows that research ethics courses have an overall modest effect on the ethical decisions of researchers and they vary depending on the approach of instruction (Antes et al., 2009). On the other hand, Antes and colleagues (2009) found that research ethics courses with a cognitive decision-making approach to instruction are the most effective, only surpassed by courses that focus on the social-interactional nature of ethical problems. A cognitive decision-making approach encourages students to discuss and reflect using real case scenarios of ethical dilemmas, where they have to ponder different values and interests. Along these lines, other studies show that exposure to ethical training does not necessarily translate into a better understanding of how to address ethical dilemmas working with historically marginalised groups of populations (Fisher, Fried and Feldman, 2009) and nor to avoid research misconducts per se (Hoffman and Holm, 2019). In fact, some scholars argue that many of the research ethics courses depict an image of research ethics as it were imposed from outside – as a process of compliance that troubles the research activity (Pennock and O'Rourke, 2017).

Given these findings, how can doctoral education infuse a culture of ethical, responsible researchers who understand the multifaceted roles of researchers and their responsibilities in increasingly more complex social realities? Should doctoral programmes include formal and specific courses on research ethics based on a more cognitive decision-making approach? Should doctoral supervisors be recognised for their responsibility in transferring ethic knowledge?

Aware and respectful of the broad range of doctoral-education models (course structural, semi-structured, supervision model) and the different nature of research knowledge production in place, our proposal moves away from prescriptive recommendations and rather suggests a framework that can inform conversations about ethics in doctoral education. In this regard, Pimple's heuristic framework (2002) of research ethics offers three inquiries that illuminate the multiple responsibilities of doctoral researchers – (a) What is true? (b) What is fair? (c) What is wise? – as well as the contested and contextual nature of research ethics.

The first question – What is true? – relies directly on aspects of what some scholars call *research integrity* (reproducibility and trustworthiness of research, including aspects of research design, manipulation, analysis and representation of data). As several scholars have shown, current pressure for publishing in academia seems to have triggered several incidents in which researchers falsified or manipulated data (Hoffman et al., 2019). An inquiry about what is true in a particular field inevitably exposes doctoral scholars to examine the codes imposed by the larger (multi)disciplinary community and their role of expanding certain bodies of knowledge.

The second question – What is fair? – entails the protection and respect of research subjects, including the wellbeing of humans and animals, and fairness in issues associated with authorship. This question also includes the dimension of conflict of interests with funders and institutional support, the relationship with other colleagues as well as the role of supervisor and mentor in the process of formation of postgraduate research scholars. The question about fairness is significantly more complex and multivariate because it requires doctoral scholars to keep in mind the several parties involved in their research, beyond the existing regulatory frameworks on research ethics and traditional understanding of research.

In fact, most of the regulatory policy frameworks of research ethics in the mentioned countries above included a statement that recognises that research with indigenous groups needs a special review, due to the many abuses that researchers have committed against indigenous populations. Yet, indigenous groups in some regions of the world have developed their own statements of what constitutes research ethics, whose principles vary from the ones established by the national scientific authorities.

This is the case with the Assembly of First Nations of the Pacific Northwest (AFNP), which has a statement of research ethics that requires at least three conditions: (a) share power of the many decisions of research, (b) self-determination, (c) access and possession of their knowledge. As described by the AFNP, any research study that involves indigenous people has to be conceived entirely through the worldview of their peoples. ANFP's understanding of research ethics invites researchers working with indigenous populations to move beyond the formal requirements dictated by regulatory frameworks of research ethics and, instead, embrace a notion of research ethics that situate indigenous self-determination at the centre of all research decisions, even when these decisions change or limit the original purposes of research.

The last question in Pimple's heuristic framework of research ethics (2002) – What is wise? – concerns the value of the research for the *common good* of society at large. This last question touches upon the role of science in favouring the interests and priorities of different societal groups and requires doctoral scholars to interrogate how their research projects relate and contribute to larger goals, such as justice, democracy and economic growth, among others.

Having frequent discussions and conversations around these three questions throughout the doctoral programme does not guarantee the formation of ethical researchers but will enable doctoral scholars to at least recognise that research ethics is an overall principle of their multiple responsibilities as a researcher, colleague and supervisor.

The limited possibilities of guaranteeing research ethics in the Middle East

Our argument so far has pictured the image of an individual doctoral researcher who, having been socialised in doctoral programmes that recognise the contextual and contested meaning of research ethics, is able to assume the multifaceted roles of doctoral researcher with integrity. Yet, this image of a responsible ethical researcher supposes certain research conditions where researchers have at least some conditions of free speech and autonomy to conduct research inquiry. Nonetheless, a vast body of research shows that these socio-political structures and conditions are not present across all regions of the world (Cantini et al., 2019b).

In fact, across the Middle East, there are many countries in which the practice of research is severely constrained, either by direct conflict (currently in Afghanistan, Iraq, Libya, Syria and Yemen), political unrest (Algeria, Bahrein, Sudan), military occupation (the Occupied Palestinian Territories) or repressive governments (Egypt, Iran, KSA, Turkey, the UAE, among others). Even in countries in which there is currently no particular restriction on the practice of research (Jordan, Lebanon, Morocco, Oman, Pakistan, Qatar, Tunisia, at the time of writing), some issues are difficult or impossible to research without putting researchers and their research partners at risk. Ethical considerations in this context mainly revolve around the difficulty of assessing the risks that potential research carries, including in the medium term, and there are currently some attempts at discussing such dilemmas openly.

The largest association for those studying the Middle East, the MESA (Middle East Studies Association) based in the US, decades ago created a Committee on Academic Freedom (CAF), which seeks to foster the free exchange of knowledge as a human right and to inhibit infringements on that right by government restrictions on scholars. The United Nations' Universal Declaration of Human Rights, Covenant on Civil and Political Rights and Covenant on Economic, Social and Cultural Rights provide the principal standards by which human-rights violations are identified today. Those rights include the right to education and work, freedom of movement and residence, and freedom of association and assembly. The CAF offers state-of-the-art indications of security alerts in the region – alerts that deal specifically with threats to research and researchers based in the region, in the US or elsewhere. Issues discussed in recent years include the sudden termination of an endowed chair at the American University in Cairo, the ongoing repression of Turkish academics in Turkey and the subsequent discussion of whether to collaborate with the Turkish Council of Higher Education (YÖK), threats against Iraqi academics that highlight cases of corruption, limitations and restrictions to foreign nationals teaching at Palestinian universities and the ongoing investigation (or rather the lack thereof) into the murder of Giulio Regeni, an Italian PhD candidate at Cambridge University abducted, tortured and murdered in Cairo in 2016.

The conditions of researchers working in the Middle East region powerfully demonstrate that ethical research cannot be prescribed in policy nor guaranteed in ethics educational training. Research ethics are, in fact, a responsibility and a right, whose meanings need to be interrogated in their diverse contexts and in the light of the multiple roles that doctoral researchers embody. A doctoral education attuned to the current crises across the globe – be they social, political, sanitary or environmental – should understand research ethics as an integral part of any doctoral curriculum. This is never a settled issue, particularly for research carried out with human beings, animals, and recently the environment as well, and it needs constant scrutiny, both external and internal to the disciplines, an understanding of past and present realities and an imagination of what the future should look like, as well as a constant, relentless self-reflection, to be directed particularly at issues of power imbalances.

Academic self-regulation plays a key role when it comes to shaping the forms, cultures and conditions of ethical doctoral education worldwide. However, such intrinsic forces reach their limits when research and doctoral education get politicised. Political or state actors do not always have the will or means to support the freedom and flourishing of research and doctoral education. As the example of Middle Eastern countries above or the below-mentioned case study on Turkey show, they are on the contrary seeking to hamper and suppress specific research topics, fields or methodologies by prosecuting those who pursue them.

The impact of neoliberalism and authoritarianism on higher education in Turkey
Yasemin Karakaşoğlu and Betül Yarar

De-democratisation impacts of neoliberal policies and recent authoritarian attacks on higher education

Following the military coup of 1980, the administration of higher education (HE) in Turkey was comprehensively rebuilt with all institutions tied to a newly established Council of Higher Education (CoHE, YÖK in Turkish). The council aimed to administer all universities directly, allowing for more direct state intervention, for example by the appointment of university rectors by the president.[5] It is also under these conditions that neoliberal austerity rules became prevalent in Turkey: in 1981, a new Higher Education Law (2547) was ratified and HE services, which until then were seen as a public domain, became redefined as *semi-public* services. This resulted in an increase of private universities with higher tuition fees in the whole sector (Önal, 2012; Aslan, 2013). Upon the amendment of a related law in 1984, so-called non-profit HE institutions appeared on the scene (YÖK, 2014). Later, the University Law of 1991 'enabled private investors to establish *foundation universities* with loans at low interest rates and up to 45 per cent state subsidies from the education budget. At private universities, students who fail to attain the required grades in their entrance examinations for state universities can take up a course of studies for a relatively high fee' (Karakaşoğlu and Tonbul, 2015: 836).

However, in the late 2000s, civil society reactions against these policies have expanded and social consensus around the government's neoliberal agenda has dissolved. Again, the regime reacted to all these upheavals with authoritarian measures. In January 2016, after the publication of a petition by a group called Academics for Peace Petition (BAK), more than 1,000 scholars who had signed the petition were put under investigation and faced dismissals, expulsions and arrests. The situation worsened dramatically after the failed coup attempt followed by the government's declaration of a State of Emergency in July 2016. At the time of writing, more than 7,500 higher-education employees have been targeted directly by this backlash, and over 60,000 higher-education scholars, administrators and students are affected by massive government and institutional actions.[6] Post 2016, 15 universities were closed, students were displaced due to shut-down programmes, academics have lost their jobs. To give a concrete example, as of 2016, at the Faculty of Political Science (Mülkiye) at Ankara University, 38 undergraduate and five graduate courses were closed and 50 dissertations stopped, and in the Faculty of Communication, 40 undergraduate and 29 graduate courses were closed and 99 dissertations couldn't be completed (Cumhuriyet, 2017). One must conclude that in Turkey, the speed of transformation of HE has reached an extreme and the impact on the freedom of research cannot be overestimated. On a regular basis, we witness direct and indirect attacks against allegedly *critical disciplines* and academics working on topics like the Kurdish problem or gender issues are institutionally marginalised and threatened.

Impacts of recent changes in higher education on doctorate programmes in Turkey

Despite some statistics showing an increase in the number of universities and doctoral programmes, the educational outcome of the current Turkish system is quite poor: only 25 per cent of the 24–65 age group is described as well-educated (ISCE 1–3), and only 14 per cent of the population in this group had attained a university degree in 2011 (OECD, 2013: 37). This is the lowest level of all OECD countries (Karakaşoğlu and Tonbul, 2015: 831). While the quality of education in securely sponsored and internationally well-connected private (or foundation) universities[7] has improved, in most of the state universities, government educational policies generally lead to lower academic quality. The Union of Employees in Education and Science (Eğitim Sen) recently criticised this dual higher-education system, presenting current figures on rising tuition fees at private/foundation universities, some of them reaching up to a 30-per-cent increase in only one year.[8] Furthermore, as a result of the increasing political pressure on universities, academic censorship and self-censorship has had a massive impact on the academic climate, limiting the freedom doctoral projects need to unfold. It is also true that under the radical attacks of the government, many academics have lost their jobs, which negatively affected the doctorate programmes of various universities.

Despite all these critical developments, the government has continued to open new universities. According to statistics from 2016 to 2019, the number of universities has increased from 183 to 207. However, a continuous increase in the number of doctoral students registered in PhD programmes (2018: 5,295 total; 4,827 in state universities) is not mirrored by an increase of qualified PhD programmes (Şen, 2013).

Many of the above findings and assumptions are underlined by an evaluation of the Summer School on Women and Gender Studies in Turkey (2019) held at the University of Bremen. The meeting was attended by 11 graduate students (8 of whom were PhD students) from Turkey, and all of them were asked to anonymously fill in a semi-structured questionnaire. Taking into consideration the limits of this small qualitative exploration both in terms of the subject (women and gender studies) and in terms of the number of attendees (11 female-identifying students), the outcome can be summed up as follows:

1. The students stated that finding a qualified programme and supervisors for their specific research interests on women and gender studies is difficult. Some of them assumed this is presently more the case than in the past, as many of the subject experts among their supervisors with international reputation had left the country.
2. The students observe a stigmatisation of certain topics in more conservative disciplines like economy, law and so on. Dealing with women and gender studies seems to endanger the scientific career of early-career researchers, as the topic both in a political and economic sense is not broadly accepted as a valuable research issue or theoretical approach. Finding interdisciplinary programmes (with an approach specific to women and gender studies) is also not easy.
3. As supervisors of some students have been dismissed or had to resign due to recent political pressures over universities, some PhD students now lack a qualified process of supervision and counselling of their thesis. Professors who are not familiar with the subject have been ordered to supervise the PhD thesis. As they are not interested in the issue, they do not spend much time supervising the candidates or helping them in their careers. The appointment process for supervisors to PhD students at some Turkish universities is organised top down with deans or PhD counsels of the departments deciding on the supervisor. Thus, the matching process is not part of a mutual negotiation process between the PhD student and a potential supervisor. However, in some cases, there were students who had control and power over their PhD studies in terms of choosing the title and content of their

thesis or their supervisors and thesis juries. But there were also cases in which the students did not have any means to influence these processes at all according to their interests.

4. The quality of supervision was evaluated by many of the summer school attendees as quite low due to the high workloads of their supervisors. Students sometimes felt abused by being asked to adjust themselves to the needs of the supervisors who themselves were incapable of balancing work–life distinctions due to a general work overload. ('She/he calls me to meet at her/his home, where I am waiting for the time to discuss my thesis while she/he is looking after the children.')

5. Some of the students have faced stigmatisation and exclusion due to their critical political positions ('If you are politically active, critical against the government you will have problems to be appointed to assistant positions, to get tenured positions.').

6. The hierarchies in general are very strong in the relationship between professors and PhD students. This is especially the case in more traditionally oriented universities and newly established provincial universities, less so in well-established universities in big cities and some of the foundation universities known for their more liberal atmosphere. Showing respect to professors is understood in the traditional way of being expected to accept the advice of the supervisor without discussion or critical reflection. This hinders an open discussion on controversial issues.

7. All students underlined in the interviews the financial problems they face. The burden is put on the shoulders of students who have to rely partly or totally on being sponsored either by their parents or their partners. Many of them have to work to earn their living. A state system that would grant PhD students access to financial support according to transparent criteria is missing. Transparency is missing as to the parameters and categories that are the basis for decisions on the granting of a fellowship or a stipend by the respective state institutions such as TÜBITAK or YÖK.

8. There seems to be also little support for PhD students from universities in terms of funding the students' attendance of (international) conferences and programmes.

It is not by coincidence that authoritarian movements and regimes around the globe fear the power that arises from the independence of thought, the freedom of research and the persons who undergo research qualification, limited only by ethical boundaries. The subsequent section aims, thus, to derive cross-cutting normative conclusions and to formulate exemplary suggestions of what value-based doctoral education should include. It also seeks to specify qualification outcomes and derived expectations vis-à-vis those who have been qualified with a leap of faith and who are supposed to give back to society by working towards a sustainable future. That is to say, those who qualify doctoral candidates trust that the candidates will meet their (and society's) expectations in their later careers.

A normative vision for doctoral education and the future role of the researcher in contested times
Christian Peters and Beate Scholz

In this section, we are discussing the future role of doctoral education, of the researcher in general and particularly of the key outcome of doctoral education, that is, the doctoral graduate, from a normative perspective. As in some of the previous chapters, our focus is on the intended outcomes and impacts of doctoral education, namely research results and highly qualified persons. Referring to and building on some of the arguments regarding the *thinking doctorate* of the Prologue to this book by Jansen and Walters, we are emphasising the future roles and responsibilities of doctoral graduates regarding society at large. We argue that doctorate holders are exponents and advocates of social, ethical and cultural responsibility as core values of doctoral education in the twenty-first century.

At the same time, we stress the role of doctoral education in realising a broader concept of education in the sense of *Bildung*; that is, integrating 'political, social and ethical dimensions to prepare engaged and wise global citizens working to extend and translate knowledge for the public good' (Hannover Recommendation 1). Accelerated by the COVID-19 pandemic, the specific challenges of our time urge us to rethink the role of doctoral education in conjunction with a thorough value-based reconfiguration of its contents and implementation. Consequently, we see as one of the key targets the qualification of doctoral graduates who have the potential to act as *transformative leaders*.

The changing role of doctoral education

Throughout the first decades of the twenty-first century, doctoral education has continued its expansion around the globe (see Chapter 1 on the doctoral-education context). At the undergraduate level, most of the OECD Member States are seeking to reach the 40-per-cent goal of tertiary education graduates within their respective age groups. Especially in countries with emerging economies as in, for example, South Africa or Malaysia, governments have defined target numbers for PhD graduates. Doctoral education seems to be a guarantor for societal wellbeing and economic competitiveness. We therefore argue that now is the right time for policymakers from local to international levels to relate doctoral education, its advancement and accessibility with the United Nations' Fourth Sustainable Development Goal (SDG), 'Ensure inclusive and equitable quality education and promote lifelong learning opportunities for all' (https://sdgs.un.org/goals/goal4).

Coinciding with growing academisation and the expansion of the doctorate, digitalisation and its impacts on higher education and research as well as the acceleration of global threats to health and the environment, wellbeing and peace, we are facing new challenges with respect to the next generation of doctorate holders. Throughout this book we have argued that a *global doctorate* is no longer the appropriate frame for educating scientists and scholars who are able to master the demands of our times or for generating *game changing* research results. However, more urgently than at the beginning of the twenty-first century, we perceive the need to seek for global research and evidence-based answers and solutions underlining that a return to mainly national or disciplinary approaches to doctoral education would not be appropriate either. If we aim to reconcile convergence and diversity in doctoral education, we need to reach global agreement (Nerad and Evans, 2014) or at least consensus concerning key values of doctoral education as well as the outcomes and impacts it is supposed to entail:

- Given its *endless frontier*, science is a truly global process: not only its topics and concepts but researchers' networks and the relevant communication and dissemination strategies have become transnational. Yet, we are far away from commonly agreed rules of fair interaction and appropriate assessment of research findings appreciating the diversity of thought and knowledge, their benefits for scientific progress and the significance or impact the research most likely achieves.
- With the change in the pace and range of data processing, research seems to become ever more borderless. This not only raises ethical issues, but also prompts more fundamental questions, for example, what we define as valuable knowledge and who has the right to define what we count as knowledge in diverse contexts. The endeavour underlying this book has prepared the ground for

deliberating on such issues in an inclusive discourse.
- The *Humboldtian paradigm*, that is, the integrated approach of research and teaching in academia, has for two centuries been a guiding principle for universities around the globe and has also given rise to doctoral education. Given its specific historical context and related Global North approach, we see the need for an updated concept which accommodates (intellectual) traditions of different cultures and world regions. We also make an argument for achieving a common understanding on the desired main outcome of doctoral education: the trained researcher and their specific role in and obligations towards society.

Implications for the scope and performance of value-based doctoral education

What we stated above will have significant implications not just at the levels of research systems and institutions in charge of doctoral education, but first and foremost at the level of persons concerned with the implementation of doctoral education, meaning doctoral candidates/graduates, their supervisors, advisors or mentors, the wider community of researchers and particularly persons who at managerial level oversee, design and execute doctoral programmes and develop or revise corresponding institutional structures. With the subsequent, non-exhaustive list we aim to provide examples and give input where we see room for development:
- Select doctoral candidates not just in view of their intellectual competencies, dominant research paradigms and streamlined scientific success parameters. In line with Hannover Recommendation 2, we ask research institutions in their recruitment and appointment procedures to 'embrace the full spectrum of people and be open to and for all on equal terms, giving those with suitable creative, critical and intellectual potential the opportunity to participate in doctoral education including protecting those who are at risk in countries where they are striving for freedom of thought and creativity', also considering their motivation for doing a doctorate. Scientific progress, ethical awareness and *social sense* rely to a great extent on individuality, independence of thought and the appreciation of diverse cultural and normative backgrounds of doctoral candidates and of different culturally dependent knowledges. An inclusive approach to admission based on appreciation of previous academic and personal achievements in combination with prognostic

instruments regarding their potential will give candidates access to doctoral education irrespective of their backgrounds.
- Develop supervisors' awareness in this direction and only appoint as supervisors those researchers who identify with the full range of responsibilities associated with supervision (for example, reachability, a critical but constructive attitude, acceptance of the leadership role) and who fully comply with highest standards of research ethics and scholarly integrity. Meanwhile, it has been widely understood (see Chapter 5 on supervision) that the competence to supervise does not inherently come with a research qualification but is a pivotal element of dedicated leadership development. As role models, supervisors, advisors and mentors need to provide room not only for research creativity but equally for the development of doctoral candidates' selves.
- Include measures of *Bildung* in the broadest sense and the appreciation of emotional and social intelligence throughout doctoral education. By *Bildung*, we wish to understand the political, social and ethical dimensions of education, where education is more than learning knowledge and skills, but also about becoming an educated person who cultivates an active inner life, self-reflection, empathy and subjectivity (Biesta, 2002). This concept of *Bildung* is not limited to doctoral education alone, but we see it as a core concept to achieve 'inclusive and equitable quality education and promote lifelong learning opportunities for all' in accordance with the United Nations' Fourth SDG.
- Overcome the concept of *knowledge production* in an industrialised (that is, parameterised) sense and sharpen the focus on research outcomes, innovation and the (societal) impacts they generate. This requires, in line with the Hannover Recommendations 1, that 'we consider as knowledge that which is defined and assessed by international and intercultural peer communities,' and Recommendation 7 to 'foster a culture where doctoral candidates undertake research with integrity, recognise the issues of reproducibility and the importance of negative results, and see beyond bibliometric and other quantitative parameters as means to value success'.
- Define a new concept of academic merits results from the above. Recognition in the academic system needs to rely on a scientific qualification in a broad sense that expresses itself through creative spirit, critical attitude to conventionalism, personal motivation and professional commitment. A just system of merit assessment should

acknowledge that individual outcomes are not separate from the conditions of historical inequalities that underlie the positions of nations and their respective scientific systems as well as of individual identities (gender, race, ethnicity, class, disability status, sexual orientation, religious background and so on) of those who are or were researchers at a given time. We argue that, as for any kind of research, the outputs, outcomes and impacts of doctoral research should be reviewed in accordance with the principles of *Responsible Research Assessment*: 'This is an umbrella term for approaches to assessment which incentivise, reflect and reward the plural characteristics of high-quality research, in support of diverse and inclusive research cultures.' (Curry et al., 2020: 5). Doctoral achievements should as well be seen in relation to the personal circumstances and the environment in which they are attained (European Commission, 2012; Scholz, 2017). For the evaluation of research results, this also implies fully acknowledging open science practices (O'Carroll et al., 2017).

The role of the researcher: doctoral graduates and the concept of transformative leadership

In the critical phase of global challenges described above, we need to rely on and qualify a new generation of ethical citizens to become *reflective*, but not self-referential contributors to public discourses. Hence, we expect doctoral graduates to be 'creative, critical, autonomous and responsible intellectual risk takers' (LERU, 2010; Council of the European Union, 2016), and correspondingly to become *transformative leaders*: 'Transformative leadership is, at its heart, a participatory process of creative collaboration and transformation for mutual benefit.' (Montuori and Donnelly, 2017). In view of the future roles and responsibilities of doctoral graduates vis-à-vis society, this implies:

- They are dedicated to working for or towards open (self-)critical societies, where politics and social cohesion function according to the principle of trial and error, by constantly questioning and adapting approaches to solutions, by reforms rather than revolutions. To ensure plurality of interpretative patterns both within the realm of research and at societal level, doctorate holders need to be alert to any attempts limiting the freedom of opinion, unless such opinion might undermine or threaten essential human rights.
- They can provide guidance for progress and orientation. Knowledge and opinion leaders in open societies have to both validate and

communicate the complexities that inherently structure our lives, thereby making them understandable and potentially less terrifying. As researchers, they are able to explain the significance of their results, be it with a view to stimulating further curiosity-driven investigations and/or in terms of societal impacts. This requires a mindset combining accuracy in analysis with pragmatism in conclusions or actions derived. Especially in times of crises, it is key for policymakers and citizens to be able to take informed decisions acknowledging there will always remain a level of uncertainty.

- They understand research as a search for knowledge and orientation with binding standards of scientific progress in line with the United Nations' Human Rights Charter, internationally agreed Research Ethics Codes and Standards of Good Scientific Practice (see the section by Cantini and Chiappa in this chapter).
- As *transformative leaders* they oppose any noticeable kind of discrimination, violence, bullying or harassment in the institutions to which they belong or their surrounding environments. As *resilient researchers*, they are prepared to defend the freedom of research within ethical boundaries, for example, by insistently communicating the value of research to society based on reliable, reproducible and provable results and by taking political action, if necessary.
- They 'promote open science where research data and other research results are freely available in such a way that others can collaborate and contribute, with just access to data, research resources and ownership of intellectual property' (Hannover Recommendation 1). While they contribute to advancing open science, they make provisions to limit its potential dangers resulting, for example, from accelerated progress in artificial intelligence research/genetic modification/combining of behavioural sciences and big data exploration.
- They understand that individual and collective wellbeing is critically endangered as a consequence of the destruction of our ecological environments and cultural diversity. We trust that researchers have the potential to anticipate the conceivable consequences of human activities in longer time frames than their own lives/generations. Doctoral education should, thus, 'instil social and ethical responsibility in doctoral candidates as well as a desire to stand up for their own ideas and to take them forward for the benefit of society' (Hannover Recommendation 7).

The challenge of a normative approach is to formulate wide-ranging assumptions or recommendations for a future that is yet to come. Therefore, it is essential for this book to give the future a voice. The subsequent chapter presents the reflections of early-career researchers who have completed or are still in the process of achieving their doctorates. They have been and still are invaluable contributors to the joint endeavour underlying this book, that is, understanding and attempting to advance the forces and forms of change of doctoral education worldwide.

References

Assembly of First Nations of the Pacific Northwest (AFNP). n.d. 'First Nations ethics guide on research and aboriginal traditional knowledge'. Accessed 9 June 2022. https://www.afn.ca/uploads/files/fn_ethics_guide_on_research_and_atk.pdf.

Anderson, M.S., Horn, A.S., Risbey, K.R., Ronning, E.A., De Vries, R. and Martinson, B.C. (2007) 'What do mentoring and training in the responsible conduct of research have to do with scientists' misbehavior? Findings from a National Survey of NIH-funded scientists'. *Academic Medicine: Journal of the Association of American Medical Colleges*, 82 (9), 853–60.

Antes, A., Murphy, S.T., Waples, E.P., Mumford, M., Brown, R., Connelly, R. and Devenport, L. (2009) 'A meta-analysis of ethics instruction effectiveness in the sciences'. *Ethics & Behavior*, 19 (5), 379–402.

Aslan, G. (2013) 'Neo-liberal transformation in Turkish higher education system: A new story of a turning point: Draft proposition on the higher education law'. Extended version of the paper 'Neo-liberal transformation in Turkish higher education system: A new story of a turning point: Draft proposition on the higher education law' presented at the 3rd International Conference on Critical Education, 15–17 May 2013, Ankara, Turkey.

Bauer, T. (2018) *Die Vereindeutigung der Welt: Über den Verlust an Mehrdeutigkeit und Vielfalt*. Stuttgart: Reclam.

Beckett, A. (2019) 'The age of perpetual crisis: How the 2010s disrupted everything but resolved nothing'. *The Guardian*. 17 December. Accessed 10 September 2021. No longer available. https://www.theguardian.com/society/2019/dec/17/decade-of-perpetual-crisis-2010s-disrupted-everything-but-resolved-nothing.

Bell, M., Berry, D., Leopold, J. and Nkomo, S. (2020) 'Making Black Lives Matter in academia: A Black feminist call for collective action against anti-blackness in the academy'. *Feminist Frontiers*, 1–19.

Biesta, G. (2002) 'Bildung and modernity: The future of Bildung in a world of difference'. *Studies in Philosophy and Education*, 21, 343–51.

Cantini, D., Chiappa, R., Karakaşoğlu, Y., Manathunga, C., Peters, C., Scholz, B. and Yarar, B. (2019a) 'Expert report: converging diversity: New frames for 21st Century doctoral education'. Accessed 9 June 2022. https://www.doctoral-education.info/dl/Workgroup-5_Societal-Political-and-Cultural-Change-and-the-Role-of-Researcher.pdf.

Cantini, D., Kreil, A., Naef, S., Schaeublin, E. and Akçınar, M. (2019b) 'No country for anthropologists'. Allegra Lab, 18 July. Accessed 9 June 2022. https://allegralaboratory.net/no-country-for-anthropologists/.

Connell, R. (2019) *The Good University: What universities actually do and why it's time for radical change*. Melbourne: Monash University Publishing.

Council of the European Union. (2016) 'Draft Council conclusions on "Measures to support early stage researchers, raise the attractiveness of scientific careers and foster investment in human potential in research and development" – Adoption'. Accessed 9 June 2022. https://www.consilium.europa.eu/media/24214/st14301en16.pdf.

Curry, S., de Rijcke, S., Hatch, A., Pillay, D., van der Weijden, I. and Wilsdon, J. (2020) 'The changing role of funders in responsible research assessment: Progress, obstacles & the way ahead'. RoRI, Working Paper No. 3. Accessed 9 June 2022. https://rori.figshare.com/articles/report/The_changing_role_of_funders_in_responsible_research_assessment_progress_obstacles_and_the_way_ahead/13227914

Dedeurwaerdere, T., Melindi-Ghidia, P. and Broggiato, A. (2016) 'Global scientific research commons under the Nagoya Protocol: Towards a collaborative economy model for the sharing of basic research assets'. *Environmental Science and Policy*, 55 (1), 1–10.

Devi, S. (2016) *Open Innovation/Open Science/Open to the World: a vision for Europe*. Luxembourg: Publications Office of the European Union.

Dutfield, G. (2004) *Intellectual Property, Biogenetic Resources and Traditional Knowledge*. London: Earthscan.

European Commission: Expert Group on the Research Profession. (2012) 'Excellence, equality and entrepreneurialism: Building sustainable research careers in the European research area'. 1–44. Accessed 9 June 2022. https://cdn5.euraxess.org/sites/default/files/policy_library/expertgrouponresearchprofession.pdf.

Fisher, C.B., Fried, A.F. and Feldman, L. (2009) 'Graduate socialization in the responsible conduct of research: A national survey on the research ethics training experiences of psychology doctoral students'. *Ethics & Behavior*, 19, 496–518.

Harding, S. (ed) (2011) *The postcolonial science and technology studies reader*. Durham: Duke University Press.

Hofmann, B., Helgesson, G., Juth, N. and Holm, S. (2015) 'Scientific dishonesty: A survey of doctoral students at the major medical faculties in Sweden and Norway'. *Journal of Empirical Research on Human Research Ethics*, 10 (4), 380–8.

Hofmann, B. and Holm, S. (2019) 'Research integrity: environment, experience or ethos?'. *Journal of Empirical Research on Human Research Ethics*, 15 (3–4), 1–13.

IPCC (2021) 'Summary for policymakers'. In: Climate Change 2021: The Physical Science Basis. Contribution of Working Group I to the Sixth Assessment Report of the Intergovernmental Panel on Climate Change. Accessed 9 June 2022. https://www.ipcc.ch/report/ar6/wg1/downloads/report/IPCC_AR6_WGI_SPM_final.pdf .

Juergensmeyer, M. and Peters, C. (2019) 'On hegemony and global doctoral education'. *Global-e* (online), 12 (49). Accessed 9 June 2022. https://www.21global.ucsb.edu/global-e/november-2019/hegemony-and-global-doctoral-education.

Karakaşoğlu, Y. and Tonbul, Y. (2015) 'Turkey'. In W. Hörner, H. Döbert, L. Reuter and B. von Kopp (eds), *The Education Systems of Europe: Global education systems*. Cham: Springer, 825–50.

Levitsky S. and Zieblatt, D. (2019) *How Democracies Die*. New York: Penguin.

Löfström, E. and Pyhältö, K. (2020) 'What are ethics in doctoral supervision, and how do they matter? Doctoral students' perspective'. *Scandinavian Journal of Educational Research*, 64 (4), 535–50.

Loudun, S. (2021) '"It was a great battle" – Michael Ignatieff, president and rector of Central European University, on the lost fight against Viktor Orban, his new home in Austria, and the miracle of the Viennese tram'. *Datum magazine*, March 2021. Accessed 12 September 2021. No longer available. https://www.ceu.edu/article/2021-04-13/it-was-great-battle-michael-ignatieff-president-and-rector-central-european.

Lulat, Y.G.-M. (2005) *A History of African Higher Education from Antiquity to the Present*. Westport: Praeger.

Manathunga, C. (2014) *Intercultural Postgraduate Supervision: Reimagining time, place and knowledge*. London: Routledge.

Manow, P. (2018) *Die Politische Ökonomie des Populismus*. Berlin: Edition Suhrkamp.

Montuori, A. and Donnelly, G. (2017) 'Transformative Leadership'. In *Handbook of Personal and Organizational Transformation*. Cham: Springer.

Müller, J.-W. (2016) *What is Populism?*. Philadelphia: University of Pennsylvania Press.

Nakata, M. (2007) 'The cultural interface'. *Australian Journal of Indigenous Education*, 36 (Supplement), 7–14.

Nerad, N. and Evans, B. (eds) (2014) *Globalization and Its Impacts on the Quality of PhD Education: Forces and forms in doctoral education worldwide*. Rotterdam: Sense Publishers.

Nowotny, H. (2016) *The cunning of uncertainty*. Cambridge: Polity.

O'Carroll, C., Rentier, B., Cabello Valdez, C., Esposito, F., Kaunismaa, E., Maas, K., Metcalfe, J., MacAllister, D. and Vandevelde, K. . (2017) *Evaluation of research careers fully acknowledging open science practices: Rewards, incentives and/or recognition for researchers practicing open science*. Luxembourg: Publications Office of the European Union.

Önal, N.E. (2012) 'The marketization of higher education in Turkey (2002–2011)'. In K. İnal and G. Akkaymak (eds), *Neoliberal Transformation of Education in Turkey*. New York: Palgrave Macmillan, 125–43.

Pennock, R.T. and O'Rourke, M. (2017) 'Developing a scientific virtue-based approach to science ethics training'. *Science and Engineering Ethics*, 23, 243–62.

Pimple, K. (2002) 'Six domains of research ethics: A heuristic framework for the responsible conduct of research'. *Science and Engineering*, 8 (2), 191–205.

Rangel, P. and Dultra E.V. (2019) 'Elections in times of neo-coupism and populism: A short essay on Brazil's right-wing presidential candidates' plans for governance and their proposals for gender and Afro-Brazilians'. *Irish Journal of Sociology*, 27 (1), 72–9.

Reagan, T. (2004) *Non-Western Educational Traditions: Alternative approaches to educational thought and practice*. 3rd edition. New York: Routledge.

Rose-Redwood, R., Kitchin, R., Apostolopoulou, E., Rickards, L., Blackman, T., Crampton, J., Rossi, U. and Buckley, M. (2020) 'Geographies of the COVID-19 pandemic'. *Dialogues in Human Geography*, 10 (2), 97–106.

Rudolph, T. (2019) 'Populist anger, Donald Trump, and the 2016 election'. *Journal of Elections, Public Opinion and Parties*, 31 (1), 33–58.

Santos, B.D.S. (2014) *Epistemologies of the South: Justice against epistemicide*. Boulder, US: Paradigm Publishers.

Santos, B.D.S. (2018) *The end of the cognitive empire: the coming of age of epistemologies of the south*. Durham: Duke University Press.

Scholz, B. (2017) 'Creating equal playing fields: How to foster international competitiveness through better gender balance in research and higher education'. In *Internationalisation of Higher Education*, C 4.2, 3.

Şen, Z. (2013) 'Türkiye'de yüksek lisans ve doktora eğitimi kalitesinin iyileştirilmesi için öneriler' ('Recommendations for improving the quality of masters and doctorate education in Turkey'). *Yükseköğretim ve Bilim Dergisi (Journal of Higher Education and Science)*, 3 (1), 10–5.

Shaw, D. (2019) 'The quest for clarity in research integrity: A conceptual schema'. *Science and Engineering Ethics*, 25, 1,085–93.

Smith, L.T. (2012) *Decolonising Methodologies: Research and Indigenous peoples*. London: Bloomsbury.

United Nations. (n.d.) 'Sustainable Development Goals'. Accessed 9 June 2022. https://sdgs.un.org/goals.

Whataoro, H. (2011) *The Lore of the Whare-wānanga or Teachings of the Māori College of Religion, Cosmogony and History*. Cambridge: Cambridge University Press.

Willinsky, J. (2005) 'The unacknowledged convergence of open source, open access, and open science'. *First Monday*, 10 (8).

Notes

1. We thank all the participants of both the Hannover workshop and conference for their invaluable advice and input that helped to form the ideas expressed in this chapter. Special mention should be made of the support of Prof. Reinhard Jahn, Emeritus Director of the Department of Neurobiology at the Max Planck Institute for Biophysical Chemistry and former President of The University of Göttingen, who helped us before and after the conference to test our concepts against the research reality, especially against an interdisciplinary background.
2. We must also consider that after the end of the Cold War and with the Pax Americana coming to an end another major confrontation is emerging for the world of science: the rise of China, its economic investment and intervention policies in many states of the Global South and the worldwide run on resources is accompanied by a renewed West–East conflict over knowledge and technology. With an increasing geopolitical competition between the US and China, the latter will continue to challenge the hegemony and the predominance of the Western model in research, academia and technological development. The course of this confrontation is unclear at this point but a more multipolar world order mirroring the economic powershift to the East may be one plausible scenario.
3. This essay is based on a conversation between Mark Juergensmeyer (UC Santa Barbara) and Christian Peters (University of Bremen) at the annual meeting of the Global Studies Consortium in Leipzig, Germany on 13 June 2019. An online version (Juergensmeyer/Peters 2019) was first published in *Global-e*, the weekly online magazine of UC Santa Barbara's research cluster on twenty-first century global dynamics.
4. Italian Marxist philosopher Antonio Gramsci (1891–1937), author of a widely received theory of cultural hegemony, is considered one of the most influential political theorists of the left. From 1926 until his death, Gramsci was kept as political prisoner by the fascist Italian regime. In the famous Prison Notebooks, the author describes how the state and the ruling class use culture to maintain power in (capitalist) societies. In Gramsci's view, the ruling class develops hegemony by using ideology and knowledge rather than force. The hegemonic culture propagates its own norms and knowledge standards so that over time they become 'common sense' and thus cannot be circumvented, maintaining the status quo.
5. In January 2021, Turkish president Recep Tayyip Erdogan's appointment of a new director at Istanbul's renowned Boğaziçi University was the main reason for massive student protests resulting in violent confrontations with police forces. In a follow-up statement, Erdogan called students and staff at Boğaziçi University 'terrorists'.
6. See reports by The Union of Employees in Education and Science (Eğitim Sen) http://egitimsen.org.tr/wp-content/uploads/2015/08/%C4%B0dari-ve-Teknik-Personel-%C3%87al%C4%B1%C5%9Ftay%C4%B1-Rapor_bask%C4%B1.pdf and http://egitimsen.org.tr/ohal-sonrasi-turkiyede-universiteler-raporu/.
7. Some of these private universities are positioned among the 10 academically best-performing universities according to University Ranking by Academic Performance/URAP.
8. Sun, Y. (2019) '30% increase in Private Universities Tuition Fees'. In the daily newspaper *Cumhuriyet*, 4 August 2019, 6.

PART III
Ways forward

10
Reflections from early-career researchers on the past, present and future of doctoral education

Shannon Mason, Maude Lévesque,
Charity Meki-Kombe, Sophie Abel,
Corina Balaban, Roxana Chiappa, Martin Grund,
Biandri Joubert, Gulfiya Kuchumova,
Lilia Mantai, Joyce Main, Puleng Motshoane,
Jing Qi, Ronel Steyn, Gaoming Zheng.

Early-career researchers (ECRs) played a unique and explicit role in the development of the Hannover Recommendations 2019. We, the ECRs, were the recipients of competitive travel scholarships generously funded by Volkswagen Stiftung, whose support brought us together from across the globe. Attendance at the culminating conference in Germany presented an opportunity for some that would have otherwise been inaccessible without that support. Our role was to work alongside established scholars to design and develop a set of recommendations to provide a foundation for the future of doctoral education internationally. We each participated in different capacities, with some members of the group joining preliminary pre-conference online meetings and contributing to group discussions at the workshop in the days prior to the conference, which also involved the drafting of written reports. Others joined later in the process, participating in the discussions that were a central part of the conference proceedings. During the events we also had informal opportunities to discuss issues related to various aspects of doctoral education. Although we participated in varying degrees and contexts, we each contributed to discussions on the current status and future directions of doctoral education globally.

We come from a diverse range of cultural, racial, ethnic, professional and educational backgrounds, with representation from all continents. Countries include, in alphabetical order: Australia, Canada, Chile, China, Finland, Germany, India, Japan, Kazakhstan, Romania, South Africa, the United Kingdom, the United States and Zambia. This diversity was not only reflected in the wide-ranging debates, but there was also diversity across our initial starting points, assumptions and experiences in doctoral education. For example, at the time of meeting in Hannover, some ECRs were in the middle of their doctoral programmes, while some were on the cusp of graduation and others had recently conferred their degrees. Some were based in their home countries, while others were far from home, in both established and emerging higher-education systems. The majority of the group were not native speakers of English and thus were navigating international academic discourse, including during the conference and the events leading up to it, in a language other than their mother tongue. For some, their field of inquiry was focused directly on higher and doctoral education, while others had an interest through their various other disciplines, but were equally invested in the state of doctoral education and the success of future doctoral researchers. The diversity of the group allowed the boundaries of discussions to be expanded and allowed open dialogue about doctoral education in its varied international contexts.

The goals of the Forces and Forms in Doctoral Education Worldwide initiative are indeed ambitious, but the advancement of doctoral education is not possible without a future-oriented perspective. Indeed, it was the explicit role of the ECRs involved in the 2019 phase of the initiative to provide a unique perspective as future leaders of doctoral education. As ECRs we are primed to be constantly thinking about, worrying about, imagining and hoping for the future (Bosanquet et al., 2020). We look forward to the time when we can finally submit our dissertation, we wonder if we can actually make it to the end, and beyond that we worry about whether or not we can gain secure and satisfying employment. We imagine where our professional lives might take us, and we hope to become the 'ideal' researcher that we imagine ourselves to be (Osbaldiston, Cannizzo and Mauri, 2019). Through various opportunities to engage with established scholars and with other ECRs, we have been encouraged to consider (perhaps more critically and deeply than before) what an 'ideal' future might look like for doctoral education across the world. Complementing this future-oriented lens, we also bring in a certain amount of hindsight, as some time has passed since the experiences we are reflecting on in this chapter. As McGovern (2020) advises, for emerging scholars, sometimes the best place to look for advice is to our younger selves as we are engaging in an often steep process of professional and personal development throughout our advanced higher education. Not only has some time passed, but it may seem longer than it has actually been, as we have had to adapt to the realities of the COVID-19 pandemic which is, as we write, impacting every corner of the globe. Through this challenging time we have been placed in positions that may encourage deeper reflection about what it is that is truly important for doctoral education and beyond. With this temporal lens, we consider the future for doctoral education while reflecting on our past experiences and lessons learned from our immersion in doctoral-education issues and the exploration of a set of core values for doctoral education around the world.

Gathering our words

It has now been more than 18 months since we gathered in Hannover for the Forces and Forms in Doctoral Education Worldwide 2019 conference. Even without the extra challenges of the continuing pandemic, it was always going to be difficult to gather reflections on the varied experiences of almost 20 ECRs undertaking various roles in different parts of the world, each with their own busy schedules in disparate time zones. Thus, we designed our approach to be as flexible as possible. In order to reach our goals for this chapter, we conducted a reflective exercise based loosely on the principles of collaborative autoethnography, a process through which participants reflect on a shared experience, and in comparing and contrasting each other's perceptions and perspectives, develop a deeper understanding of the experience at both an individual and group level (Hernandez, Chang and Ngunjiri, 2017).

Central to the process of gathering information is an 'intentional and purposeful dialogue' (Blalock and Akehi, 2018: 89), and so our exercise began with the development of a number of purposefully broad questions aimed at eliciting initial reflections related to our experiences through the development of the Hannover Recommendations 2019. These questions were added to an online document and shared with all ECRs. ECRs were requested to access the document at least once but more regularly if possible and to add their responses to the initial questions, to comment on other ECRs' responses, to pose follow-up questions and/or to add their own inquiry questions. This virtual, written, asynchronous and informal 'conversation' continued for the month of March 2021, with reminders sent weekly to allow as many ECRs as possible to contribute.

At the end of this time, 15 ECRs had added their contributions, which totalled 18 pages and more than 9,600 words.

A smaller group of ECRs then engaged in a process of reading and analysing the responses to identify themes that recurred throughout the document. We drew on our experience in qualitative content analysis (Braun and Clarke, 2006), but as this is a reflective exercise rather than an empirical study, we were more casual in our approach, drawing out themes that would be of interest to readers of this volume.

Through this exercise, we identified five themes that resonated across our experiences, indicated in italics. The first two themes relate to the discussions that made the strongest impression on the members of the group. On the one hand we raise our surprise at the sheer *depth and diversity of practices, norms, policies and debates surrounding doctoral education* and the challenges faced in coming to terms with this reality. On the other hand, we were struck by the fact that some of the *challenges facing doctoral education are shared across the diversity of contexts,* albeit in different ways and to different extents. The next theme relates to the recommendations themselves. Through our discussion there was a definite tension that was evident between the broad nature of the recommendations and a desire for the development of concrete and actionable policy, although in the end we recognise that the *recommendations provide a valuable set of guiding principles that can be applied to various contexts,* and as we have seen, are robust enough to withstand even a global pandemic. Next, we reflect on the dedicated space we were given through this initiative and our experiences *engaging in the doctoral education community*. Finally, in *looking to the future,* we hope to see the recommendations translated to practical application and real change in our particular contexts and consider what our roles in that process might be.

In reporting each of these themes below (and throughout this chapter), we have opted to use the pronoun 'we' to capture the essence of the collective narrative, but we note that this does not infer consensus among all members of the group. Indeed, our group is highly heterogeneous and to reflect this we have included the words of individual participants directly from the shared document, as indicated in quotes. These words may have been slightly paraphrased so that they fit grammatically into the narrative, while taking care to retain the original meaning. The quotes are included to explain and illustrate the five themes, as well as to ensure the voices of the ECRs remain central, something that is a priority within this participatory exercise (Corden and Sainsbury, 2006). In making our chapter as close as possible to the words presented in the shared document, we hope to retain the ECRs' voices, and efforts were also made to ensure that all participating ECRs were represented in the chapter. In order to confirm this, all ECRs were given a chance to review the resulting report and to provide comments if the interpretation of their words was not captured accurately or fully. Where we make reference to the Hannover Recommendations 2019, we use italics.

Theme #1: reflections on the depth and diversity of doctoral-education discourse

One of the strongest impressions that remained with us was the sheer breadth and depth of the discourse as it pertained to doctoral education. We were exposed to many 'trends and changes/reforms taking place in doctoral education worldwide' which allowed us to 'broaden our knowledge' and 'expand our understanding'. During the course of the proceedings, it became apparent that 'doctoral education can be so diverse in terms of perspectives and research questions'. Being exposed to the 'many different research streams that were presented and discussed at the workshop' proved a 'valuable experience to gain a big picture of doctoral education as a research phenomenon', helping to build our 'confidence and understanding about the field'. While trying to 'grasp so many issues' was at times somewhat 'overwhelming', our learning was facilitated by ample time in a relatively "isolated place" where we could 'dive into the topic'. As one ECR also noted, 'the beautiful location' was an ideal space to process our thoughts as we wandered through the magnificent gardens.

It could be said that the greatest asset of the 2019 Hannover conference was its seamless congregation of minds from across the world, 'bringing together and recognising diverse voices and perspectives'. Beyond our shared expertise in the field of doctoral education, pedagogy and knowledge building, our contribution stemmed from an innate understanding of doctoral education as we experience it in our 'many different contexts and locations' as described earlier. As ECRs, we were poised to contrast our unique experiences with that of others and within the broader worldwide matrix. Thought-provoking differences were certainly seen from each other's immutable national circumstances and challenges. As a diverse group, we have 'different lenses through which to view doctoral education and its role in society, which governs what we want to and can achieve'. As one of the ECRs explains, 'A lot of time was necessarily and fruitfully spent in sharing our contexts and changes in our contexts, our unique experiences of those contexts as well as our own particular interpretations of these contexts, informed by the various roles we play in our institutions and our various levels of experiences.'

Because of this diversity, we 'had an opportunity to probe issues to ensure that all group members were on the same page'. At times we struggled even for the right 'words that allowed us to share consensus while at the same time maintaining and respecting differences'. We held differing views on 'seemingly self-evident concepts such as "improving" or "optimising" or making doctoral education more "efficient"', along with 'different notions of what counts as "quality" and "excellence"'. We grappled with the implications of using words such as 'produce', 'educate', 'train' and 'cultivate'. Not even the term to indicate the person undertaking doctoral education is universal. Within our sharing document there are varied references to 'doctoral student', 'PhD student', 'graduate student', 'doctoral researcher', 'doctoral scholar', 'doctoral candidate', 'junior researcher' and 'early-career researcher'. These wide-ranging distinctions in title reveal implicit biases with regards to our perceived 'professional identity' within institutions and among other more established faculty members. Is it indeed fair to brand those engaged in doctoral education as 'students' when they are pursuing their own uniquely designed research project as part of their thesis? Are they not working alongside their professors in their quest for scientific insight? This 'suggests there is still a long way to go to enhance the recognition of the professional identity of doctoral candidates as junior researchers'.

On the status of a doctoral researcher, we were found to have among ourselves a disparate understanding of postgraduate education, ranging from our expected responsibilities, workloads and priorities. We came to realise the lack of international consensus regarding whether or not 'the doctoral phase should be paid' or on 'rights to visas for doctoral researchers looking to transition after completion'. For one ECR, the discussions surrounding the 'position of doctoral scholars and how they are treated as students/staff/other in different countries' left a particularly strong impression. There were specific discussions around the 'Ph' of the PhD that 'really resonated', leading many to consider the very 'nature and purpose of doctoral education' and 'the fundamental purpose of a PhD'. Indeed, has the 'philosophical thinking' of the degree been lost to the dissertation itself? This is explicitly reflected in the Hannover Recommendations 2019, which ask us to *support and acknowledge the contribution of the arts, humanities and social sciences*. While practices, norms and circumstances may vary, we have been able to 'reflect on the role of a doctoral education in our societies worldwide', and perhaps what we have in common is a will to advance doctoral education toward a more human, compassionate and united experience, readily accessible and, we hope, broadly valued.

Theme #2: reflections on shared challenges that cross contexts

Among the diversity of issues discussed, interestingly, there were a number of shared challenges that ECRs brought to light that impacted us all in our various contexts (albeit sometimes in different ways). Particularly, 'conversations regarding doctoral graduates to employment ratios in academia' were common. The value attached to higher education (specifically the doctoral degree) left the 'biggest mark' and 'biggest impact' for some ECRs and issues of global mobility were also a shared concern. It was unavoidable for these matters to come up in our reflections because they touch on real issues that personally affect us as ECRs, and as one of us intimated, 'it may be due to my personal bias as a doctoral candidate on the cusp of graduation'. Nevertheless, these are also challenges that are facing doctoral and early-career researchers across the world and will likely continue to influence the coming generations.

Another shared challenge was the misalignment between the number of and demand for doctoral graduates. In some contexts, lack of 'doctoral graduates' employability' is a common concern, noting that, 'unlike some years back, there has been an influx of doctoral graduates across the world, yet these highly educated fellows are unable to easily fit in the world of work, especially outside academia'. This ties up well with one ECR who stressed that in their context, 'very few faculty positions are available to a growing number of qualified candidates'. In addition, 'outside academia, it's also difficult to find employment when not from the STEM (science, technology, engineering and mathematics) fields'. 'This means that more work needs to be done in helping students "sell" their skills outside academia' and also to acknowledge the 'slew of transferable skills' that are gained through doctoral education, including in the humanities. In essence, it means that 'doctoral education needs to be reimagined and to take into account the precarious nature of academia'. However, not all contexts were concerned with an 'oversupply' of doctoral graduates. Other regions face a reality where 'more PhD holders are needed to build research and supervision capacity'. This is exacerbated further by unequal resource distribution across institutions, leading to 'a few "world-class" institutions that produce world-class researchers and many historically disadvantaged universities where research capacity often remains underdeveloped'. This raises concerns about 'equal access to quality doctoral education', 'overall supervision capacity' and how 'emerging supervisors can be developed and supported'.

'Continual casualisation and contract roles offered to doctoral graduates globally' was also highlighted in the conversations. For example, one ECR noted that in their context, 'only 10 per cent of PhD graduates will achieve an ongoing (tenured) academic position', a reality for many across the world. There is a changing landscape within higher-education institutions and shared across our narrative is a fear of the marginalised position that emerging researchers have in this landscape. As explained, 'it reflects a turn in the management of professors in universities from mostly tenure positions (with some part-time support from graduate students or early-career researchers), to a majority of class loads being taken on by perpetually renewed part-time contracts with a few, select tenure professors as figureheads of departments'.

This leaves 'most of the academic workforce in this uncertain, unstable place', aptly described as placing an 'increasing pressure on PhD holders in a volatile job market', forcing some to consider 'for how long working in academia will remain an option'. Thus, questions requiring answers were posed: 'Should candidates be told straight away that academia is unstable – and reinforced during candidature – and that their career pursuits should be beyond academia?' These sentiments caused one ECR to 'reflect more broadly on the value we grant advanced studies' because 'it is expected that more education means more value'. More critical questions were therefore asked: '. . . shouldn't the public sector and other workplaces seek out highly trained workers? Or at the very least, individuals who have proved determined, hard-working, articulate and skilled, even if not in the specific area of work that they apply for?' Such questions surrounding 'job security', 'graduate employability' and 'diversification of the job market for PhD holders' still have no 'clear answers'. However, these are issues discussed at the conference that many of us, from our diverse academic environments, are 'still pondering'.

Global mobility matters were also touched on focusing on 'brain drain/gain', a concept that appears to 'dehumanise' the movement of scholars. Emphasis was placed on the 'need to talk more about mobility and its current disembodied approach'. Changing the conversations that focus on 'brain drain or gain' to 'a 'more human' perspective was emphasised because it is not 'the brains that move from place to place but human beings who have emotions and families, etc.'. In reality 'people might not be able – or willing! – to move every couple of years with very little job security', and certainly, 'it's not sustainable to maintain the casualisation of work and temporary contracts'. Unfortunately, in this debate, early-career researchers across the world 'are often seen as disposable human capital'. However, 'to quote PhD Comics – we are not just 'brains on a stick''. There is a need for a paradigm shift to 'influence policy and practice positively' so that 'issues around scholar mobility can be handled and researched from a more human point of view'. A commitment to *diverse forms of mobility to develop multiple careers and ensuring a more balanced distribution of talent around the globe* is indeed one of the recommendations that was set forth.

Reflections on employment and global mobility and the position of doctoral researchers within these discussions coincided with musings on the 'value' attached to doctoral qualifications and encouraged further 'reflection on the nature and purpose of doctoral education'. While this is something that we are all inevitably thinking about, 'we have different assumptions about the purpose and features of doctoral education', as we discussed in the previous section. What we value 'depends on what we consider to be a good society', and there may be individual and societal differences at play when considering the answer to this complex and foundational question. However, as one ECR recalls the words offered by Professor Jonathan Jansen in his keynote address entitled 'The Thinking Doctorate: The PhD in a Global Culture of the "Mass Production" of Higher Qualifications', perhaps 'we should also pay attention to the "H" in PhD: Humane. After all, the goal of education, including doctoral education, is to address the social needs and serve the development of human beings as a whole'.

Theme #3: reflections on the recommendations as a valuable set of guiding principles

While some initial concerns were expressed about the 'broad', 'overall' and 'abstract' nature of the recommendations, influenced by a desire for more immediate and 'concrete policy recommendations', there is a clear acknowledgement of the vital role of and need for a set of guiding principles from which to 'derive concrete actions'. The Hannover Recommendations 2019 'capture the needs of doctoral education broadly' and the 'complexity of the issues', and in doing so they 'acknowledge that there will perhaps never be concrete policies that could be useful for the variety of unique contexts'. And while ECRs from a diverse range of contexts were represented, we 'were not necessarily "representative" of doctoral education in our contexts'. As one ECR pondered, 'our perspectives are based on our individual identities as researchers, scholars, practitioners and students in different disciplines and locations'. The tension between the individual and the collective was certainly felt by many of us during the proceedings and since. However, in the end there is perhaps a shared sense that the nature of the recommendations, having been developed through a 'collaborative' process, is that the 'principles hold true despite the pandemic' and that they can be 'translated to diverse and specific contexts and times', making them 'relatively timeless', 'relevant today' and beyond. For example, one ECR wrote, 'I have come to think that these basic principles are necessary to reflect on and have a shared understanding of what the purpose of a doctoral education is for the individual, for the local community and for society in general.'

Certainly, the past 18 months have put the recommendations to the test. As lockdowns and other social distancing measures have led some higher-education institutions to move online, there continue to be major interruptions and disruptions to doctoral education and to individual research studies. 'Admissions and graduations have been either delayed or cancelled.' 'Some students have had to change their data collection strategies', others have had 'severe disruptions to their fieldwork', while others have 'lost access to support networks and childcare and have had to take on extra duties in home schooling'. Doctoral researchers have had to make 'adjustments and find alternative ways to keep learning'. Indeed technology has helped to overcome some of these challenges, through 'online supervision meetings, online data collection, online conferences, etc.', but 'the technical advanced knowledge is not enough to address big societal problems'. The recommendations aim for the *fostering of diverse ways of operating*, but at the same time they require us to *recognise and seek to overcome existing inequalities*. And indeed, as one ECR notes, 'doctoral education is a very good field to understand how inequality operates among a group that typically appears as an exception of the educational system'.

The Hannover Recommendations also ask us to advance continuously and continually review doctoral education; these explicit terms serve as a reminder of the need to be responsive to any situation that may unfold and who could have imagined less than two years ago how much our professional and personal lives would change. The pandemic reminds us that with the guidance of the foundational principles, 'there is a need for doctoral education to be continually reimagined'. It is clear that the pandemic will 'set back many positive developments' and has 'intensified specific areas of inequality and inaccessibility', but there is also an opportunity to think about the big lessons we have learned that can encourage us to think *more* strategically about creative and innovative ways of offering doctoral education'. There is a potential for more imaginative and creative pathways to 'ensure doctoral researchers are not being disadvantaged and that they can continue with their research with as little disruption as possible'. Indeed, 'the pandemic has shown us that many things we considered impossible before are actually not so impossible'.

Theme #4: reflections on engaging in the doctoral-education community

The conference and the activities leading up to it (and since), presented a 'remarkable' opportunity for the ECRs 'to get to know the large international community of doctoral education'. Some of us were 'not aware of the international research community' and were 'incredibly heartened by its existence'. In meeting face-to-face, we were able to engage with 'all of these big names' in the field, with 'the cited works in my dissertation becoming real'. As one ECR wrote, 'meeting so many brilliant minds from all over the world on one subject was such a memorable occasion'.

However it was not merely being in the presence of 'well known and established scholars' that we valued, but the fact that we were 'welcomed into the community' and were 'part of the conversations with experts in the field of doctoral education'. This is why we have named this theme 'engaging in' the doctoral-education community and not 'engaging with'. Throughout the process of 'deliberating recommendations in the collective group', the 'ECRs were defined in the agenda and programme'. The process involved 'the voices of experts and ECRs from different parts of the world being taken into consideration'. The format of the conference was 'very collaborative' and there were 'various opportunities – prior to and during the conference – to interact with different participants'. Some of us noted just how 'rather rare' this is. It must be said that in some contexts, 'doctoral students are usually not given much space to make themselves heard. But during the conference I saw how welcome and helpful everybody was'.

This is also captured in this comment: 'Something notable was that I felt senior researchers gave junior researchers a lot of space to have their voices heard in discussions and panellists engaged with questions in non-dismissive ways. This is something I feel requires celebrating. My experience in my field is that it is not like this very often.'

Unfortunately, not all ECRs were involved in the working group sessions preceding the conference, but for those who were, they presented a 'wonderful opportunity to share and debate'. These small group discussions, with each focused on a particular aspect of doctoral education, were particularly 'conducive to critical reflection on the topics of the conference'. Through interaction and engagement in involved conversations, both during the working groups and then later in the conference proceedings where all ECRs were involved, we were able to make 'personal connections to members of the broader higher education community'. That included both other ECRs and more experienced researchers. For many, the relationships formed in Hannover have continued to develop and in some cases have led to ongoing discussions and fruitful collaborations. This community continues to provide an important source of support, for example: 'It was great to know that so many people are in the field I like! During the meeting, I had opportunities to interact with a few experts that have done extensive research in the area. So, whenever I need help or am stuck in any way, I don't worry that much anymore because at a click of a button, I can ask for help and get it.'

The 'importance of collaborating beyond your institution and country' was clearly evident, and for one ECR, the biggest impact of this opportunity has been 'realising that I am not alone'. After many months moving our lives more and more online, 'the world has understood and shown that we can be very well connected and collaborate across the globe without blowing the budget'. The writing of this chapter has provided an opportunity for the ECRs to interact again, and it has been a poignant time to consider what our hopes for the future are, for doctoral education more generally, but also for ourselves, both personally and professionally, as the current global situation has forced us to re-prioritise and reconsider what is truly important, and this leads us to our final theme where we look to the future.

Theme #5: reflections on future directions

Our engagement in the doctoral-education community has given us a 'picture of doctoral education from the past, present and future point of view'. The Hannover conference 'set an important research agenda in doctoral education for the years to come', and in that way it can be seen as a new beginning, rather than an end-point. One of the common hopes that is clearly evident through our sharing exercise, is to see 'practical application' and 'concrete action' derive from the recommendations, that is, 'Action action action is what I would like to see'. Now that we have a blueprint for doctoral education internationally, we ask the question, how can these recommendations now be 'translated to specific contexts' to bring about 'actionable change'? Questions remain unanswered about 'how far the set of recommendations developed will reach and what the impact will be', and indeed 'how this impact can be captured' is one area of potential future discussion.

In working with the tension between the collective and the individual mentioned earlier, we see that 'some of the issues that doctoral education faces affect us all', but that we 'can learn so much from those who contribute to research conversations from different countries and across research disciplines'. There is a need to acknowledge the unique and varied contexts in which doctoral education exists and to acknowledge contextual realities when applying the recommendations to a specific national, institutional or disciplinary context: '. . . not only the variety of contexts in which doctoral education takes place, but also the extent to which different people approached the subject with completely different lenses. Not only is the way in which we practise doctoral education itself context-based and historical, but so is our understanding of it.'

Whatever action or change may look like in a specific context, we strive toward the pivotal goal of doctoral education, that is *the development of original, responsible and ethical thinkers and the generation of new and original ideas and knowledge*. Striving toward this universal ideal requires the involvement of a range of interested parties including 'policy-makers and key practitioners in discussions on developments in doctoral education'. As the Hannover conference involved ECRs explicitly in the conversation, this practice should be replicated: 'doctoral scholars need more spaces to hang out with policy-makers and public audiences'. One question asked by a member of the group, 'why not connect doctoral candidates with policy-makers and big scholars? On Zoom everyone is (almost) equal. There is no reason not to attempt connections'.

Not only does progress in the doctoral-education space need the contribution of various parties, but the discussions also need to be ongoing. In essence there is no end-point where it can be said that the recommendations have been 'reached'. On a personal level, some ECRs are 'looking forward to a time when I shall work with some of the experts I met in Hannover', with one ECR sharing that they had 'worked on different projects with two of the experts I met' and another has 'started discussing possible joint research projects'. There are also ongoing and planned collaborations between the various delegates, including specifically among the ECRs, facilitated by the experience of working together in close collaboration: 'The trust and communication among the group is high... I also continue working with some senior researchers... the Hannover conference indeed provided a helpful opportunity for us to meet and sustain our communication and collaboration, for which I am very grateful.'

While broad discussions about the 'forces and forms' of doctoral education are ongoing, we also reflect on our own contributions to the issues surrounding doctoral education that were grappled with and note that we certainly have 'more space to learn how the skills and knowledge that we have could better be used at this time'.

Final remarks

Although we were selected as the 'future leaders' of doctoral education, for many of us our future in academia is unknown and unpredictable, and this is a reality we share with ECRs across the world. We may continue to contribute our own research with direct and indirect links to doctoral education. We may be involved in supporting the next generation of doctoral researchers either formally as supervisors and administrators or informally as alumni, colleagues and friends. We may contribute the knowledge and skills that we have developed during our doctoral training and early career to influence fields within or outside of academia. Whatever our contribution may be, the opportunity to meet with like-minded professionals to discuss, consider and debate complex and fundamental issues surrounding the nature of higher education has been formative and memorable. We wish to collectively offer our gratitude to all of the funders and organisers for providing this opportunity and for explicitly including our voices as early-career researchers in the proceedings.

As a unique group of individuals, we each have our own distinct areas of developing expertise, as well as avenues of inquiry that we may wish to pursue in the future. In the interest of *supporting more research on doctoral education for evidence-based decision-making* and of continuing collaborative discussions, we conclude our reflective chapter with a list of our areas of interest as it relates to doctoral education, noting that many of us also work in other fields beyond higher education. We hope that we may be able to engage with the doctoral-education community on these issues that are of particular importance or interest to us, as well as continuing the broad and wide-ranging discussions that sprung from the development of the Hannover Recommendations 2019.

Table 10.1
Early-career researchers' areas of interest

Initial	Areas of interest
SA	Doctoral education (experiences and support); Higher Degree Research writing; learning analytics for doctoral education, writing analytics
CB	Internationalisation of higher education; mobility; marketisation; neoliberal governance and accountability; knowledge production; societal impact of research in the social sciences and humanities (SSH); organisational and professional identities; ECRs
RC	Inequalities of higher education and scientific systems; internationalisation of higher education; academic elites; doctoral education; decolonisation
MG	Neural correlates of conscious perception; brain-body interactions; evidence-based science policy; mental health; equality
BJ	The development or inclusion of non-traditional research methodologies in legal research at doctoral level; developing techniques for communicating PhD research in an accessible manner across disciplines and faculties
GK	Research competences development; research methods courses in doctoral education; supervision practices
ML	Continuing education for older students/seniors; graduate and doctoral education for older adults across the world
LM	Doctoral education (experience and support); ECR employability and transition; PhD skills; researcher careers; undergraduate research; higher education forms and trends; academic identities; curriculum development
JM	Academic and employment pathways of science and engineering students
SM	The experiences and ethics of doctoral researchers publishing during candidature; research communication within and beyond academia; internationality of higher education scholarship; the experiences of doctoral researchers who are also navigating motherhood
CM-K	Internationalisation of higher education; experiences of doctoral students in host countries; experiences of foreign educated doctoral graduates in home countries upon their return and the 'foreign' skills they (returnees) bring home
PM	The role of the institution in developing and supporting emerging supervisors; supervision identity development
JQ	Internationalisation of higher education; Indigenous and transcultural doctoral education; community and teacher education; digital and online education
RS	Changes in doctoral education practices and purposes; doctoral education and its relations to macro social structures; social justice; social realism; history of education
GZ	International joint doctoral education provision; international doctoral students; quality and quality assurance of doctoral education; Europe-China higher education cooperation; institutional logics perspective

References

Blalock, A.E. and Akehi, M. (2018). 'Collaborative autoethnography as a pathway for transformative learning'. *Journal of Transformative Education*, 16 (2), 89–107.

Bosanquet, A., Mantai, L. and Fredericks, V. (2020) 'Deferred time in the neoliberal university: Experiences of doctoral candidates and early career academics'. *Teaching in Higher Education*, 25 (6), 736–49.

Braun, V. and Clarke, V. (2006) 'Using thematic analysis in psychology'. *Qualitative Research in Psychology*, 3 (2), 77–101.

Corden, A. and Sainsbury, R. (2006) 'Using verbatim quotations in reporting qualitative social research: Researchers' views'. University of York, Social Policy Research Unit. Accessed 9 June 2022 https://www.york.ac.uk/inst/spru/pubs/pdf/verbquotresearch.pdf.

Hernandez, K.C., Chang, H. and Ngunjiri, F.W. (2017) 'Collaborative autoethnography as multivocal, relational, and democratic research: Opportunities, challenges, and aspirations'. *Auto/Biography Studies*, 32 (2), 251–4.

McGovern, V. (2020) 'Great advice is closer than you know'. Inside Higher Ed. Accessed 9 June 2022. https://www.insidehighered.com/advice/2020/03/30/advice-overcome-career-challenges-listen-your-younger-self-opinion.

Osbaldiston, N., Cannizzo, F. and Mauri, C. (2019) '"I love my work but I hate my job" – Early career academic perspective on academic times in Australia'. *Time & Society*, 28 (2), 743–62.

11
Ways forward

*David Bogle, Ulrike Kohl, Maresi Nerad,
Conor O'Carroll, Christian Peters, Beate Scholz*

Doctoral education lies at the heart of the mission of the research university. It is the highest level of university qualification and as such commands the attention of university leadership as pivotal in the unique mission of training future leaders who drive our research and innovation across society within and beyond academia. In our book, we have highlighted the growth in numbers, the wide range of ways for achieving high-quality doctoral education and the increasing scrutiny of the quality of the training experience. As we outlined at the start, we see doctoral education both as a process of training to undertake research by encouraging curiosity-driven, creative doctoral research, and as a passport into better employment prospects within and beyond academia. Both developed and developing countries see research and innovation as key drivers for increasing prosperity which needs trained researchers. Our conference demonstrated that there is a common vision as to what is important in the education of doctoral candidates across the globe while practices varied as to how to achieve it.

A key element of the success of the Hannover Conference was the bringing together of researchers, practitioners, leaders (graduate deans) and early-career researchers to develop working papers and to discuss and debate about doctoral education across the world. The chapters in this book that developed from the preparation for the conference discuss the many reforms in recent years. So much has changed recently: the pandemic, the growth of nationalist agendas and, most concerningly, the consequences of the climate crisis and the need for greater sustainability.

The pandemic and the sustainability crisis have made society more aware of the role of research and researchers in tackling these existential challenges. To prepare them for this role, Jonathan Jansen asks us to ensure a 'thinking doctorate', where we train our candidates to give an articulate account of their work, to be able to make a case for its significance and to give a convincing account of its conceptual framework. Rising divisions in society and fear of an uncertain future have made many lose faith in authority, political and scientific, and to turn to nationalist or other extremist answers and belief systems based on prejudice and not on evidence. Openness and debate, fundamental to research, are the bedrock of democracy. They challenge authoritarian administrations. The values of openness and constructive debate must be sustained and built into doctoral education worldwide. This should be done in an open and inclusive way to embrace all knowledge systems. There still remains a degree of colonialism in the dominance of Western knowledge systems. The dominance of the English language could be seen this way, but it has become the vehicle for common understanding around the world.

Our argument here is that research training should be based on a joint value system rooted in the universal principles of the United Nations Human Rights Charter. It should be based on respect for the individual and aim for an equilibrium of knowledges from South, North, East and West including indigenous knowledge systems in an 'ecology of knowledges'. Doctoral graduates should be able to see their work in this context and be able to make a clear case for the significance of their work to the public beyond the traditional peer group.

In this way, we can train doctoral graduates to be not only 'creative, critical, autonomous and responsible intellectual risk takers' but also to bring the intellectual community into closer contact with the users of research so that we can jointly develop ways forward to tackle the existential challenges that confront society. Researchers must be ready to engage fully with society to bring the case for knowledge and evidence while remaining balanced and able to articulate how to handle the uncertainty which is inherent in research results.

Science has always been a global collaborative activity, and the advent of open science brings the potential to provide access to data and results without barriers and enhance global collaborative efforts to address major problems like climate change. The obverse of these developments has been an increase in research misconduct, lack of reciprocity in some countries that are less open and threats to research themes that do not fit with official government policy. The twenty-first-century doctoral candidate and PhD graduate must now deal with these new issues, and this underlines the need for good training and mentorship to support them.

The challenge for the employment of PhDs is well recognised especially as the majority are still trained as academic apprentices, a profession where the number of jobs cannot match the graduate numbers. The precarity of employment for PhD graduates (as researchers) is a global issue, and the academic research system must broaden employment opportunities through training and career development support.

The researchers that we train will be driving future research agendas. They must be prepared for closer working with society. We believe the value system that we are proposing here will help build trust and ensure that the resources go towards tackling the challenges that our societies consider most important.

So, what are the ways forward? Here are some views and hopes of the editors.

The Hannover workshop and conference offered a unique setting and framework for experts from around the globe, from different ethnicities, religious backgrounds and beliefs, different sexes and gender identities, political attitudes, research fields and disciplines and across generations to enter into an open debate and eventually to agree on core values of doctoral education worldwide. This gives us hope that it might serve as a model for future deliberations beyond doctoral education to address the joint challenges the world is facing. These encounters, which allow for the respectful perception of otherness, can help to realise inclusive concepts of *Bildung* and work towards research-based solutions for today's problems while relying on diversity as a key asset.

The conference has shown that to cope with the increasing complexities of professional research environments across disciplines, countries and research systems, it is essential that, beyond technical or disciplinary knowhow, PhD training, and also researcher training across a career, includes more human and social aspects. A way to enhance this will be to develop research collaborations in creative open spaces, inclusive and full of respect for human and social diversity, between researchers, research professionals and research users, making sure that core values form part of the collaborative agenda. This would enable larger visions beyond a narrow disciplinary academic scope. Stimulating these types of collaborations can be possible at a local, regional and global level, according to the reach of the research agenda. It requires original ways of organising research that can be imagined by several individual collaborating researchers at a small scale or by institutions or research actors and stakeholders at a larger scale. We imagine learning environments where traditional disciplinary and academic barriers are overcome, bringing together different communities of learners with their diverse and enriching contributions.

We believe that doctoral candidates should all be required to reflect on the ethical dimension of their work, the impact that it might have and how it fits into the 'ecology of knowledges'. Many systems now assess the impact of research but sometimes in a rather narrow way. Doctoral candidates should be trained to consider the very broadest impact that their work might have on society and, during the formulation and execution of the research, to engage with those who might be affected.

We believe that mobility is good for you as a researcher! *International mobility* can be an enriching experience, broadening research and perhaps more importantly cultural horizons. *Intersectoral mobility* enables you to experience a much broader working environment. *Interdisciplinary mobility* takes you out of your thematic silo to access different disciplinary approaches to research challenges. *Virtual mobility* can drive greater equality by, for example, enabling those in disadvantaged regions to collaborate internationally.

We, the editors, are committed to continue working with the early-career researchers, bringing them together, supporting them in forming peer groups, and acting as mentors encouraging them and standing by their side in the task of carrying the core values forward. It is most encouraging that such an international group of junior colleagues who wrote Chapter 10 has already started uncovering hidden norms that may lead to self-censorship and stand in the way of open communication among doctoral candidates, among junior colleagues, between early-career researchers and supervisors, and among supervisors and their academic peers and professionals working in doctoral education. We stand here ready to support early-career researchers who are the future of the research system.

Index

Page numbers in italics are figures; with 't' are table.

Al-Azhar University (Cairo) 209
Antes, A. 220
applied doctoral degrees 23–4
approach of the book 45
areas of interest 254–5t
artificial intelligence (AI) 185–7, 204–5
arts/humanities/social sciences 53
Assembly of First Nations of the Pacific Northwest (AFNP) 221–2
Association of American Universities 68–9
attrition 29, 38, 67–8, 79, 112
Australia 20t
   and COVID-19 34–5, 120
   funding 114, 120, 125–6, 158
   and geopolitics 160–1
   and quality assurance 61, 62–6
   and race 210
Austria 178

Bates, G.W. 33
Beckett, Andy, 'The age of perpetual crisis' 202
Bildung 25, 47, 49–50, 212, 222, 231, 259
   in the Hannover recommendations 51
Birmingham, Simon 161
Black Lives Matter (BLM) movement 203, 209–10
Black Tax 138–9
Bogner, Alexander 206–7
Bologna Process 26
brain drain 130, 134–5, 144, 148, 162, 248–9
   Asia 150
   Australasia 150
   Eastern Europe 149
   India 143
   and virtual mobility 152
Brazil 20t, 157, 179, 191
Brexit 160

Canada 20t, 77, 125, 146–7
capacity building *see* mobility
career tracking 29–30, 60, 66, 67, 174–80
challenges 247–9
changes in doctoral education 229–30

Chile 20t, 125, 147, 155, 157
China
   capacity-building policies 136
   and ethical research 219
   funding 115, *116*, 117, 128
   and geopolitics 159, 160–1
   political control/influence 155, 156
   and the precarity of academic research careers 174
   and quality assurance 61, 69–71, 128–9
   trends/growth 2, 20t, 171
climate change 31, 188, 203
Coalition for Next Generation Life Science (US) 69
cohorts 105–6
collaboration 183, 193–4, 252, 258, 259
collective supervision 104
colonialism and colonisation 209, 214, 215, 258
Committee on Academic Freedom (CAF) 223
communication, as a skill 183
conceptual framework 45–6
coursework 23, 84, 85, 105, 124
   Australia 62
   Germany 97
   Japan 87–8, 105
   South Africa 90, 92, 105
   United States 101, 105
Coventry University (CU) (UK) 91, 92
COVID-19 23, 33–7, 159, 201, 202–3, 217–19, 243, 250
   and funding 119–20, 127, 158
   and international students 161
   and the labour market 173, 174
   and mental health 32–3
   and virtual mobility 135, 144–5, 152, 162
culture sensitivity 137
Czech Republic 73

digitalisation 18, 54, 79, 171, 184, 204–5, 229
dissertations 24–5, 60, 84, 105
   Australia 62, 63–5
   China 70
   Germany 75
   United States 67, *100*, 101–2
diversification, forms/outcomes of degrees 23–5

diversity 52, 215–16, 242, 259
    and capacity building 138, 143
    in doctoral-education discourse 245–7
    quality assurance, United States 67
dual/joint doctoral degrees 25
Dutfield, G. 213

early-career researchers 241–5, 254–5, 255t
    on depth and diversity of doctoral-
        education discourse 245–7
    engaging in the doctoral-education
        community 251–2
    future directions 252–5
    on the recommendations as guiding
        principles 249–51
    reflections on shared challenges 247–9
ecology of knowledges approach 46, 51,
    210–12
employment 31, 247–9, 259
    preparation for 28–9
engagement of the doctoral-education
    community 251–2
English 29, 139, 158
Enlightenment, European 209
environments 259
    and employability 191–2
    institutional 54, 57–8, 107
epistemocracy 207
era of digitalisation 205
ethics 54–5, 201, 212, 230
    research 217–24
    and the thinking doctorate 9–13
EURAXESS 183
Europe/European Union
    and Brexit 160
    capacity-building policies 136
    and COVID-19 35
    doctoral schools 26
    and ethical research 219
    EURAXESS 184
    European Charter and Code for
        Researchers 174
    funding 113–14, 113, 155–6, 157, 191
    and geopolitics 158–9
    industrial doctorates 190
    labour market 177, 178
    mobility trends 149–50
    political control/influence 155
    professional doctorates 189
    quality assurance 71–3
    skills development 186–7
European model 84
European Science Foundation 176
European University Association (EUA) 72
    Council for Doctoral Education (EUA-
        CDE) 176
evidence-based decision-making 53
examinations
    Australia 62, 65
    China 70, 209
    Germany 75, 96, 97
    Japan 88, 89
    South Africa 5, 90
    United States 66–7, 67, 68

fairness, research ethics 221

#FeesMustFall 2
First Nations 213
    Assembly of First Nations of the Pacific
        Northwest (AFNP) 221–2
    see also minorities
Floyd, George 209–10
Forces and Forms in Doctoral Education
    Worldwide initiative 242
France 177, 190
Frick, Liezel 89
funding 110–14, 113, 172
    and capacity building 155–8
    concerns 119–30
    global trends 115–19, 116
    and mobility 133–4
    and political control/influence 155–6
    sources 156–8, 188
future directions 252–4

gender 208
    studies 12, 161, 225–7
geopolitics 158–62, 160
Gerber, Ferdie 89
Germany
    funding 115, 116, 117, 120–1
    growth/trends 20t, 171, 175
    industrial doctorates 190
    labour market 177, 179
    and the precarity of academic research
        careers 174
    quality assurance 74–6
    Goethe University of Frankfurt am Main
        78
    supervision 84–5
    Max Planck Institute-University of
        Göttingen (Göttingen, Germany) 94–9,
        104, 105, 108
Global Studies 214, 216–17
goals of the book 43–4
Goethe University of Frankfurt am Main
    (Germany) 78
Gould, J. 129
Graduate Record Examination (GRE) (US)
    66–7
graduate schools 26–8

Hannover Recommendations 49, 51–5, 110,
    201, 241, 243, 249–51
    Recommendation 1 51, 188, 201, 211–12,
        228, 231, 233
    Recommendation 2 52, 84, 230–1
    Recommendation 3 52, 133–4, 163, 170,
        248–9
    Recommendation 4 53, 108, 188, 246
    Recommendation 5 50, 53, 179, 254
    Recommendation 6 54, 107, 170–1
    Recommendation 7 45, 54–5, 201, 231–2,
        234, 253
Hayashi, Yasuhiro 85
hegemony, in higher education 214–17
Humboldt traditions 65, 230

identity, professional 246
Ignatieff, Michael 204
implications, and value-based doctoral
    education 230–2

imposter syndrome/phenomenon 139–40
India 20t, 141–2, 219
indigenous doctoral students 24
industrial doctorates 190–1
inequality 248, 250
   and creating just research systems 208–13
   see also hegemony
innovation 187
   Waseda University (Japan) 85–6
Innovative Training Network (ITN) 22, 25
input (defined) 60
institutional structures, graduate schools 26–8
intellectual property (IP) 212–13, 233
intercultural peer communities 211
interdisciplinary mobility 135, 152, 154
intersectoral mobility 135, 151–4, 192, 260
ITN (Innovative Training Network) 22–3

Japan
   funding 114, 115, *116*, 117, 120, 122, 157
   increase in PhD production 20t
   industrial doctorates 190
   political control/influence 156
   and the precarity of academic research careers 174
   supervision 84–9, 104, 106, 108
joint/dual doctoral degrees 25
Journal Impact Factor (JIF) 139
just research systems 208–13

Kazakhstan 122, 127, 129
knowledge
   open 207
   as a resource 206
   traditional 213
knowledge production 50n2, 104, 203, 205, 207, 208, 219, 221, 231
knowledge systems 46, 51, 208, 210–12, 258

labour markets 170–1, 194–5
   doctorates for 176–80
   growth in 171–3
   professional/industrial doctorates 189–91
   and research environments 191–2
   skills development 180–9, 181–2t
   trends 173–6
Latin America 146–7
   see also Brazil; Chile; Mexico
League of European Research Universities 72
Levecque, K. 33
local knowledge 127–8

Mackie, S. A. 32
Maintaining a Quality Culture in Doctoral Education (LERU) 59–61
Malaysia 20t, 76, 120, 155, 156, 157–8
Marie Skłodowska-Curie Actions (MSCA) 35, 126–7, 129, 177, 188
   European Industrial Doctorates (EIDs) 190–1
   and mobility 192
massification 17, 30–1
Max Planck Institute-University of Göttingen (Göttingen, Germany) 94–9
Max Planck PhDnet 75–6

mental health 32–3, 233
mentoring 139–40
merit assessment 232
MESA (Middle East Studies Association) 222
Mexico 20t, 147, 156
Middle East, and research ethics 222–4
migration see international students; mobility
minorities 259
   and capacity building 136–40
   and intellectual property 213
   and knowledge systems 212
   and research ethics 221–2
mobility 4, 21, 22–3, 31, 52, 133–5, 143–6, 248–9, 260
   capacity-building policies 136–7
   challenges to capacity building 137–40
   and diversity 143
   and English language 29
   and funding 126–8, 155–7
   and geopolitical influence 158–62, *160*
   international mobility 146–7
   Africa 148–9
   Asia 150
   Australasia 62, 150–1
   Europe 149–50
   Latin America 147–8
   intersectoral mobility 151–4
   and massification 30
   policies 162–3
   political influence 154–5, 162
   and research environments 192
   reverse migration 140–2
Moses, D. 161

National Academies of Science, Engineering and Medicine (US) 68
Netherlands 175
   funding 125
New Zealand 20t, 76
normative perspective 228, 234
North America
   capacity building 146–7
   graduate schools 27–8
   see also Canada; Mexico; United States
North American model 84

OECD (Organisation for Economic Co-operation & Development) 19
   and AI 186
   on funding 111, 115, *116*, 117–19, 157–8
   and precarity of research careers 174–5
open knowledge 207, 258
open science/scholarship 139, 186–7, 205
   and intellectual property 212
outcomes (defined) 60
outputs (defined) 60

pandemic see COVID-19
PEP (power, energy and professions) programme (Waseda University, Japan) 85, 86–9
philosophical thinking 246
Piccini, J. 161
Pimple, K. 221, 222
political theory 214–15
politics 133–5, 154–5, 205–6

INDEX   263

and funding and control 155–6
influence on the PhD 154–5
and mobility 146
and the thinking doctorate 9–13
positionality 11
postdoctoral funding 128–9
priority research, and funding 118–19
private funding 117
process, doctoral 14
professional doctorates 190–2
project funding 118
projectification 118, 123–4
publishing 174
and Australia 65–6
purpose, of the university 21–3

quality assurance 57–9, 78–80
basic concepts and elements 59–61
country examples 61–76
and employability 194
importance 58–9
university cases 76–80
Quality Assurance Agency (QAA) (UK) 73–4

R&D spending 156–7
racial essentialism 11
racism 9, 10, 11, 203, 211
Black Lives Matter (BLM) movement 203, 209–10
research 37–9, 205
environments 191–4
research commons, global 212–13
research ethics 217–24
research integrity 220
Responsible Research Assessment 232
risk taking 258
intellectual 23, 43, 179–81
in the Hannover Recommendations 54, 79
ross, kihana 210
Russia 20t, 115, *116*, 122, 195

Saini, Angela, *Superior: The return of race science* 10
Salzburg Principles 72
Santos, Boaventura de Sousa 210–11
scholar–practitioner approach 136
scientist–practitioner training 136
self-awareness 9–10
significance 6–8
skills development 172, 180–9, 181–2t, 196
social consciousness 9, 10, 13
social theory 214–15
South Africa 1, 3–4
and COVID-19 36
funding 122, 125, 129, 158
and geopolitics 161–2
international mobility 148–9
Stellenbosch University 9–10, 89, 91, 92, 149
supervision 84–5, 89–93, 104, 105, 106, 108
trends 2, 20t
South Korea 20t, 115, *116*, 117
stakeholders (defined) 211–12
standardised experiences and outcomes, and supervision 106

Stellenbosch University (SU) (South Africa) 8–9, 89, 91, 92, 149
structured PhD education 105, 136, 192–3
student learning outcomes (SLOs) 68
subsidies, government 2–3, 5
supervision 25–6, 28, 82–5, 231
Czech Republic 73
and ethics 218
and relationship with the candidate 30
vignettes 102–8
Germany 94–9
Japan 85–9
South Africa/United Kingdom 89–93
United States 99–103, *100*, 104, 106
systems thinking 184–5

tenure 63, 118–19, 137, 248
Germany 174
India 142
Turkey 228
US 99
theory, and the thinking doctorate 8–9
thinking doctorate 5–6, 13–14, 227, 258
ethics and politics 9–13
and significance 7–8
throughput 60
timeframes 29, 30, 54, 136
and funding 112–13, 124–5
professional doctorates 189–90
traditional knowledge 213
transcultural 211
transferable skills 25
transformative leadership 232–4
trends 1–4, 19–21, 20–1t, 229, 247
true, research ethics 221
Turkey 161, 223, 224–8

UNESCO International Standard Classification of Education 76
United Kingdom
and COVID-19 36
funding 115, *116*, 120–21
growth 20t, 171
labour market 177–8, 179
professional doctorates 190
quality assurance 73–4
supervision 89–93
United Nations
Fourth Sustainable Development Goal (SDG) 229
Universal Declaration of Human Rights 223, 233, 258
United States
capacity building 136, 137, 144, 146–7
and COVID-19 36–7, 120
and ethical research 219
funding 114, 115, *116*, 117, 120, 121, 124–5
international students 159
labour market 177, 179
and the precarity of research careers 174
professional doctorates 189, 190
and quality assurance 61, 66–9
supervision 84, 99–103, *100*, 104, 106, 107, 108
trends/growth 1–2, 20, 20t, 171, 175–6

Universiti Sains Islam Malaysia (Malaysia) 76
University of British Columbia (Canada) 77
University of Otago (New Zealand) 76
University of Washington (Seattle, US) 99–103, *100*

value systems 51
virtual mobility 52, 133–4, 135, 144–5, 152, 154, 162, 260

Walter Sisulu University (WSU) (South Africa) 91, 92
Waseda University (Japan) 84–9
Web 3.0 204
wellbeing 32–3, 233
Wimpenny, Katherine 89
wise, research ethics 220, 222
WISE (World-leading Innovative and Smart Education) (Japan) 86–7
women 21, 173
   and capacity building 136–40
   wellbeing 31, 34, 37
   see also gender; minorities
World Education Services 67

CPSIA information can be obtained
at www.ICGtesting.com
Printed in the USA
JSHW070204150323
38889JS00022B/116